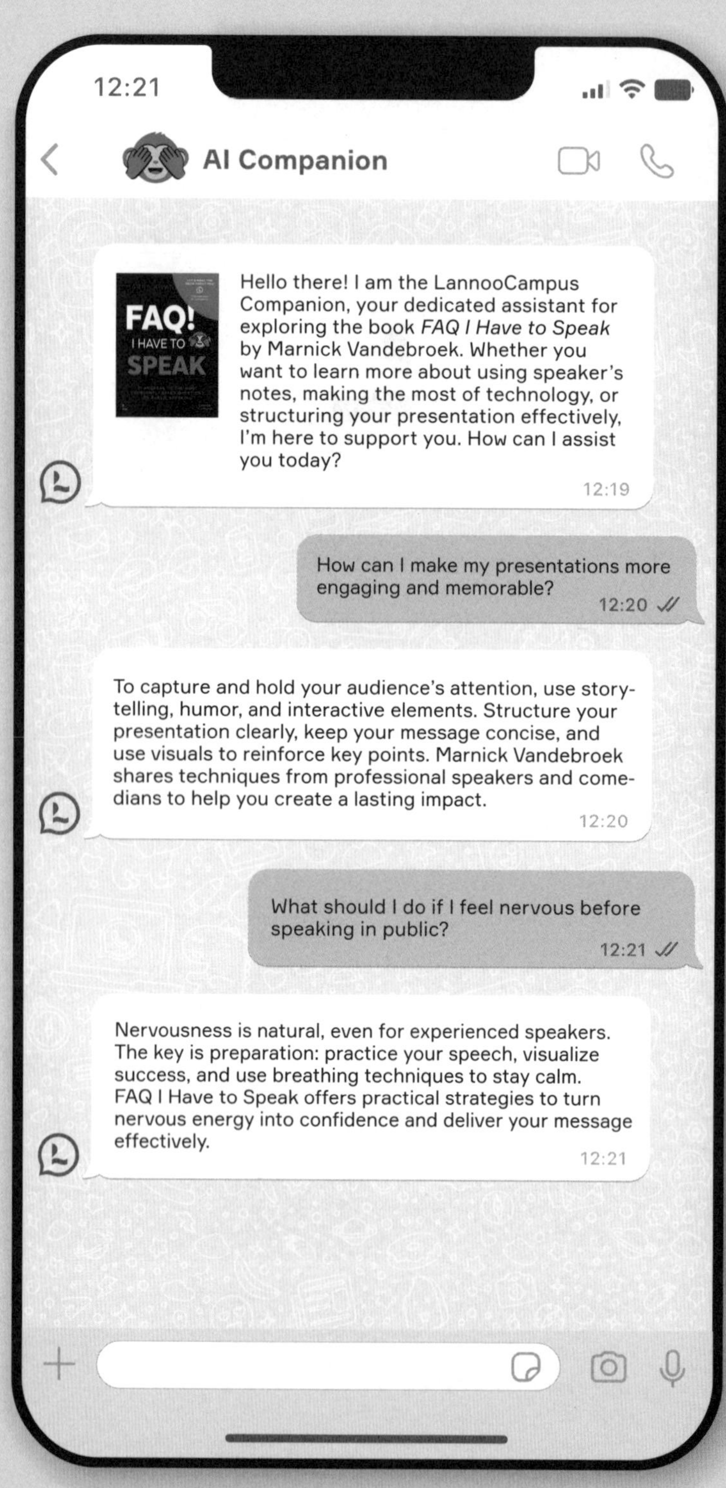
12:21
AI Companion
FAQ!
I HAVE TO
SPEAK
Hello there! I am the LannooCampus Companion, your dedicated assistant for exploring the book *FAQ I Have to Speak* by Marnick Vandebroek. Whether you want to learn more about using speaker's notes, making the most of technology, or structuring your presentation effectively, I'm here to support you. How can I assist you today?
12:19
How can I make my presentations more engaging and memorable?
12:20
To capture and hold your audience's attention, use storytelling, humor, and interactive elements. Structure your presentation clearly, keep your message concise, and use visuals to reinforce key points. Marnick Vandebroek shares techniques from professional speakers and comedians to help you create a lasting impact.
12:20
What should I do if I feel nervous before speaking in public?
12:21
Nervousness is natural, even for experienced speakers. The key is preparation: practice your speech, visualize success, and use breathing techniques to stay calm. FAQ I Have to Speak offers practical strategies to turn nervous energy into confidence and deliver your message effectively.
12:21

LET'S MAKE THE BOOK ABOUT YOU!

Ontdek je AI Companion

MEET YOUR AI COMPANION

Imagine this: you're not just reading this book, but engaging in a direct conversation with it. It feels as if Marnick Vandebroek is right beside you, ready to answer your questions and support you with his knowledge and expertise. To the left, you'll see how such a conversation with the AI Companion might look. The LannooCampus Companion perfectly adapts the content of *FAQ I Have to Speak* to:

- you as a professional;
- your team;
- your company or organization;
- and your unique situation.

Through a convenient chat feature (available in WhatsApp), you'll discover extra functionalities that go beyond the classic learning experience—such as personalized advice, real-time updates, and practical tools to immediately apply the book's insights.

Experience a new, interactive way of learning that truly grows with you in 3 easy steps:

STEP 1:
Go to: https://click.lannoo.be/ai-faq-i-have-speak or scan following QR code and follow the instructions.

STEP 2:
To activate the AI Companion you will need following unique activation code:

569236017f203a37

STEP 3:
Open the chat en start the conversation. You get free access from the moment you sign up.

In honour of my
grandfather René V.

(♥1931- 2023)

I write because you wrote.
I read because you read.
I speak because you spoke.

MARNICK VANDEBROEK

21 ANSWERS TO THE MOST FREQUENTLY ASKED QUESTIONS ON PUBLIC SPEAKING

Lannoo
Campus

CONTENTS

BEFORE YOU START READING

Yeah, but...

- **...I don't speak on big stages; I only have three people in a meeting room.**
  This book is for everybody who wants to make a bigger impact on their audience in a personal or professional context. You don't have to be a keynote speaker or politician to get value out of this book. Speaking is a skill we all need to master. If you want to take your friends, partner, colleagues, investor, board members,... along with your ideas, you need to be able to speak. Speaking is not just reserved for people who stand on big stages in front of huge crowds. You must be able to apply the same techniques in a video call at work or in front of five people in a meeting. I stand on big stages for a living, but still, most of my own speaking and coaching work with others is within companies for client, board, investor or stakeholder meetings, online and offline.

- **...speaking is not my issue; building a story and presenting my ideas in a clear way is.**
  When I use the word 'speaking' in this book, I refer to everything related to it. You can talk about performing, presenting and storytelling. One focuses more on voice and body, the other more on actual presentations and the last one more on content structure. To make it easy, in most cases I will group all these aspects of the trade under the term 'speaking'. So, when you are 'speaking', you need a solid performance, you need great content and a crisp structure, and you need to be able to present your ideas, but also to bring them across in a conversation-like way.

- **...I mainly work online and have to stand in front of a camera instead of a live audience.**
  If you mainly work remotely and spend more time in front of a camera than a live group, this book is just as relevant for you. There is not a lot of difference between online and offline speaking. Online, things will have to be enlarged, which will be discussed in this book, but all the techniques, structures and insights remain the same in essence. Online will flatten emotion and interaction and will add a bit more stress, but once you master the fundamentals of speaking, the online playing field will level itself out.

I KINDLY ASK YOU TO...

... read this book with the goal to 'teach' and not just to 'learn'. When you read a book with the commitment to teach the insights to somebody else afterwards, you will gain more from it.

> ***"To master it, you must create an obligation to teach it."***

THE QUESTION THAT STARTED IT ALL

> *"Marnick, when we have a budget cut, why do you get budget? And when we have a hiring freeze, why do you get to hire people? What do you do in the boardroom that we aren't doing?"*

I was working as a digital manager for a huge multinational company when one of my former colleagues stopped me in the office hallway and asked me the above question. I didn't have an answer and had never really thought about it. Why did I experience so much success in the boardroom, while I was responsible for a part of marketing (social media) that was in its early days and got more scepticism and push back from seasoned marketers than anything else? For most executives, my job was a fad, but somehow, I managed to take them along with my ideas. I didn't give it much thought and quickly dismissed the question with a smile, "Just lucky, I guess." But the question kept lingering and in the following days I started looking more consciously at my internal presentations. I wasn't aware of it, but I had been shaped by the hobby I had picked up two years earlier, stand-up comedy.

I realised that I was using a lot of those stand-up comedy techniques in my daily work – techniques I had acquired in comedy workshops, MC (master of ceremony) masterclasses and by performing across Flanders from dodgy bars to cosy theatres. I was unaware that I had started using these comedy techniques in my professional work – not to make people laugh, but to harvest the power of one of the purest forms of storytelling. Hundreds of people, one person with a microphone looking the other way and claiming to be funny. A person literally changing the emotional and physical state of an audience by what he is saying. People laugh, clap, move, shake and enjoy the reward. The reward that comes in the form of dopamine (The molecule of I feel good, rewarded and I want more of it). Purely by what he says and how he says it, a comedian triggers the same effect in his audience's brain as it would if they took a line of cocaine. Or in the words of famous stand-up comedian Jimmy Carr:

> ***"A stand-up comedian is like a drug dealer. The only difference with a real drug dealer is that the audience already has the drugs on them."***

I started dissecting my presentations and performances. I wanted to know what exactly resonated so well with my corporate audience. To execute my 'develop people target' in my performance review, I decided to organise an internal training for my colleagues, sharing this speaking knowledge. The training filled up in minutes and I quickly planned a second and third one. It was a big success and apparently something a lot of people got value out of. I even got asked to duplicate this work internationally within the company. The impact was so great that at a certain point I was training people more on speaking and giving keynotes myself than doing my job as a digital manager.

I come from a family of entrepreneurs and had always wanted to start my own business, but I never knew what in. Now, it was crystal clear to me. If these professionals needed these speaking insights, others would too. I quit my job, my partner Natalie soon did the same and Stand Up Company (standupcompany.com) was officially born. Now, after that one question, we are more than a decade, two books and hundreds of clients and conferences into the greatest journey of our lives. This awesome adventure makes me think of that memorable quote from Jeff Bezos:

> ***"You don't choose your passion; your passion chooses you."***

A passion that serves one purpose:

> *Helping you break through corporate walls and have you stand up for your ideas, projects, and visions in your own genuine way. For you to find your voice, be seen, heard, appreciated and positively stand out in your life by the way you tell your stories. #standuptostandout*

This dedication to the speaking trade led me to discover that speaking, our ability to express ourselves by telling stories, goes to the core of who we are and want to become. There is so much more to speaking than meets the eye. It's not just about controlling nerves and finding the right words. It's about mastering the skill that makes us human, the power of telling stories to others, bringing across value, insight and emotion and to do it in such a way that these stories get retold by others for days, weeks, years to come.

Being able to stand up for what you believe in gives you power, attention and appreciation. It boosts your confidence, energy and eagerness to engage with others. As you will notice in the examples in this book, it affects all aspects of your life. My clients discover that they can do more than they imagined possible. They start walking more upright, start eating more healthily, dressing differently. Not that I have told them to – I'm not a personal trainer or a style guru – but when you are able to express yourself and people listen and take action on your ideas, it will trigger a whole new version of yourself. Still completely you – just an improved and more powerful version that was always there, but has now, through speaking, found a way to literally and figuratively express itself to the fullest.

I have seen a person tear up and shake when asked to introduce themselves in front of a group, only to give their first TV interviews confidently, after a few sessions. With an entrepreneurial couple who had been together for years, I had one of them express amazement at how the other performed during a business pitch: "OMG, I don't know you like this; I love it." I have had a seasoned leader experience the difference between being comfortable speaking in front of their team and genuinely inspiring them. I had the shyest engineer become one of the most highly rated speakers at a major technology conference after their first ever speech. Just a few examples of how teaching people to speak is worth every second of the time I have on this earth.

All my keynotes, coaching, and training on public speaking around the world presented me with thousands of questions from people who were not heard, understood or appreciated. After a while, I started seeing a pattern in these speaking challenges. The same questions kept coming up in every workshop. I gathered and simplified them. The result is this book: a collection of the 21 most frequently asked questions and their answers. I hope you have already browsed through the table of contents and said: "Yes, those are exactly the questions I have."

This book will grant you access to all the techniques you come across from interviewing top speakers, reading many books, or notching up a lot of speaking miles yourself. You are holding the most important insights nicely bundled together in your hands. Presented to you in logical order, but in such a way that you don't have to read them in that order. You can start with your prominent questions and cherry pick your way through the book. It is however advisable to read chapters 10 –15 in chronological order for maximum value.

It's now up to you to read them, to become aware of their use and impact. I guarantee they will work and make your next presentation so much more engaging and influential. The very reason they are the universal blueprint for the world's most successful speakers and the most complete answer to my former colleague's question.

Now, let me kick off this book with a question for you:

> *"How much dopamine are you triggering when you speak?"*

Are you just transferring a message, or literally changing the emotional and physical state of your audience, leaving them thinking, "I understand it, I feel it and I want more of it!" Whatever the answer, after reading and applying the insights from this book, you most definitely will. You will no longer think, "Fuck, I have to speak!", because you will know exactly what to do. Time for you to stand up for your ideas and stand out in life and business by the way you share them with the world. Enjoy the read, embrace the journey and welcome the applause.

MINDSET

BASIC PRINCIPLES & BELIEFS OF GREAT SPEAKERS

1

WHY SHOULD I LEARN TO SPEAK BETTER? I'M NOT IN SALES.

SHORT ANSWER:
"EVERYTHING IS SALES."

"Do you even know how smart I am in Spanish?

A quote from Modern Family actress Sofia Vergara, pointing out during an argument that English is not her native language. She needs to translate everything from Spanish to English in her head. This makes her less effective in heated conversations. This book is not about speaking in different languages, but the quote does capture the essence of this entire chapter: why it is of the utmost importance that each of us spends time and energy on learning and improving our speaking skills and taking away every possible barrier that stops our audience from understanding and embracing an idea.

We are fluent in our own business language (also referred to as nerd language), but fail to translate it into plain English for outsiders (e.g. board, IT, sales,...) due to our curse of knowledge. This makes us sound like a genius in our community, but we are perceived by others as difficult to work with, unclear or even unfit for the job due to an ineffective presentation. The world is full of people who are very good at what they do. People who work hard and are an expert in their trade. Technically they excel, but still run around frustrated:

> *Management doesn't see the added value of the project.*
> *We are already at meeting five for simple budget approval.*
> *Marketing doesn't understand how important it is that they clean up their data.*
> *Our product is the best, but we aren't getting any investment money.*
> ...

Change projects are in a rut, promotions are missed, budgets aren't approved, and knowledge is lost. All because these messages weren't properly presented. They weren't properly sold to the audience.

Not everybody is in sales as a function or department, but if you know that 85% of people's jobs revolves around communication (convincing, feedback, leading, inspiring,...) and we ignore this skill, we ignore a big part of what determines our professional success. Only 15% is our technical knowledge, our actual expertise. Your ticket to play. A strong statement for some, but a harsh reality for us all. Everything in this world depends on the success of its presentation. TV commercials, political speeches, movie trailers,...They are all designed to convince and inspire people to take action. The same goes for your projects, ideas, job applications. We are constantly selling. Even our love relationships are based on sales conversations, e.g. selling your idea for a ski trip to your partner who loves beach holidays.

"85% of your job is communication. 15% is technical skill."

I'm not saying everyone needs to share the same passion for speaking as me, but they should at least acknowledge the added value, no matter the activity they are in. Moving a solid block of a couple of tons with hand and rope will take thousands of people. Put a layer of ice under that block, lower the friction and you will only need a handful of people. Speaking skills are that layer of ice under the block of work we all try to move every single day. It makes our life easier and our impact greater. Billionaire investor Warren Buffett summarised it well when he said: "Learn how to speak and increase your professional value with 50%."

In case you are still a bit sceptical, being a good speaker is not about claiming the spotlight everywhere you go, – boosting your ego and selling people ideas that aren't backed by data, experience or research. There is a wide spectrum between stroking your ego, artificially inflating your image and really making a difference with your stories at the right moment for the audience and yourself. The main purpose is to make yourself and particularly your work visible. No matter how hard it is for some to hear, 'good and hard work is often invisible'. What is easily visible are mistakes. So, it is our responsibility to make speaking a vital part of our day to day lives. It is making your work stand out in such a way that people learn from it, because they understand it. They act after hearing it, because they felt inspired.

People who accept this and are good at it are seen, grab the attention and often get what they want. This doesn't mean that everybody who is good at speaking identifies as a Slick Rick, has watched Wolf of Wall Street a few too many times and is a clear extrovert. These are people who understand the significance of transferring ideas in the right way. Mastering this skill is not just meant for keynote speakers, comedians, politicians or sales professionals. It is a must for everybody, of all ages, in all lines of work and all stages of life.

It will take time and effort. A strong story will demand preparation and a solid performance with voice and body will take a lot of practice. Standing in front of people takes courage. But no matter how big the speaking mountain seems, it will always take less time and effort than having to go through meeting after meeting, struggling to take people along in your story. Getting the boardroom door slammed in your face time after time. Missing opportunity after opportunity because nobody sees that you are immensely gifted in your trade and they do not understand why you are of value to them – due to the absence of the right speaking skills = "Do you even know how smart I am in Spanish?"

The fact that you are reading this book tells me that you belong to the group that really wants to work on the development of this skill. If you started reading with the title of this chapter in the back of your mind, I hope you now realise you were right to pick up this copy. You just increased your chances for success in anything you will do in life or business. You do great, hard work and now it is up to you to show this to the world and to inspire people to follow your ideas.

> *A new client of mine was sent to me by his manager. He was an analyst, and his manager wanted him to improve his speaking skills, because he lacked conviction and influence in meetings with his stakeholders. His work was mostly being ignored. When he entered the first session, his face said it all: "This is mandatory. I don't want to be here." He barely looked me in the eye and had a very closed posture. The first sessions were spent purely on discussing this chapter – the relevance and use of this skill for, in this case, an analyst. "My job is analysing data and reporting it, that's it."*

He thought that taking the stage in meetings and bringing his conclusions across in a more enthusiastic and convincing way was dirty and manipulative, which was against his core values. "The work needs to speak for itself; I'm not in sales." This conviction held him back in his work and in his ability to develop this skill. Step by step we progressed from fierce discussion to meeting preparation, story structuring and voice/body work. With every small positive reaction from a colleague on his new way of presenting the data, the negative conviction was replaced by a positive one. The figurative applause started to have its effect.

Then came the big day when he was asked by the top management of the entire holding (200 people) to present his predictions for the next year and his personal advice. Of all the analysts, the fact that he was asked was a visibility win. It will probably not surprise you, since this story is in the book, that he completely rocked it. Afterwards the CEO of the holding came to him and shook his hand, saying: "I didn't know data could be this interesting." Another board member said, "I have never seen this side of you before. Who knew you could do this." Two weeks later, he was asked to a smaller board meeting of a member company to do a deep dive.

The next session, a new person walked in: big smile, shoulders back, glowing. He started the conversation with: "Marnick, now I understand what you meant with 'This will make your life so much easier. You will be seen, heard and will pluck the fruits.'" By the time I started writing this book, he was speaking at conferences and regularly sits at the podcast mic as a guest expert.

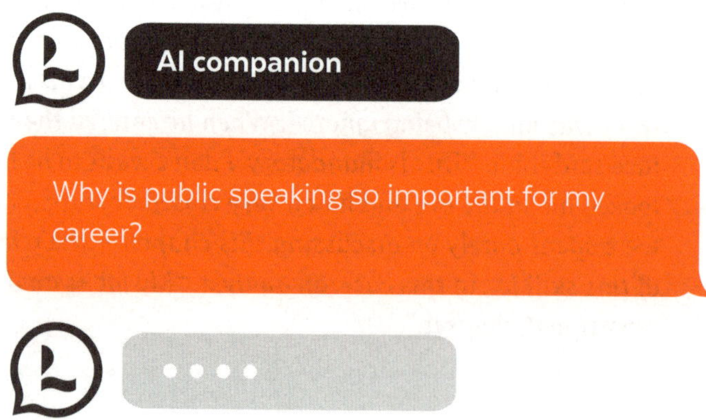

CORE INSIGHTS:

- Strong speaking skills aren't for boasting or manipulating. They exist to make your messages understandable and inspiring. They are the layer of ice under your block of work. They start from a positive intent.
- Influential presentations and strong speaking skills take time and effort to build. Having five meetings about the same decision because of a sloppy story takes even more time and effort.
- Everybody is in sales. 85% of your job consists of convincing people of your ideas.
- Great presentations make you and your work visible.
- You don't have to develop a passion for speaking but should understand its value. If not, you will never break through your own development wall and therefore your stories will not break through the corporate wall, or the wall of your audience.

2
IS IT SOMETHING YOU CAN LEARN OR IS IT JUST A GIFT SOME PEOPLE HAVE?

SHORT ANSWER:
"IT'S NOT A GIFT, IT'S A CHOICE."

I didn't grow up with musicality. Few people in my environment played an instrument. I didn't get further than playing 'cuckoo' on the recorder in my first year of high school. So, when I recently decided to sign up for piano lessons, I soon heard people saying: "You are too old to learn." "The theory alone is going to be a struggle." We are now two years on, and I'm reading scores, gave my first class concert in front of 150 people and play quite a few pieces. In all honesty, I didn't expect it myself. I'm amazed how quickly you can learn something if you really want to. With the right mindset, you can master a skill. The same goes for speaking. Your level of mastery will depend on your ambition, effort, experience and interest. As my piano teacher said, "Marnick, you might not become the next Elton John, but you will be able to play 'Candle in the wind'."

Once you master something, it is fun to get compliments about it. When I translate people's stories back to them or show them what their talk could become, they immediately tell me how impressive they find it. "Can't you do the presentation for me?" "Can you do it again, so I can record it?" Everybody loves compliments, but those compliments are often followed by, "Speaking is really a gift, something you are born with. It's a real talent to talk like this." I understand where this comes from. As kids, we all heard that you need a knack for languages or maths to really excel at them. To me it's not about being born with a talent, but about interest and exposure too. A friend of mine was applauded for his knack for maths, but people ignored the fact that both his parents were engineers. People see me as a speaking talent, but don't know that my grandfather was an incredible speaker. Another friend of mine was seen as a promising athlete, but no one considered the fact that her dad had been a successful soccer player.

It's a gift, something you are born with, is a limiting thought. You are saying to yourself that the chances you will master this skill are non-existent. You are giving the other person a compliment, while at the same time closing the door for yourself to ever receive a compliment for your speaking. Think back to my analyst friend from chapter one and how he went from being shy to being applauded. Or read about my grandfather and my piano adventure.

My grandfather, who this book is dedicated to, was in his nineties when he was still asking me about technology he read about in the newspapers. He pronounced things incorrectly, and didn't quite grasp the purpose of the innovation he talked about, but he didn't care. He stayed curious, and wasn't afraid to make a fool of himself and ask questions. He stepped out of his comfort zone and exposed himself to everything new at an age that most people don't get to or decide the new is no longer for them. It kept his brain sharp, and he could easily talk along with his grandchildren.

"To master something, you need to be willing to be bad at it for a long time," my piano teacher said. "You have to put in the 10.000 hours, or at least stick with it for about four years. After that you will notice a leap in progress." She was right. I felt like a retarded monkey when I was playing my first pieces. I cursed my hands, piano and brain many times, but I stuck with it and now I'm slowly getting the hang of it.

Or listen to the words of Professor William James of Harvard:

> ***"Most of us are only half awake and only use a small percentage of our resources (body, voice, brain). Most people live very comfortably within their own set limits."***

Speaking has always been something mythical. It appears to be something only for the happy few that are blessed with it. There are three reasons for that:

1. **TONE DEAF:** Our brain justifies most of what we say as 'well said'. This is the reason very few of us listen to and critically watch our own way of speaking. We all think we are rocking it, but our audience doesn't feel the same, and is too polite to tell us. We think we know what we are doing, but don't get any results, so it must be the audience that is not smart or driven enough to act. It can't be me.

2. **COMFORT ZONE:** We don't like stepping out of our comfort zone. We are hard wired that way to protect ourselves. Mastering a new skill means being bad at it for a while. "Oh, how I have cursed at my piano and stood in front of many silent stand-up comedy crowds." We don't like to fail, to be confronted with ourselves, to listen to our own voices or see our awkward movements. We avoid consciously analysing our own speaking behaviour. I'm fine.
   What I do now, I know and it feels like me. Even if deep down we know it doesn't work or could be better.

3. **PUBLIC HUMILIATION:** One of the biggest fears in the world is public humiliation: other people laughing at us or making us feel like the odd one out. Our ancestors needed to be accepted by the tribe to survive. Acceptance was king and it still is. How do you increase the chance of public humiliation? Right – stand in front of an audience.

Mix these three together and you have a recipe for not being good, not growing and, in general, completely avoiding speaking opportunities. What is hard or unknown is undesirable for some and changes into something mythical that only a few blessed by the speaking gods master. What do these three reasons have in common? They are all in your head.

Critically and consciously looking at yourself and your current speaking ability is a choice. It's a matter of courage. Once you start becoming more aware through this book and show that courage, the public humiliation will quickly be replaced by applause and that scary spot in front of people will become your new comfort zone. I often say, "The best seat in the house is always on stage."

No matter how big or small, online or offline that stage is. To master all the techniques in this book, not a single shred of talent is needed, only some will power, persistence and self-reflection. The only one who has a valid excuse is my cat. She will never self-reflect or question her actions in the name of growth. Cats don't have that ability, but luckily humans do.

In short, my answer to the question that titles this chapter "Can you learn how to speak even if you are starting from scratch?" is "Yes, you can." You just have to want it, show interest (you are already reading this book, well done) and expose yourself to it. Who knows, you might just become the next Barack Obama or Brené Brown of speech and I will become the next Elton John of piano.

"Expressing yourself in a powerful way is not a gift; it's a choice."

Even if you are an introvert? Yes, I'm a big introvert myself. Ask my wife; she is the extrovert in the family. Being an introvert has nothing to do with whether you are a good speaker or not. Most successful comedians, actors and rock stars are introverts. Sometimes hard to believe when you see them rocking a stage or owning a meeting room. Expressing yourself in a powerful way in front of an audience is about mindset and skill. Being an introvert or extrovert is linked to energy management, to knowing when your batteries charge and deplete. Simon Sinek describes it as follows:

"An introvert starts the day with five coins and loses a coin with every interaction. An extrovert starts the day with no coins and gains a coin with every interaction."

Being introverted is about energy management. "But why then do introverts appear to struggle more with public speaking than extroverts?" Exposure. When you get your energy from being silent and closed off, you don't get much social practice. Extroverts don't necessarily know what they are doing, but they seek social connections, so they grant themselves that exposure. It becomes their comfort zone. Just being shy is about lack of self-confidence and skill. Shyness is not a personality. Most people – and of course there are exceptions – are a mix of all these traits and they even vary depending on the context. Strong traits to keep, weaker points to develop.

The question is: "Is being too extroverted, introverted, shy,... going to limit you in the development of your speaking skills?" Only you can decide. Will you use it as an excuse or a push forward? Get to know yourself and determine what you need, but don't let any of it be a blockade to your personal growth. I could quote entire scientific research reports to prove everything I have shared so far in this chapter, but you chose to pick up and start reading this book and are still at it. You made your choice and need no further persuasion. Kudos! For me the most important reasons that I wholeheartedly believe that everybody can master the art of speaking, are:

- **GROWTH** - I have seen so many street pigeons starting to sing and fly like nightingales in the last decade.
- **BLUEPRINT** - All the techniques, structures, insights in this book are not things that I invented. They are the universal blueprint that is being used by every great speaker in the world. From early days of theatre and politics to current times.
- **PRESENT** - Without being aware of it, you are already using some parts of this book at this very moment. Imagine what you could do once you are aware.

You wouldn't be good at your job if you hadn't mastered some speaking skills. You wouldn't have been able to get the job in the first place if you had bombed your job interview. You wouldn't be running your own company if you hadn't succeeded in securing investments, clients and personnel. You wouldn't have any friends or a partner willing to listen to your latest game victory, if you weren't able to share it with enthusiasm. Some are already better at it than others due to upbringing, education or training (= exposure), but we all have the fundamentals in us. Humans are social animals, no matter how introverted or shy some might be. We thrive on connection and acceptance, and you can only acquire this by communicating and therefore speaking, sharing your ideas and experiences with others. According to various studies, social connection is one of the biggest keys to a long and healthy life. If it has that power, imagine what mastering this skill will do for your career.

I'm sure that, just like many of my clients, when reading the following chapters, you will say: "Oh, I'm already doing that." "I have seen or heard that before." Chances are you have and that you are already applying many of the techniques from this book. But you weren't aware of it, until now. You know very well what presentations you like but can't quite pinpoint the exact elements that make it so captivating. Awareness is step one in learning any new skill. Noticing in yourself and in others what works and doesn't work, and then starting enhancing, stopping or optimising.

If many of the techniques from this book are already in your speaking kit, whether deeply buried or already surfacing, why then would it be such a stretch to master this skill? Let's clear the fog over your previous top performances during job interviews, strategy meetings or conferences and reveal why you owned those stages. Let's analyse those techniques and make them a conscious part of your skill set. Just as my instructor said when I nervously stepped onto a motorcycle for the first time, "Marnick, just do everything exactly as I tell you to and practise between sessions and you will pass your exam on the first try and will be cruising the sunny streets in no time." Two months later, I got my licence and was riding my dream Harley Davidson out of the dealership. The same goes for speaking.

It is not a gift, it's a choice. A choice you made by picking up this book and hopefully many others like this, including coaching, training and practice. You might not have been exposed to it during your childhood, but start surrounding yourself with people who have mastered this skill. Observe, learn, try and you will catch up in no time if you really want to.

EXERCISE

Film yourself telling a two-minute story.

If you are now thinking: "Forget it, I don't like to speak in front of a camera. I even get nervous during video calls with colleagues. I don't like watching myself and hearing my voice. I will not watch it or I will delete these videos immediately. Or I'm not going to do the exercise, because the author will never find out."

Then this is a perfectly normal reaction, but also a moment to step out of your comfort zone and show that courage we talked about. You are reading this book to learn. Film yourself telling a two-minute story. It doesn't matter what it is about. Just imagine somebody asking you how your weekend went, what you like about your favourite hobby, a new project at work, a concert you are excited about,... Don't overthink the content, just choose a topic and go. I recommend that you stand while doing this.

After you have recorded yourself, do something active, like jumping around, going for a run, dancing to your favourite song, playing rock paper scissors with your partner, doing some squats and push-ups,... As long as you are having fun and you are really moving around. Now, once you have done something active, take your phone out and start filming yourself again. You can tell the same two-minute story or come up with a new one. It doesn't matter. Tell the story standing up.

Now re-watch both videos and let me know how it went in chapter 8 on page 91. Here I will explain the purpose of this small exercise and why you are already a good speaker. And I will build further on the concept with some fundamental techniques. If you want to get the most out of this exercise, don't just film yourself but do it with a partner. Let this person film you, dance around with you and film you again. As I said in this chapter, it's hard for us to look at ourselves and make an objective observation, so the video comparison together with the feedback from an observer will amplify the outcome of this exercise.

AI companion

What are the reasons for people not being good at public speaking?

••••

CORE INSIGHTS:

- Speaking is not a gift, it's a choice. A skill you can learn. Expose yourself to it.
- Becoming good at speaking has nothing to do with being introverted or extroverted, or shy.
- You are already applying many techniques from this book; you are just not aware of it.
- Surround yourself with people who have mastered the skill you are trying to learn. Observe, and foremost, try.
- How good you become at speaking will be determined by your own ambition, your persistence and courage to be uncomfortable for a while.

3
HOW CAN I TELL STORIES WHEN EVERYTHING IN MY COMPANY HAS TO BE TO THE POINT?

SHORT ANSWER:
"TELL A STORY. IT WILL BE MORE TO THE POINT THAN 99% OF THE PRESENTATIONS IN YOUR COMPANY."

For me, speaking is the collective term for everything that has to do with conveying a message in an engaging and inspiring way. This goes from content, voice, body, and visualisation to interaction and energy. The content is a part of this whole that eventually wins the hearts and minds of the audience. This content is built in a certain way, so it becomes a story, and when that story is told, you are 'storytelling'. Storytelling is, for me personally, about the way content is shaped, structured, built up to certain points and glued together. Telling stories is often seen in business environments as 'beating around the bush', 'making messages longer than necessary' 'a lack of ability to get to the point'.

A good story can be 60 seconds long, but could just as well be 60 minutes. Transferring a message is sharing information with your audience and hoping it will land. Storytelling is the art of shaping that message in such a way that it sticks, triggers emotion and takes your audience by the hand so that they can't do anything but agree with what you are saying or act positively upon it. Storytelling is not making messages longer than necessary or telling anecdotes about your last holiday or project that nobody really cares about.

> **"A message hopes for action. A story leads to action."**

Why do I get this question a lot in training? Why does it seem as if am I purely discussing a definition? Because people are being discouraged to invest time and money in learning how to build stories due to a misperception. They are too afraid to try anything besides what they have been doing so far or what seems to be expected by their environment. Fear of standing out, being beaten with the 'keep-it-short stick' or even losing their job for doing things differently.

I am not a fan myself of making messages longer than necessary. The shorter, the simpler, the better. This is the reason this book isn't very long; it could easily have been 500 pages without significantly amplifying the value for you. But short and simple doesn't equal boring and dry. Millions of messages and pieces of information are presented every day, but in most cases, they are nothing more than that. Pieces of information. Therefore I feel little connection to my content; there isn't a nice flow, and it completely leaves it up to the audience to draw the right conclusions and interpret the content, as you as a speaker, hope they will. The reason so many conference talks fall flat. So many meetings that really matter, end with discussion, tough questions, no decisions or conversations completely beside the point. Signs that you lost control over the narrative.

Information that is moulded into a story sticks together, flows in a logical order, builds up, surprises at certain points, inspires and literally takes the audience by the emotional hand and leads them to your prepared goal, without the audience realising they are being led. As they say in stand-up comedy:

> ***"You lead, the audience follows. They always need to have the feeling that they need to catch up to you. Not the other way around, or you will lose the room."***

That is storytelling, that is telling stories versus just sharing information. Like a good joke that triggers laughter in seconds, a good story can secure approval, applause or a hire in minutes. In chapter 13, we discuss in depth how you can build these stories yourself. An interesting side effect of storytelling is that your audience loses track of time. I have often started meetings where they told me I had only ten minutes. Only to hear at the end that they will move the next meeting or reschedule a longer meeting immediately. When people are absorbed by a good story, they want to hear more; they forget about time. Just a like a great three-hour movie will be over before you know it. My workshops are always eight hours long, but every survey features the response, "I thought eight hours was going to be long, but the day was over in a heartbeat." Again, the goal is not to talk for a long time if it doesn't add value or fit the context. The goal is to make people want to listen to you for the time that you are talking and leave them with the feeling, "I want more!" The famous elevator pitch is a great example of this. You only have one minute to convince a person, go! My reflex is to tell my story in such a way that this person asks to step out of the elevator, because he wants to know more. If only one minute is what I have and no more, no problem; you will discover in chapter 13 that a one-minute story is more to the point than what people think to the point is.

If you are reading this book in chronological order, I will share the following with you now, to ease the anticipation of the last-mentioned chapter.

Example

A client of mine got exactly 60 seconds to tell his story on the big stage at one of the most prestigious logistic conferences in Europe. One minute is a very limited amount of time. His goal: convince as many decision makers in the room to visit his fair stand after the pitch. He presented me with three whiteboards, dozens of pages of information about his clients and products. All that information needed to be filtered, reduced and shaped into a compelling one-minute story that triggered action. Three sessions later, he formed the story below and brought it to the conference. It was a huge success and became one of the pitches that created momentum for the company and kickstarted a beautiful growth journey.

You have 60 seconds, go!

(Walks on stage after introduction by the conference host)

When I talk to logistics professionals, I notice two main concerns:

1. *They are losing control over safety, which worries them a lot.*
2. *They have too many misplaced pallets, which generates extra cost.*

Despite using all the current modern technology of scanning & RFID, they just leave too much room for error.

Our answer is simple.
We put a 3D model, a digital twin, of your entire warehouse in this small device.

(holds up device)

and install it together with this tiny camera on your vehicles.

Resulting in:

(shows slide with live environment of all moving parts in a warehouse being tracked)

You know the exact location of every vehicle, every pallet, every movement, 24/7, without scanning, without RFID. At the same time, the machines talk to each other, so they can take control when needed, which reduces your safety issues to close to zero.

Do you want to know how we can do this for you?

Come and see us at our booth and with our ROI-calculator you will instantly discover how much time, money and worry you will save in your own operations.

Thank you!

What makes this short pitch so strong:

- **IT'S SIMPLE.** Even if you are not in logistics, you understand what this product does. No fancy words or technical terms. The audience is active in the sector, but in such a short amount of time they have very little time to process, so it must be quick to grasp.

- **IT'S A STORY, NOT A FAIRY TALE.** This story has a clear structure (see chapter 12). It doesn't waste time on details, fluffy descriptions or unnecessary explanations. It takes the listener by the hand from A to B to C without distractions.

- **IT'S RECOGNISABLE** (see chapter 10). The two most important challenges in the sector are loss of pallets and too many safety incidents. They are all dealing with these issues and have tried many things, and invested a lot of money in the latest technology, but the numbers are still too high concerning loss and accidents. This is the moment in the story the audience starts nodding and decides, "This is a message for me."

- **THERE ARE ELEMENTS OF CONTRAST AND SURPRISE** (see chapter 14). They just heard the speaker talk about their own world. A world where things aren't yet optimal despite their efforts in the past. Suddenly a man stands in front of them on stage and claims to put their entire warehouse, forklifts and pallets into one small device (surprise 1). Then he shows them a live tracking blueprint of a warehouse with all the moving parts (surprise 2) due to this little device. This is the moment the audience literally thinks, "Wow, that is impressive, I need this product."

- **EMPHASISING VALUES** (see chapter 11). The previous points lead us to the values that are offered, and that the speaker knows the audience craves. 24/7 control, no more time-consuming scanning, human error at almost zero. He doesn't literally mention the extra value, but what becomes clear when he shows the device is that the installation is plug and play versus what they currently have installed in their warehouses.

- **SPECIFIC CALL TO ACTION.** The pitch ends with the 'goal' of the speaker. The goal of getting these decision makers to the stand to start the conversation, because he only had 60 seconds. But instead of just saying, "If you want to know more, visit our stand." He offers them a clear incentive to act, "Calculate your ROI on the spot with our calculator," knowing very well that this ROI number is the big internal value this audience needs to get approval for the purchase. So, people will not just learn more about the product, get a deep dive demo, but immediately know what it will mean in financial benefit.

In case you now have the feeling that this pitch isn't that spectacular despite its success, you are right. Pages full of information about the product, clients, research, nerd-language,... All downsized to these measly 60 seconds. When you hear it, the simplicity stand outs. That is the power of a good story. When the audience thinks, "I could tell that story, that doesn't seem so hard." (the re-tell value of a story) Then you have yourself a good story. Look up the famous shark tank elevator pitch for

Quikflip Apparel that turned a backpack into a hoodie and vice versa. It's short, almost childlike in its simplicity and kept the investors asking for more. Years after the initial pitch, this video is still being shared as best practice and is frequently re-told in workshops and at conferences.

That is how some stories in our world have survived for centuries. The simple ones always last. People who really master their trade, make others think "this looks and sounds easy". What you are witnessing is mastery. Hours of preparation, killing darlings, linking, practising,...coming together in that one moment. When I watch Novak Djokovic play tennis, I believe I can play like him. I forget that he makes a forehand look so easy and effective due to years of practice and experience. Be honest with yourself and ask yourself if you could give a solid 60 second story about your business right here on the spot. Most clients, when asked to do this in a session, start serving me a word salad and one minute quickly becomes five. A whole lot of words, but zero points are made. Making something sound and look easy is hard, if you don't master the techniques to do it. The purpose of this book is to simplify this practice for you, and fast forward your process towards speaking mastery.

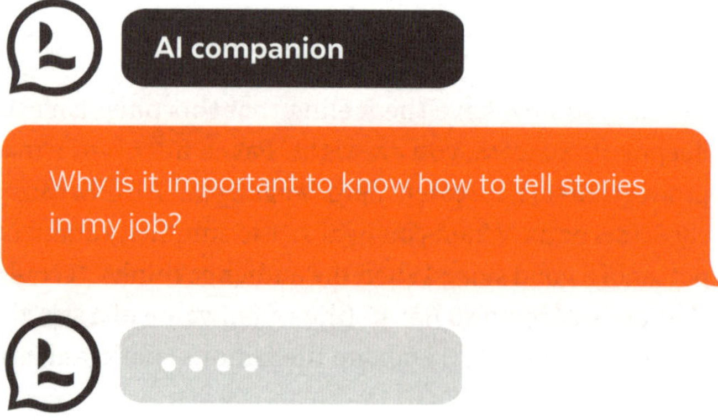

CORE INSIGHTS:

- Speaking is the all-encompassing label for all elements that contribute to bringing a story across with impact.
- Storytelling is the art of structuring and shaping your content.
- A great story can be 60 seconds or hours long.
- A message hopes for action. A story leads to action.
- Adding an anecdote to a presentation doesn't turn it into a story.
- The easier a story can be re-told by your audience, the better.

PERFORMANCE
OWNING YOUR STAGE LIKE A PROFESSIONAL

4
HOW CAN I BECOME LESS NERVOUS?

SHORT ANSWER:
"DO IT A LOT."

Being nervous in front of a group is perfectly normal. No matter whether this is three people or three thousand. Our reptile brain equates it with being in a vulnerable position. All eyes on you and if this was a pack of lions back in the day, that would not be a great situation to be in. We are herd animals; we like to be protected by the group. Standing out from the herd means being unprotected and visible. Visible to predators, but also to the group. As previously discussed, we crave acceptance and therefore shy away from standing out, being different. Public humiliation is one of the biggest fears in the world and speaking to an audience only increases the chances of that humiliation. Combine all the above, and no wonder people claim the fear of speaking is worse than the fear of death. I can assure you, having seen people who looked death in the eyes and lost, public speaking doesn't even come close to that experience. Speaking…"My sweet boy, there are worse things in life," my grandmother would say. Apply what you learn in this book and after two or three talks, you will even start to find it one of the most fun things to do.

> ***"You will get addicted to the applause."***

Still, I don't want to downsize the stress. Nerves will be present, even with experienced speakers like me. The difference lies in where these nerves are coming from. Is your stress coming from your R-complex (reptile brain, fight/flight, instinct), telling you this is not a good idea, triggering the emotion of fear in your limbic system and shutting down your neocortex? This means no thoughts will come and blackout, stuttering or panic will follow. Or are the nerves from wanting to perform, do good and give the audience a great experience – a state where the R-complex is silent, because it doesn't see the upcoming situation as threatening? You feel excitement, anticipation, and your neocortex is ready to take over and have you speak with impact. For most rookie speakers, nerves are linked to the first state (primal state), due to lack of experience, training and belief in oneself. The goal is to practise, learn, get comfortable with body, voice and audience and move to the second state (performance state).

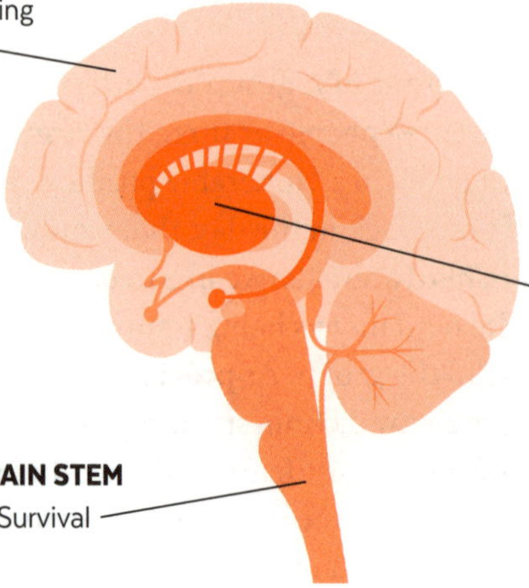

After 15 years on stage, I'm still nervous for meetings, keynotes or trainings, but I'm always in a performance state and my training and experience take over the moment I start talking or jump on stage. I experience the above in other aspects of life and the principle stays the same.

> *I had never fought before but decided to challenge myself to dive into the world of violence and self-defence. In the first session, my mentor immediately put me in a threatening position that I could encounter on the street. My reaction? I froze up completely, even though I knew that this was role play and there was no real threat. I had always thought that I would be Rambo in these situations, but I became a statue. My mentor said, "This is your R-complex taking over. You feel fear and the instinct to freeze or run. You are not used to this type of situation. Your neocortex has completely shut down. There is just instinct and emotion." In the next sessions he confronted me with more and more aggression and showed me how to react (= a skill, just like speaking). After session five, I noticed that I was still nervous for the session – he remained an intimidating man – but those nerves were no longer the same. They felt more like excitement – getting ready to perform – and a bit of confidence started seeping through. I had seen this situation before (experience + recognition); I had the techniques (skills) to fight instead of freeze or flight. It grew with every training. I'm not John Rambo yet, but I am no longer a victim of my instinct.*

Moving from state one to state two (primal state to performance state) takes some time, so what can you do with the excess of reptile stress? How can you keep it under control and to an acceptable level in your journey towards a performance state? The following 12 tricks are a list of techniques that work 100% for everybody, in any situation. Even world-famous performers use them from time to time for situations where they are stepping out of the speaking comfort zone once again. Let these tricks have a calming and uplifting effect on you, so you can work your way to that performance state.

"But isn't stepping out of the comfort zone a good thing and confronting yourself with pressure a way to grow?" Yes, it is, but there is no point in piling up so much pressure that you become averse to speaking and quit before you get to experience the fun in it. To find balance and enjoyment, these 12 tips will help.

1. SHAKE IT OFF

A singer never sings her first notes on stage. An athlete doesn't warm up his muscles during the game. All professionals get themselves in a performance state before they run, sing, speak. Speaking, winning the hearts and minds of people on stage or in a meeting room, is peak performance and therefore requires you to act like an athlete. What do they do? They get themselves in the zone and so should you. I'm not saying you should take ice baths just before a meeting, but I am saying you should build in a moment where you consciously connect with your current state. Where are you at mentally, emotionally and physically? In a good place, nice, amplify it. In a bad place, get yourself out of it. Create a routine for yourself – a routine in which you prime yourself positively for performance. By making it 'a routine', it will turn into an anchor for future presentations.

You spend a lot of time in preparing your content, in practising your presentation at home, so put the same effort into getting your mind, body and heart in the right state before you start talking.

- Move around, pace, jump, swing your arms
- Go outside, breathe fresh air
- Play your favourite song that gets you going
- Pull your shoulders back, make yourself big
- Do breathing exercises
- Warm up your voice
- Talk to people from the audience upfront or colleagues backstage

Whatever you do, don't sit somewhere curled up on a chair, reading through your speaker notes (if you still have them, read chapter 6) or altering your slide deck. Don't hide somewhere in a corner, being silent until you have to speak, eating dry cookies or drinking coffee (dries out your mouth),... Keep yourself moving, pump dopamine, serotonin, adrenaline and a healthy portion of cortisol in your body. Make yourself big, warm up that voice and be present in the room instead of losing yourself completely to your internal fears. Video call, small meeting or big stage: in each case you need to perform, speak, energise, so make sure your entire body knows that is what is expected, and get in that zone beforehand.

I will be on location one hour before it is go time. I acquaint myself with the room and talk to the people who booked me, the technical crew if present and some people who are already there. I want to know I can connect with people. I don't want to have my first interactions in front of the group. I will keep moving, pacing, drink water and consciously breathe. I'll find some solitude just before showtime and focus on my first lines. I do this for workshops and big keynotes. You can also do this at work, for meetings and video calls. Make this a priority; see this as an important part of your preparation and foremost, feel the paralysing nerves changing to drive, excitement and adrenaline. More on energy management in chapter 8.

2. BE ON TIME

Arriving on time is a seriously underestimated technique for strong performances. Being on time isn't only respectful and doesn't only have the obvious advantages, like not having to worry about traffic, a delayed train or technical hiccups before a call. It gives you the room to become one with your speaking environment. It offers you the time to be alone in the space where you tell your story – a meeting, stage, online call, studio – and get the chance to feel the room, test tech and check or remove all elements that could interfere with your talk.

Use this time to stand in the empty meeting room, on the big stage, in front of the camera. Experience what it will feel like when it is go time. Remove the initial shock of the camera, your voice sounding through the speakers, the big room, the bright lights,... You will downsize your nerves tremendously. Also take a moment to sit in the seat of the audience, get a feel for their perspective. How will they experience your talk? At bigger conferences I see people arrive too late or just in time, stressed, full of excuses, with their speaker notes in hand or flipping slides on a laptop. Just as with an exam in your student years, your brain will no longer absorb any content. The time of content preparation is over. The time for energy management and grounding on stage or in the room has arrived.

Being on time will take away the stress of rushing that you don't want to add to your already nervous state. It gives you the opportunity to check, remove, experience, feel literally everything upfront. That feeling of control, recognition, comfort will reduce your nerves and inject confidence. You will forget to be lost in your head and signal your body that you are focused on the task at hand and not on what you might forget to say, or what people might think of you. It will help you and will come across as very professional to your audience, client or event booker. Do this for every speaking opportunity you have, big, small, online or offline. You don't have the time, you are too busy? A couple of minutes less doom scrolling on your phone and you just found that time.

I arrive at any location for a training, keynote, or coaching, at least one hour in advance. Most of the time I arrive before my client or the event booker are even in the building. This gives me time to socialise with the tech crew or remodel the training room to how I want it. By the time my contact or audience arrive, I will be relaxing and going through my routine. I will then get questions like:

"Do you want to test the microphones?" Already done, tech crew is fully briefed.
"Do you need markers or some materials?" Got them already, receptionist helped me out.
"You need help with setting up the room?" All set up, tables moved, chairs placed in a half circle.
"When do you want lunch for the group?" Already agreed with the catering that this will be around 12:15; they were just here for coffee and breakfast.

Response of my contact: "Oh, nice, then we just need an audience and we are good to go. Convenient, then I still have some time to do some other work. Great, see you in a bit." = Contact can relax and feel confident, I feel relaxed and in control, tech crew (if present) doesn't feel stressed. Your credibility and professionalism go up, your nerves go down.

The same goes for online sessions where I have to present or train: one hour before people log in, the virtual room is up and chat, screen share, lighting in my office... have been tested. Anything that can cause unnecessary stress needs to be eliminated. And you can do that, if you are on time.

3. ENJOY THE MOMENT

You have a routine, arrived on time, the tech works, and you are fully accustomed to the on- or offline room. You are still nervous, but it is time to start. Find peace in realising that most people are happy you will speak and not them. In general people want to see you succeed, because a great presentation means you didn't waste their time. They learned something or got some inspiration. People will forgive your nerves – certainly when they know you aren't yet that experienced. Take your time, enjoy the moment and appreciate the fact you are asked and allowed to speak and people are there to listen. It is a privilege. Accept the applause you will get for just walking on stage (figurative applause in meetings).

At events you will even have a host who will introduce you, break the ice and warm up the crowd for you (for how to do this yourself as a host, check chapter 20). You also don't have to start speaking immediately; silence can add to the anticipation of the audience. Take a few seconds, even if they feel like minutes to a nervous speaker. Get used to the audience, the room and check your breathing. The audience is ready when you are ready. (Note that I said seconds; longer will feel awkward for everybody, so then the audience is of course more than ready, and I recommend saying something.) Have fun!

4. FOCUS ON THE BEGINNING

"I hope I don't forget anything," is a sentence that I frequently hear when a nervous speaker is about to present. You will forget things, but with the right preparation it won't be the most important points. Your audience doesn't know what you are going to say, so they also don't know what they aren't hearing. Don't break your head over it; it will only increase your nerves and downsize your confidence.

Let's assume you did proper preparation, then instead of focusing on the big chunk of content that will be your presentation, focus purely on the beginning. What is the first thing you are going to say or do at the start of your presentation? Imagine yourself landing that start. This creates space in your head, because no matter how nervous you are, you will manage to remember those first sentences. This new peace of mind will open the door for the rest of your preparation to kick in. Your excess nerves will leave your body the moment you make that start and receive some positive reactions from the audience. The audience uses your start to rate the experience they are expecting to get and the ending to shape their memory of that experience. Focus on your beginning and, before you know it, you will be at your mic drop.

5. BEFORE WE START

An extension of the previous point is the 'before we start...'- technique. Many professional performers use this in their talk. Saying 'before we start' at the beginning gives the audience the feeling that the presentation hasn't really started yet and some unprepared, incoherent improvisation will follow. As if the speaker is saying, "I'm first going to casually talk to you and then I'm officially going to begin." The audience will therefore look at the content less critically and grant the speaker a couple of minutes to freestyle.

For you as a speaker, this means taking some of the pressure off and getting a free hall pass simply by saying, "before we start". You know the audience will give you a couple of minutes, so it won't matter if I make a mistake or lose my train of thought. The audience is thinking, "he said we haven't even started yet", so I can relax and don't have to listen too critically. This idea will calm you down. In reality, you are going to start bringing your prepared content from the first second and everything after the "before we start" is officially part of your presentation. You prepared it. The only thing this magical sentence does is remove the pressure from speaker and audience. Pay close attention to the next conferences or comedy shows you will attend. This technique is wide spread amongst professionals. Guilty as charged, but with good reason: it works.

6. NAME THE ELEPHANT IN THE ROOM

Those are some tough cookies, these nerves of yours. Despite everything you are still anxious and short of breath. Remember that the audience wants to see you succeed and is more forgiving than most people think. Use that insight to apply the following when a meltdown seems unavoidable. Just name the elephant in the room. The elephant technique will be mentioned multiple times throughout this book, because things that are festering in people's minds become less severe when they are laid out on the table. Simply start mentioning to the audience what is happening:

> *"This is my first time speaking in front of a group. I'm very nervous."*
> *"There are so many of you, I'm a little overwhelmed."*
> *"I'm looking for the point I was going to make. Grant me a second."*
> *"Are you also warm or is it just because I am nervous?"*

In my many years of experience, most people who have the courage to mention what is flaring up inside them get applause, support from colleagues or other audience members and an understanding energy. Of course, immediately afterwards you need to pick yourself up and continue; people don't have an endless amount of patience. In case you are still in meltdown and can't continue, then we need to look at your preparation and other techniques, because then there is more causing these paralysing nerves than just a lack of experience.

> *A client of mine was a couple of months pregnant and her shortness of breath didn't help her existing speaking anxiety. She asked me what she could do if it became too hard for her to speak fluently, which would make her even more nervous. I said, "Just mention it." People will notice, but if you mention that you are pregnant, a bit short of breath and nervous, they will understand. Later she told me that her presentation went super smoothly. She decided to mention it at the beginning of her talk and people were appreciative and understanding. She felt respected because she had stood in front of the group – despite the inconvenience linked to her pregnancy and her speaking inexperience – while others would have passed up the opportunity.*

I'm not a fan of starting presentations with excuses, but there is a difference between mentioning you are nervous because it's your first time or you are short of breath due to illness or pregnancy versus your clicker not working because you didn't test it, you are out of breath because you arrived too late, or you forgot to change your first slide due to the busyness of your agenda,... Those are excuses you need to avoid by taking ownership. In this point we are talking about mentioning things the audience will understand.

This also means not minimising yourself and your content. People who are inexperienced or overly nervous tend to downsize themselves and their expertise. You are nervous, yes, you are a first-time speaker, okay, but that doesn't mean you need to make yourself smaller. Believe in yourself and the audience will too, despite your nerves. Be convinced that your content is the best content ever presented, and the audience will be convinced too. What I do recommend that you downsize is the distance.

7. DOWNSIZE THE DISTANCE

Small meeting room, video call or big conference hall – the following principle stays the same in any context. The less figurative and literal distance there is between you and the audience, the better. The smaller the distance, the less the nerves. It will make building a connection between you and the audience easier, because there is less distance to bridge when you are asked a question. This is the reason so many workshops are given with the chairs positioned in a half circle. Downsizing the distance means literally removing unnecessary tables and other physical barriers in the room, which you can do when you arrive on time. It's putting on camera and chat functions in a video call (if you have trouble getting people to do this, see chapter 19). It means leaning and stepping towards the audience on a big stage, or standing up and walking around in a smaller meeting room. "I can do this in a small meeting?" Yes, you can. You are the speaker, you control the room and the experience.

Downsizing the figurative distance is asking the audience a question, engaging in simple interactions with the people in front of you, small talk before a webinar or easy interaction in the chat. Limit the space between you and the audience as much as possible. You are nervous and you will feel much better when that scary monster, the audience, suddenly becomes a friendly bunch of people listening to stories around a campfire. You can do this with two people in front of you or 5.000. Same principle. Also, the audience may be just as nervous as you if they need to interact. Make sure they can do this in a comfortable way.

If we combine this insight with point 4 from this 12-point list, you have an effective combo. Focus on the beginning of your talk and make it a very easy interaction with the audience. Preferably with added value for your story (see chapter 14). A simple question, greeting, riddle,...that can't go wrong. An interaction you know you will be able to remember, no matter how much pressure you feel. Lower the physical distance between you and the audience and from the moment the audience reacts, your nerves will leave your body like hot chocolate from a freshly made moelleux. I guarantee it.

In my opinion, this is one of the most fool-proof ways to becoming less nervous once you are on stage.

8. TALK TO YOUR ALLIES

Once you have decreased the distance between you and your audience and you have gained enough confidence to keep your eyes open while speaking, you will notice that there are friendly faces in the audience. You can call them your 'allies'. At work presentations, these allies will most likely be colleagues, team members or a supporting manager. If you are speaking to an unfamiliar audience, then speaking to people up front during your warmup routine or having an easy interaction with the audience at the start of your talk will create those allies.

There are allies in every audience – people you know or are excited and want to participate and see you rock. When you are nervous, just talk to them as much as possible. In a small setting, you will catch their eye every couple of seconds and see them nodding or smiling. In a bigger setting, they will be friendly anchor points for you to look at. If they are spread out across the room, you can present to them, and the rest of the audience will get the feeling you are talking to everybody. Allies boost confidence, make a large audience small and support you with a smile, nod, reaction or sparkly eyes. When you are really a rookie speaker, you can ask colleagues or friends to sit strategically in a certain audience for your first presentations. This might seem a bit artificial, but why not do it if it helps to deliver a better performance? We talked about grounding in the room, checking the tech, removing obstacles; why not give yourself an extra confidence boost by placing some allies in the audience?

In training or smaller meetings, I use the people I talked to when everybody was arriving as my allies the moment the session starts. Or I use my client contacts if they are also present. Then perhaps I will link to the little conversation we had when relevant, or just use them for my first interactions. At bigger events, I use the people I talked to during my warm-up routine. If that isn't possible, I talk to the people who speak to me with their eyes or stand out in some way. Or I ask a simple question at the very start of my talk and work further with those who reacted most enthusiastically.

9. BUILD IN 'STOPS'

Embrace the silence. All those eyes staring at you, waiting for you to say something smart. You will want to fill up that silence, because as long as you hear the sound of your voice, you will probably be okay, and nobody will notice that you are nervous. Or at least that is what your mind tells itself. When you are very nervous, you are in your emotion and easily lose yourself in a word cloud, dry mouth and shortness of breath. You get caught up in your own spaghetti of content and no longer see a way out and continue to speed up. The more insecure you are, the more repetition, the more filler words (see next chapter) will arise, and any form of silence will be banned. While silence is exactly what you and your audience need.

> ***"To speak with impact, you need to learn how to be silent."***

People who are nervous either close up or start rambling. In the first case, focus on your beginning. If you are 'getting ready to ramble', those first sentences can come out too fast and once that rambling train has left the station, it might not stop. If you are likely to talk too fast, build in 'stops' for that train: prepared moments where you know you have to come to a halt for a few seconds, for example, a video during which the audience is distracted, you can breathe and drink. (And take that drink break, don't rush it. Take your time to take a good sip. The silence will feel awkward, but the audience won't mind or notice. Better a good sip than a smacking sound in the microphone from a nervous dehydrated mouth.) A question the audience needs to think about, a riddle on a slide,... – obligatory stops that give you a few seconds to break the rambling and grant yourself a second slower start.

If you haven't prepared these stops, you can create them on the spot by using stock sentences. Let's say you are losing yourself in a lengthy anecdote or straying away from your actual point, then at any given moment you can say: "The point I want to make is..." "What I'm actually saying is..." "What it all comes down to is..." and then follow these points up with your crystal clear point or fact. These stock lines will help you break through the ramble and force you to come to a stop. Even if you are completely lost, these sentences will allow you to get a hold of yourself, and make a complete U-turn back to your actual point. The audience easily forgets, and they will be grateful you just did this. For more on making solid points without these stock lines, see chapter 13.

If the prepared stops and stock lines don't do it for you, try a trick I once heard from a talented voice and speaker coach, Stefanie Van Moen: put a cork in your mouth. Practise your presentation in front of the mirror with a cork in your mouth. The goal is to practise articulating properly. Something you no longer do when rambling. The more articulation, the more slowly you are going to talk. This also prevents over-breathing while speaking – filling your lungs with too much air – which causes words to fly out too fast, like a balloon you accidentally let go of while blowing it up. Breathing is key to controlling nerves, but too much air is also not advisable.

10. IT'S NOT ABOUT YOU

This realisation might seem a bit abstract, but it is probably one of the most important points to remember for the rest of your speaking days. This entire book is written for the sole purpose of teaching you all the fundamental techniques of speaking, so you can serve your audiences in the best possible way. It's all about them. Being nervous, not wanting to forget content, fear of bombing, hoping you will shine is normal, but all focused on 'you', on your experience, your image, your ego. While all the focus should be on them.

> ***"It's not about you; it's about the audience and their experience."***

The more you accept this and consciously start preparing, researching, interacting, and speaking in service of your audience, the better the talks you will deliver, and the better the response you will notice from your audience. And, linked to this chapter, you will be less in your head and have a lower chance of a fight or flight response. You will no longer be 'fighting' the audience monster, but you will be ready to 'help' the audience leave in a better state than when they walked in. Rethinking that mindset might sound fluffy, but it's a differentiating approach. How do you prepare your story, practise your speech and appear in front of the group? "I'm nervous, will I do well? I hope I don't mess this up, what will people think of me?" vs. "I know the audience will love this story, I have some cool interactions prepared for them and I'm excited to speak and deliver a valuable experience."

When I'm at internal client events or big conferences, I can immediately spot which speakers are focused on themselves and which ones are focused on the audience, by observing their warmup routine and way of talking backstage. It's normal when you are taking your first steps to be focused on yourself, but when you can switch that mindset, it will give you an early edge. The audience and your nervous system will thank you.

11. TELL A STORY

Many presentations are just a collection of information in a certain order. They have the purpose of transferring a message by literally passing on the information to the audience. Not a very sexy thing to do and in combination with stress and little experience, there is no incentive to speak with impact. Many speakers start a presentation with these thoughts: "I just want to get it over with." "My content is too boring." If only the audience knew this is what they made time for. You want to get it over with, share that dry content that you may have tried to cheer up with a GIF or cartoon. But what if you tried to tell a story instead of sharing information? What if you built your content in function of a clear goal, your specific audience and the value that you hold for them? Wouldn't that motivate you to step up your game and be less anxious about speaking? (For how to build this, see chapter 11.)

If I asked you to tell me about your favourite holiday destination and what to do there, I'm not going to get dry information. I will get a passionate story through the highlights of that location. There will be emotion, inspiration, belief behind every word. In the professional world, we often believe business topics can't be sexy and are boring by default. While you could build a story about your latest quarterly review and have finance managers worldwide see you as the speaking messiah of numbers. You must put in the work of turning pieces of information into a story you can get behind. A story you can't wait to share, just like talking about your favourite holiday destination. If you are now thinking, "I don't feel that way about the business I'm in," maybe you are not in the right business.

Start building stories and the more figurative or literal applause you receive for telling these stories, the more ambitious and eager you will become. Most people have never experienced what it is to truly rock a presentation, because they are stuck in the conviction that sexy and interesting topics are just for the happy few who are lucky to already be in a context that is seen as sexy and interesting.

Coaching clients walk into my office saying, "I'm here because I have an important internal presentation to give." They walk out saying, "I can't wait to try this tomorrow. I'm curious about how everybody will react." The difference? They walked in with a box full of information, they walked out with a story. Imagine going to your next presentation with that feeling; your nerves will be a whole lot more manageable. You will be in the 'performance state', excited like a kid on Christmas eve.

If you look forward to doing something, you stress less about it. If you love to do something, you will want to do more of it. The audience will feel it, love it and copy it. (See chapter 9).

12. PREPARATION & PRACTISE

The above insights are great, practical and effective, but if you want to go to that performance state as a default, the way to achieve this is by: preparing, preparing, preparing, preparing, preparing, preparing, preparing and practising, practising, practising, practising, practising, practising, practising.

Use this list of 12 to start feeling more comfortable in front of groups. You will start to enjoy speaking and will want to do it more often. Let that – doing it a lot – be the key to mastering any skill. Through experience, you will create recognition. I have seen this before, I have done this before, I have heard this before...The more recognition, the calmer you will become. Besides recognising information, your brain will also start to block out certain information that it no longer deems relevant due to the repetitive exposure. Like we always see our own nose, but our brain blocks out the image. Like the sound of trains passing by your house, that you no longer notice after a few months. Just as it blocks out many factors that were stressful the first few presentations, but you now no longer notice. Do, do, do, do; get out of that comfort zone so many times that it becomes your new comfort zone.

> *"Natalie (my wife) is a fan of everything that goes high and fast. Put her in a slingshot at the carnival and she will love it. I am less excited. Or should I say, 'was' less excited. Every day, I challenge my clients to get out of their comfort zone and step into the speaking arena, so I need to practise what I preach. A few years back, I went to Disneyland Paris with Natalie for the first time and said, "I will go on any attraction you go on. You lead, I follow." The result, no voice, primal fears, sweaty hands and literally breaking one attraction out of pure panic. I kept going and what happened to me will also happen to you when it comes to speaking.*
>
> *I was standing in line for the Hyper Space Mountain, a rollercoaster that launches you like a rocket. I heard screaming people, grinding wheels and a lot of noise. My R-complex was in full control, "I need to get out of here." But with the encouragement of Natalie, I hung in there. The first ride was hell. The second ride was a little less hell. After the twelfth time, my heart rate was still high, but I walked to the carts with a smile. Two days ago, I was praying for my life; now I was excited to step on. The reason? I kept challenging myself, experiencing it and creating recognition. I got used to the screaming people, I understood why. I knew the grinding wheels were normal and not a sign of bad maintenance. All the lights, the sounds and smells became familiar. I became calm, more confident and my primal state made room for my performance state. The same happened for the Tower of Terror, Iron Man,... This is what will happen to you when you continue to prepare, practise and experience.*

Recognition = relaxation. The audience stare, the lights, the sound of your voice through the microphone,... It's that simple but getting over that initial threshold will take courage.

Oh yeah, one more thing... I am absolutely positive that when you apply the insights from this chapter and basically everything in this book, you will deliver top performances sooner rather than later. Moments in which you think, "Wow, what a rush, this couldn't have gone any better." When you get that feeling, lock it in. Anchor it, as they teach within NLP (neurolinguistic programming). Link this feeling to a movement, smell, sound,... – something you can reproduce at any given moment. It's like me smelling freshly baked waffles every time I visited my grandmother. Now, so many years later, I just need to smell waffles and I immediately think of her and the great moments we had together. That is an anchor linked to a certain state of being. We all create these anchors subconsciously during our lifetime – and most are linked to a smell. That is the most powerful one. You can also consciously create them after a top performance. For example, play a certain song every time you ride home after a great presentation or meeting. Next time you need to pump yourself up for a talk, play that song. Do it for long enough and just like my grandmother's waffles, that song, smell, movement,... will trigger that desired state. Which brings us back to point number 1 of this 12-point list.

AI companion

What are the best techniques to become less anxious for a presentation?

••••

CORE INSIGHTS:

- Having nerves is perfectly normal, but there is a difference between those that originate out of fear and those that do so out of the desire to perform.
- It is all about the audience, not about you. Don't lose yourself in your head; focus on them.
- Don't share information but tell a story. You will be less anxious if you know you are going to tell something you love to talk about.
- Experiment with these 12 techniques and hold on to the ones that work best for you.
- Speak a lot. What you know, you will fear less. Grant yourself the recognition that comes from experience.

5
HOW DO I AVOID USING FILLER WORDS?

SHORT ANSWER:
"SLEEP AND LEARN TO THINK IN SILENCE."

Uhm, actually, like, you know, all right,... and many other filler words are stranger to no one. Even the most experienced speakers are victim to these little buggers. The good news is that you can easily get rid of them if you are aware of the five reasons that they currently pop up during your talks. I call them, 'the five killers for avoiding those annoying fillers.'

1. YOUR BRAIN NEEDS TIME

A filler word is nothing more than your brain filling up the time it needs to think. Your brain is looking for a word, how to jump to the next point or isn't entirely sure what comes next, so it needs a moment to reflect. When you are running a combination of inexperience and nerves, silence appears to be your enemy. Silence gives you an awkward feeling and a fraction of a second seems a lifetime. Maybe the audience is thinking that you have no clue what you are doing, or they lose interest the moment you stop talking. We are automatically going to try to fill up these silences. Welcome filler words. To avoid them you need to counterintuitively embrace that silence.

2. EMBRACE THE SILENCE

They say a couple has a 'good' relationship if they have strong communication. They say a couple has a 'great' relationship if they can be in each other's presence in silence without feeling awkward or needing to fill it up. The same applies to speaking. Silence is power; it helps to emphasise a point, creates anticipation, allows the audience to process information and gives you a chance to think about your next move. Embrace the silence. We all lose our train of thought sometimes, and need to process information or doubt our next words, even if you have ticked all the boxes of this chapter. Leave that silence; your audience will be grateful. I have trained myself to think in silence, to not fill up every second with little words or sounds. Not so long ago, at the end of an eight-hour workshop, I asked what had stood out most. One man raised his hand and said, "That you didn't say 'uhm' once during the whole time you talked."

In the beginning this will be a conscious act of stopping yourself from using filler words, but after a while it becomes second nature.

3. TAKE A NAP

The most common reason for the appearance of filler words in your speech is low energy. You're tired, it's the end of the day, you had a rough night, you're stressed from work. There are many factors in our lives that influence our mental and physical state. This low energy, you can't afford as a speaker. (See chapter 8). If you do appear drowsy in front of an audience, filler words will annoy them. The more tired you are, the slower your brain will work, so the more time it will need to provide your mouth with the right words. I'm very aware of the fact that when I'm drained at the end of a workshop day, those filler words start sneaking in. It's normal, but you can limit or entirely remove their appearance by making sure you are well rested and able to present yourself fresh and fruity.

4. PREPARE AND PREPARE

"I'll just wing it!", I often hear speakers say. I'll make it up on the spot. It could be that your improvisation skills are on point, but for most of us poor or absent preparation translates itself into nerves, lack of structure, lengthy anecdotes, few concrete points and... filler words. Strong preparation is crucial and the reason few professional speakers actually wing it (even if they claim to do so), but more on that in chapter 11. Improv artists master the techniques and have experience in processing new information on the spot and linking it together. When you aren't an improv artist, your brain will require more processing time and filler words, if you aren't yet used to embracing the silence. A well-rested, silence loving, and prepared speaker will rarely encounter filler words.

5. KNOW YOUR LINKS

What if you checked all the boxes of this chapter and still catch yourself using too many filler words? The missing links will most likely be the cause. You prepared yourself well, but forgot to spend time linking all your points together (see chapter 13). 'Linking' is what separates good speakers from great speakers. It helps the audience follow your story, make their own connections and gives the feeling that your entire presentation is one big whole where everything is intertwined. It helps you remember how to go from point to point without having to remember everything. "What was my next point again?" "What came after this slide?" Even with a good preparation, seconds of doubt can sneak in if that preparation didn't include link work.

"How do I go from point A to B?" – Uhm... You need to know how you can get from A to B to C to D. This assures you that when you are still talking about point A, your brain already knows how to transfer to point B. If you finish point A and still have to take a second to think about the way you are going to jump to the next part, that second will most likely be filled up with a filler word. In chapter 13, I'll share a simple exercise with you to practise linking. Every speaker encounters filler words. We are human beings and can't expect that with everything going on in- and outside our body during a presentation that our brain won't occasionally need a moment. Now you know why those moments are filled up by these annoying words and how you can avoid them.

AI companion

How do I avoid using filler words?

CORE INSIGHTS:

- Your brain needs time to think. That time will automatically be filled up with little words and sounds when inexperienced.

- Everybody encounters filler words. How frequently and intensely they present themselves is determined by energy level, nerves, preparation, experience, linking and how comfortable you are with silence.

- Avoiding filler words can be trained. Spend time on the matter, because filler words that become a habit, a part of your core speech, will turn into ticks and that will drive any audience mad.

6
SHOULD I USE SPEAKER NOTES?

SHORT ANSWER:
"NO."

I'm personally not a big fan of speaker notes, not at conferences, in meeting rooms or during video calls. You can write down as much as you like during your preparation, but I advise you to throw away this document once it is showtime. I saw this happening with myself and many other beginner comedians. If we brought our notes on stage, on a stand or for moral support in our back pocket, we were sure to forget some jokes, mess them up or reach for the paper. When we didn't bring our notes, we performed the entire set without flaw. It was as if my brain cells knew when I did bring notes: "He brought his notes; we don't need to remember everything." Just as you can more easily let go of a to-do when you write it down, when you bring notes, you are more inclined to feel the need for them, certainly when stress is involved.

It reminds me of an ex-classmate in middle school who could swim on his own when the instructor no longer walked next to him with a safety stick. The moment he lost his lifeline (stick), he could suddenly swim. As long as the stick was next to him, he grabbed it every three strokes. For many people, speaker notes are the stick they reach for, because it's there, not because they need it. Notes will stop, distract or confuse and give the audience the feeling that you didn't prepare well and haven't mastered the content. Not great in regular meetings, but definitely a big no-go at paid conferences. People pay a lot of money for a chance to hear experts talk on stage. The least these experts can do is prepare themselves, know their story and act as professionals. If you can't invest time in managing that, why should an audience invest time and money in you? The same goes for every other speaking opportunity, big or small: own it!

I'm not saying you can't take anything along for the speaking ride. Rather than long sentences and paragraphs, have only your main points in front of you. For example, an insurance client of mine had to give a talk on cyber security and the role of insurance in this. He wrote down the main points in order and trusted his skill, preparation and expertise in the topic to weave these points together on stage as he had practised beforehand. (How to come to the right points in the right order: see chapter 11).

Your possible notes:

1. Cybercrime has evolved
2. No. 1 concern for entrepreneurs is cyber security
3. Any company can be a victim of cybercrime.
4. Ransomware is the most common one.
5. One wrong click and the hackers are in.
6. More than 100.000.000 euros in ransoms have already been paid in recent years.
7. Foolproof way to protect yourself: Cyber Security Insurance.

I don't use notes as a speaker, but I do when I'm hosting an entire event. Way too much information to remember. But still, I just write down the names of the speakers and a few important points that link the show together. For the rest, I trust in my brain, skill and preparation. It hasn't failed me once. You don't have the time on stage to read everything. In stressful moments you will even lock in on your notes and forget to look at the audience entirely or get confused by the amount of information you see. Think of video calls where the speaker's eyes are looking to the side of the screen and you hear a reading voice instead of a speaking voice, a conference speaker staring at the monitor for minutes on end, reading entire slides or shuffling cards nervously in his hand, looking down in hope of enlightenment. You have no doubt experienced this as an audience member. You felt cringe, second-hand shame, disrespected... Now hold that feeling and ask yourself, "Do I want my audience to feel this during my next presentation?"

I'm not a fan of speaker notes, that much is clear. I think they are disrespectful towards the audience, certainly when you start reading. And I find it disrespectful towards yourself, because it shows lack of trust in your speaking abilities. I'm not asking you to share my opinion; do what works best for you. I can only share what I think, have experienced and seen in my career in myself and others. I only ask you to give it a try. To show courage, not for me, but for yourself. By doing this, you say:

To yourself
"I have faith in my own speaking ability. I can speak, I came prepared, I own my content and I am capable of conveying this story in a powerful way."

To the audience
"I understand that I am asking for your attention. I expect you to listen to me instead of doing a million other things you could do in this moment. Therefore I came well prepared and stand before you as an expert and a professional. I will own my stage."

If you don't yet feel confident enough to throw away your notes during your next speaking opportunity, come back to me after reading this entire book. When you apply all the techniques I'll share with you, speaker notes will not even be on your mind anymore.

> *He was very nervous. It was the first time my client, a rookie manager, needed to speak in front of the entire organisation. 400 people were looking forward to the new year's kick off. He prepared during the coaching sessions. After that, he wrote it all out, as this was the way he used to study. During the dry run the day before the event, he took his notes on stage and put them on a table in front of him. It was not a good dry run. Too much hesitation, stress and reading. The CEO wasn't happy with what he saw. The next day the room was packed, and he entered the technical room all dressed up, ready to get mic'd up. I told him that now the time had come to let go of his notes and just own it. He told me that wasn't possible and he needed his notes. I turned my heart to stone and just took his notes from him and ripped them apart. (I know, a dick move, but it was for a good cause.) His cheeks became red, his eyes teared up and his colleagues were shocked. But it was showtime and there wasn't any time to dwell on my action.*
>
> *He got on stage and started talking. After a couple of minutes of initial anxiety and a fun interaction we had prepared for his opening, he completely blossomed when the audience responded with laughter, and he performed for a solid 30 minutes. He and his colleagues had long forgotten what I had done in the technical room. He delivered more than expected and showed a side that nobody had seen before. So, instead of taking heat after his talk, I got praise and a big thank you from him and the CEO. My client was proud and totally pumped. I can't prove it, but I'm certain that if those speaker notes went with him on stage, he would have bombed again.*

(Disclaimer. This was an extreme situation where after intense one-to-one coaching, I assessed the situation and felt I could/should take away his notes. This is not a common practice for me. I normally leave the choice but advise against the use of speaker notes. Nine out of ten clients leave their notes or downsize them to mere bullet points.)

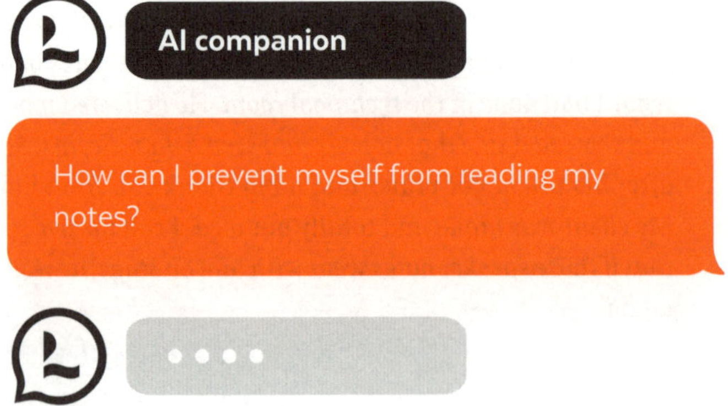

CORE INSIGHTS:

- Speaker notes are a lack of trust in one's own ability and preparation.
- Notes are not recommended, but in case you do want to use them, use points and not long sentences or paragraphs.
- Put these points on the monitor or teleprompter (big stage - live stream) or screen (meeting) in front of you. As a speaker, avoid using cards; as a host, this is accepted.
- You don't have the time, or you are too stressed, to read all your notes in front of an audience. It will only confuse or trigger you to start reading instead of speaking.
- You ask attention and time from the audience. Return that valuable gift by being a professional and owning your stage.

7
HOW CAN I BE FUNNY?

SHORT ANSWER:
"HOLD UP A MIRROR FOR THE AUDIENCE."

I wanted to put this question at number one, as it is the most frequently asked question, but it didn't match the logical order of this book. "Marnick, teach me how to be funny." I understand where this question is coming from. People who are humorous get more attention, are liked and easily make connections. Humour makes messages more digestible and, when properly dosed, stick longer in the memory of audiences. Humour is a very powerful tool to have in your speaking kit. But with great power comes great responsibility.

Humour is subjective and delicate. What cracks up one person is offensive to another. Certain words in a certain order trigger laughter; change one word or the timing in delivery and it will fall flat. Being 'funny' is what a lot of people want to be and see as a fundamental part of influential speaking, but it is actually something many people should stay away from and certainly when they are just taking their first steps in speaking. The risk of the humour tearing down the story is too big. Throw in some nerves and you aren't speaking, you are gambling, hoping something will stick.

"If you are not funny, don't try to be funny." There is nothing as cringey and nerve-racking as a joke that doesn't land. I long believed that humour could not be taught. That this was the exception to the rule of chapter 2, that anything can be learned. But I admit my incorrect belief when it comes to being funny. It can be taught. Over the years I have seen young comedians receive mere silence, open mic after open mic, where many of us thought, "Maybe comedy just isn't for you." But after a couple of years of courage and intensive training, they have their own theatre shows. Just as with speaking, you can learn to be funny.

Does this chapter have the goal of making you the next Bill Burr? Not at all. What I do aim to do for you in this chapter is present you with four rules of thumb to remember and seven techniques to practise that will work with any audience, in any situation. No risk of a joke not working, or you fumbling the funny ball due to nerves. If your ambition is to become a stand-up comedian, I strongly advise you to learn how to write and deliver jokes. Grind your way through hundreds of open mic nights and follow some masterclasses from professional comedians. Assuming this is not your main purpose in reading this book and you just want to speak with more impact at conferences or within your professional environment, the following insights will be sufficient for you to add that funny note to your stories.

What do you need to remember?

1. RELAX

In the business world people primarily expect great stories with strong insights. Humour is an aid to making that content more digestible and yourself more likeable, but it is not a necessity. When jokes are overly used they can even distract from your main message. In a professional context, it's 'connection over laughs' and 'fun' content doesn't have to be 'funny', while a comedian without funny jokes is just painful. Don't lose confidence in your speaking by comparing yourself too much with speakers that constantly trigger laughter. Good for them and you will get there too, but know you don't need it for your presentation to stand out.

2. MAKING JOKES IS AN ART

I'm not an ambassador for playing it safe when it comes to speaking. This would go against the 'stand up to stand out' philosophy. I am, however, an ambassador for a sense of reality. You can be funny in the bar with your friends, wittily responding to what is said. Turning hooks into jokes out of thin air and bringing them to an audience with expectations is a different game. A comedian needs to test and re-write a joke many times before he can be sure it will work for most audiences. Some comedians try out their jokes up to 50 times before you get to see them in the theatre. Only when the joke is shaped and stripped down to the very core will it be worthy of putting in a show. For the audience it will seem as if it is all made up on the spot, but in reality it's intense preparation and hours of practice that you are experiencing.

Most presentations that are given within companies will only be presented once or twice for a specific project, budget, strategy,… The only testing of this presentation and your potential 'jokes' will be at home or in front of some colleagues. You have one shot at convincing the board, inspiring your team or rocking the conference stage, no do overs. In those moments, you don't want to show up with something 'funny' that has never been tested before. This is what I meant earlier with 'the risk is too big'. When you have to speak within your current context about the same topic multiple times, you can start experimenting, seeing you then have room to test, analyse, adapt and retry. Like a comedian going from open mic to open mic.

3. DON'T BE LAZY

The moment you feel like you need a funny GIF, cartoon or video to make your story less boring, I recommend you head back to the drawing board and rework the whole thing. Funny elements amplify an already great story and have to add value to the point you are trying to make; it can't be a life raft for a Titanic of a presentation.

4. PLAY IT SAFE

Most corporate presentations are only presented once or twice, the chance of jokes landing is rather small, but not completely ruled out. If you got some comedy gold in your hands by accident or you are truly a funny person who knows what you are doing, surely use it. For most people, being funny is something that you can learn, but you are advised to do it in a safe way. Speaking in front of a group and public humiliation are the world's biggest fears: let's not up the pressure by 'I-hope-it-will-work-jokes'. Rather try the seven 'these-will-always-work-techniques' below when it comes to getting laughs while speaking:

What do you need to do?

1. RECOGNITION

Recognition is a recurring theme in this book. It's one of the foundations of great communication. What is the best joke for you during a comedy show? It's not the one the comedian thinks is best written, it's always the one you recognise yourself in. That's why they say storytelling is not about telling your story, it's about telling your story in such a way that your audience recognises themselves and their own story in yours. Find more on this in chapter 10.

When people recognise something, they trust it more. What we trust, we want to give attention to. A nice bonus is that recognition will often also trigger laughter, unless it's a sad story you are telling. But still, if people look into a mirror and get confronted with mistakes or challenges in the right way, even that recognition will get laughs. The use of recognition is safe and almost a certainty for entertainment. Not every recognisable piece of content will have people rolling on the floor, but during a presentation a smile or a chuckle is enough to keep the attention and create a good feeling. By simply holding up a mirror for people on their way of working, communicating or decision making, they will start to laugh while saying/thinking: "OMG, that is so true." "That is indeed what is happing in my company." "You just described 90% of our clients." It's like observing monkeys in the zoo. You laugh at their behaviour, but don't realise that the reason you are laughing is because you recognise human behaviour, exaggerated in the monkeys (see point 3 below).

The earlier OMG-reactions show you, together with a nod, that you are nailing the recognition part. The goal is not to be funny, but it happens automatically and is a welcome side effect. A speaker I saw recently described his teenage daughter's behaviour and how he was struggling to grasp it as a father. Another speaker talked about trying to get IT to help you with your computer problems at work. These were not jokes, just very recognisable observations and the crowd loved them.

This is a great way to get more acquainted with 'recognition'; watch other speakers and note when they get a laugh and what they said to get it. Chances are this is in moments of recognition or one of the other points on this list. Certainly, check out one of famous comedian Michael McIntyre's shows; you will probably relate to everything he says. When you want to create recognition, prepare yourself and be sure of your content. If you have to check with the audience if it is relatable, you didn't do your preparation right and the fun factor will lower (like laughing at your own joke).

When creating recognition, try to avoid saying:

> *I know what you are thinking...*
> *I know what you have been through...*
> *I understand that you...*
> *Is this recognisable for you?*
> *You recognise this?*

This will either make the audience think that you doubt your content or give them the feeling that you claim to know what they do, think or experience. They will think, "You don't know." Even if you do know, and you have prepared yourself well, you have to give the audience the option to decide for themselves whether they recognise what you are saying. If your preparation was done right, you know for sure that it will relate to the majority of the audience, but you can't always claim that.

So, you are going to say...

> *What I often see in this industry...*
> *What I have experienced when I attended some of these meetings...*
> *What I hear a lot of managers claim when talking about...*
> *Many entrepreneurs do it like this...*

These types of sentences give the audience a feeling that you have made general observations, but are not saying that they as an audience do this – particularly when you are making a point about a negative behaviour or failure. By introducing your observation in this manner, the audience doesn't feel attacked or singled out and they can decide if they recognise themselves in what you are saying. Normally they should, and as with monkey watching in the zoo, they will laugh at somebody else (the general observation you made), but deep down know it's really about them.

2. SURPRISE

Surprise is the foundation of stand-up comedy, with the punchline being the surprising conclusion to the setup. The bigger the surprise, the bigger the laugh. The longer the setup, the bigger the surprise needs to be, because you are creating expectations, and you buy more attention/ time with laughter. You can also use surprise in your presentations. The most common form is 'naming the elephant in the room' – mentioning what the room is thinking or what everybody has noticed, but hasn't said out loud. If you ever do an improvisation workshop, this will most likely be one of the exercises they will have you do. Standing on stage and mentioning remarkable things you see in the room, mostly accompanied by saying, "I see... and it reminds me of..." The more surprising the connection between the two, the more laughs it will get. Surprise generates laughter and reclaims attention, but a surprise can also be an unexpected twist or conclusion in your story that is relevant to the point you are making, but that nobody really saw coming. The more surprises, the easier it is to keep the attention. Read more on creating surprise in chapter 14.

3. CONTRAST AND EXAGGERATE

If you mention things that are recognisable, you will most likely get laughter. Now, combine it with an exaggeration of this point or a comparison of two extremes and the laugh will enlarge as well. This contrast or exaggeration is often made by the above-mentioned comparison between two things, mimicking behaviour or doing an impression. What is also used is looking at the strange world of your audience through the perspective of a normal person (e.g. most comedy shows where the comedian isn't playing a character) or looking like a strange person in the normal world of your audience (e.g. Mr Bean movies).

All these techniques enlarge points and make the switch between content more surprising. During a presentation about recruitment and employer branding, the speaker talked about how intensely HR teams work to get the right campaign to attract new hires, only to result in... He showed a classic stock picture with a plain slogan. (first laugh). He then said that of course recruitment is fun and sexy and Halloween is coming up, so HR gets creative and the result is... the same stock picture of people in suits in a meeting, but with a pumpkin on the table and the slogan in cheap Halloween letters. (second laugh). The build up from strategic preparation and research to a plain stock picture with crappy slogan is the contrast. The Halloween story exaggerates it even more and the audience laughs, because they recognise that this is indeed what happens a lot in the business. They accept the message because the speaker is in the business himself – he isn't saying he is better than the audience. There is another great example of this point combined with surprise and recognition in chapter 14.

4. DISCOVER INSTEAD OF CREATING

After reading the above techniques, if you still don't have a clue how to get started with humour, work backwards. Just go out presenting and be very aware of the audience's reaction to what you are saying. If they laugh, why did they? Write this down and see if you can perfect it and use it in future presentations. This way you will gradually discover possible surprises, jokes, exaggerations or recognisable content. I use this technique a lot. Certain pieces of content get a smile, laugh or chuckle everywhere. I turn them into personal stock content and use it when needed.

5. USE STOCK LINES (STOCK JOKES)

Stock lines are sentences or small jokes that all comedians can use and don't have to fear copyright infringement of another comedian. It's not stealing jokes; it's more a base package for all comedians to grab from if in need of something funny in a hurry. There are comedians who say they don't use them and all their material is original, but go to a couple of comedy shows and you will soon notice these stock lines popping up – certainly when the comedian does crowd work.

Stock lines can be as simple as saying:

"Everybody speaks English?"
"I see that the atmosphere is already pumping."
= If it stays very quiet when you just asked the audience a question or the room you enter is super quiet.

"In the coming three hours I'm going to talk to you about..."
= When you notice the audience is already tired and bored of the previous speaker or an already too-long meeting.

"We are apparently getting some live news coverage here."
= When somebody is typing mails during your presentation.

"Are you always this pumped or is it just the cocaine?"
= When somebody is overly excited in your meeting.

"Luckily my invoice is already paid."
= When you say something a bit cheeky about the company you are speaking for and people laugh in bit of a 'ooooh no he did not say that'.

"What, did you just say..."
= When somebody in the audience says something, you pretend to have misheard and repeat a funnier version of what they actually said.

"That sounded funnier in my head..."
= When you tried to say something funny, but the audience doesn't laugh and you notice they don't get the joke.

"Sorry for the rest of the audience, but I need to get to the bottom of this..."
= When an audience member reacts in a funny, surprising or weird way to what you are saying or just asked and you know it needs clarification.

"We don't have budget for a survey, so I'm going to ask the question now."
= When you want to check something with the audience.

"I'm the best speaker for this budget."
= When a host enthusiastically introduces me and sets the expectations too high or I make a mistake during my talk.

"No, sorry, you used up all your questions."
= When a workshop participant has already posed multiple questions and asks if he can pose another one.

"I always say, I'm only an invoice away."
= When somebody in a meeting asks if they can continue working with me after a presentation.

These stock lines almost seem dull or like dad jokes, but they work every single time. Stock lines don't aim to be great jokes; they are just elements that you looked up or discovered by speaking (see previous point) and notice they are simple and work with any audience. To break the ice, the silence or reclaim attention, they will do the trick. They don't have to be similar to the lines above, but can also just be part of a previous talk you gave, a remark to the audience, a piece of content and quote you came up with that really resonated with the audience, and got applause and laughter. Test it during future talks and if it works multiple times for different audiences, you got yourself a stock line or stock content.

6. CALL BACKS

Call backs are also a form of surprises you can incorporate into your story. It's something funny that happened earlier during the conference, was said in a different presentation or something you mentioned in the beginning of yours, and now you reference it again somewhere in your talk. It was funny before, but people didn't expect it to be mentioned again or woven into your story. In comedy line-ups, comedians do little backstage competitions on who can call back a certain joke, sentence or word the most with or without the audience noticing. This will then be called a running gag.

Call backs require you to be very aware of the environment you are in, listen to others speak, sense what is funny, what funny thing you said and how you can incorporate it again. Seeing the audience doesn't expect it, it surprises them and offers a speck of recognition, seeing they have laughed with it before, "Hey, that's what that other speaker said that was so funny – nice that it is referenced again here." In a workshop I gave during the writing of this book, a man made a remark that consultants do storytelling very differently. I responded, "That's the reason consultants don't get much done."

The group laughed and I made sure the gentlemen knew it was all in good fun and acknowledged that there are indeed different models, but they basically all say the same thing. During the workshop I referenced, 'consultants probably do it differently' a couple of times at the right moments and people laughed at the call backs, even the person who initially said it and was a consultant in his previous job.

7. BE ENTHUSIASTIC

In the next chapter, we dive completely into the importance of focus and energy. How do you present yourself? What energy are you giving people to copy? People feed off your energy and start copying the behaviour and feeling it creates. Being present, focused, filled with positivity and enthusiasm for your story will already get people in a good mood. It will make the audience smile and laugh at the tiniest of things during your talk. Things that you couldn't have imagined being funny yet the audience still laughs. Why? Because you are in a good place and when your mind and body are in a good place, your movements and voice will express this vibe, making the words they support become more entertaining. "If you can't put a smile on your face, don't open a shop," Dale Carnegie said in 1930. "If you can't put a smile on your face, don't speak in front of people," I say in the 21st century.

"If you can't put a smile on your face, don't speak in front of people."

Instead of giving you an example with every point in this chapter, scan the QR code below that will lead you to a snippet of one my talks at a conference in Croatia, where I got rated 'most entertaining and valuable talk' and went from laugh to laugh without really making any comedy-like joke. I could write all the jokes in this book, but seeing as 90% of a joke is its delivery through intonation and movement, they would lose their effect on paper. Better just to watch the show.

Scan the qr-code to watch the video:

How do I get away with some of these things I say? Well, by bringing the right energy, laughing and showing people that I have no bad intentions, that I am joking, not making fun of them. I also laugh a lot at myself and positively put the people I interact with in the spotlight, so the audience knows the speaker is laughing at himself without losing credibility – there is a difference between self-mockery and putting yourself down. Plus, I compliment and thank my audience allies, so they know I am on their side. You notice when you get this right: people laugh and continue to participate, because they know it's all in good fun. When you sense you went a little too far, mention it and make a mental note that this audience will only go so far and adapt your future funny inserts.

- Be 100% on top of your game. Your energy will determine whether people accept your jokes, remarks or attempts to be funny.
- Discover in a safe environment. Test certain things in coaching or workshops before using them at crucial meetings or big conferences.
- Make fun of yourself, without losing credibility.
- Build up your credits. Start off easy and win love and acceptance. The more value and fun you offer, the more you will get away with. If you are trying to be cocky or bring an attitude, realise the value you bring needs to be 20x your attitude or the audience won't accept it.
- Learn to find the right intonation, style and wording. You can't be me, and I can't be you. I can say things you can't and the other way around.
- Follow up remarks to the audience with positivity and compliments and defuse what you just said. Always make sure people feel there is only positive intent.
- Don't expect laughs or applause. Continue your talk as if you didn't design it to be funny. When there is big applause or laughter, give the audience time to acknowledge you, leave some silence, smile, but don't gloat. It needs to look like you are surprised by the laughter.

These guidelines show why being funny is so hard. As mentioned at the beginning of this chapter, everything depends on energy, timing, voice, movement, wording, intent and a style that fits with who you are. Get one thing wrong and you can turn a whole audience against you. Play it safe, practise, discover and go for connection first.

But what about cartoons and funny GIFs in your presentation?

- Read chapter 15 when we dive into making a good slide deck.

But what about culture?

There are indeed cultural differences in what is perceived as funny and what is not. There is even a difference in what is perceived as funny in every province in Belgium, one of the smallest countries in the world. That is why humour is so hard and tricky. You need a solid understanding of your audience (see chapter 11) and need to be in a high-performance state where your spider senses are on maximum alert to sense who is in front of you, what their state is and what you can or can't say, yet. Reading the room can only be done if you are in a performance state. Saying recognisable things and making points that are perceived as funny can only come from understanding, preparation and testing beforehand.

EXERCISE

- *Write down all the times people laughed during your last presentation. Be aware of it during your talk or record yourself so you can rewatch it. See how many of those laughs can be turned into funny moments you can re-use during your next presentation.*
- *Watch talks of speakers you admire and only focus on when they get a laugh or applause. Write down which technique of this chapter they used, so you learn to recognise it.*

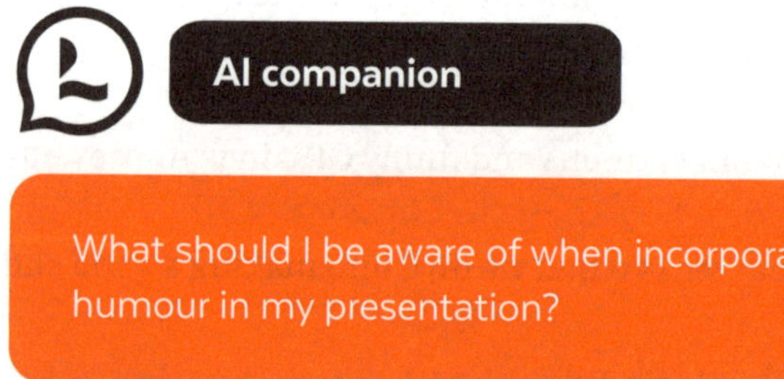

CORE INSIGHTS:

- Humour can be taught, but it will take a lot of effort and time.
- Humour helps make messages digestible and memorable but isn't a must within a business context. Connection over laughs. Fun doesn't always equal funny.
- Funny elements need to amplify your already strong story and add value, not save a boring one.
- Coming up with great jokes is a craft. Don't take the risk when presenting something only once. Rather use 'recognition', 'surprise' or 'exaggeration'.
- Rather than using jokes, fill your backpack with stock lines.
- Speak with enthusiasm and energy. This will automatically create good feelings in the audience. People copy energy and behaviour.

8
HOW DO I MANAGE MY ENERGY, EVEN ON A BAD DAY?

SHORT ANSWER:
"EMOTION IS A CHOICE."

If you are reading this book in chronological order, I asked you to do a little exercise in chapter 2 on page 31. If you haven't done it yet or haven't read that chapter, I recommend doing the exercise before you continue reading.

What did you notice? What was the big difference between the two recordings and what did your observer say?

Chances are you will have a similar response to my clients when I have them do the same exercise in a workshop. The story I asked you to tell was short and had no specific requirements. Just 1–2 minutes about anything. The brief is very simple, but for most people the execution during the first recording lacks structure, energy, emotion and is pretty colourless. A person staring into a camera like a deer in the headlights and mostly worrying about 'what' they are saying. "Am I making sense?" "Was it too long, too short?" "How long did I talk?" "Was there structure?" All in their head, focused on the content and how they are perceived by the observer. Which is a completely normal reaction, but at the same time, remarkable, because there is no pressure, no set topic, there are no requirements, and nobody will ever see this video if you don't share it. The reason? You are focused on yourself, on the content and on your reputation. You are not focused on a potential audience and delivering the story for others to enjoy.

That is why I ask my clients and you to do some crazy exercises with me that get you moving, out of your head and get the right juices flowing. I hope you went all out and had some good fun. During workshops, this is the moment other departments hear the screaming, cheering, laughing and clapping and ask their manager, "Why don't we get a workshop like that?" After these fun exercises the second recording follows, same 1–2 minutes max, same story or something else, it doesn't really matter. "How did you experience the second recording? Was there a difference?"

When I ask this question to groups across the world, the answer is always the same: "The second video was more fun to watch as an observer, a more interesting story, more movement in body and voice and you forgot you were in front of a camera." And it doesn't even have to be as elaborately executed as I requested of you. I often joke around a bit with my clients who are super nervous in front of the camera. The moment they react and start laughing at my joke, I say action and press record. That take will always make the cut, because they took that short boost of dopamine, that smile and brief moment of 'not being in their head' along in their talk before the camera. The camera loves it, and the audience can feel it through the screen. It can be that simple.

That is the beauty of these little exercises. You don't yet have a lot of techniques and insights on truly upping your speaking game. Yes, you now know how to approach speaking as a mindset, controlling nerves, etc. but we haven't dived into the technical stuff yet, unless you are reading in a different order than the table of contents. No insight and no techniques on intonation, structure, or camera work, but you and the rest of my clients have still managed to significantly increase your speaking ability by just jumping around like a headless chicken for ten minutes.

It could be that you really got out of your comfort zone with this exercise. Your reaction could be that your first video was better than the second one. It felt more natural, less rushed, more structured. I'm not saying that is not possible, but most of the time this is just a feeling, because the first version was the default mode. A way of speaking that is familiar and comfortable, but speaking isn't about the speaker, it's about the audience and how they experience it. In a workshop, when somebody says, "My first version was better," the observer will often jump in and say, "Not at all. Your second version was way more interesting and fun to watch."

The audience enjoys version two more, but some speakers like to stay with familiar number one. Those who embrace version two will soon rock their presentations. Those who keep saying it is fake will continue to do more of the same and will know little growth in the art of speaking. But why is this massive change possible in such a short amount of time? Well, if you entered my workshop or started doing this exercise at home, you are doubtful, unprepared, scared, uncomfortable and a bit hesitant. People in my workshop don't expect that they will have to do something right away. Maybe you are also facing a rough day, some traffic, a difficult meeting or rushing to pick up the kids from school. This primes you to generate cortisol, make yourself smaller and become internally focused. Just what you don't need when you have to speak and be big, full of confidence and hand out dopamine.

Then a couple of minutes of fun exercises follow. They take you out of your head and start producing the right chemicals in your body. The diffidence fades and if you did it with an observer or group, it becomes a safe environment, because everybody acted crazy. Despite not having had time to prepare yourself or knowing what techniques needed to be applied, you still presented a better story than the first version, purely by changing your focus and energy. As with everything in life, your focus is your future. Focus on yourself, the shame and what could go wrong, and it will. Focus on the audience and their experience and you will perform.

From now on, ask yourself the question every time you are about to walk into an online/offline room to speak,

"How am I walking in on a scale from one to ten?"

Ten being focused, ready to perform, aware of your environment, maybe feeling a bit nervous, but still very good. One being close to freezing, fearing a blackout, frustrated, stressed, still thinking about that last tough meeting and dreading walking in. Are you a one, a ten or something in between?

Is the answer 8, 9, 10? Great, keep it that way and ask yourself how you got to this state. If you find the answer, you can use that information to get yourself back to that number for future presentations when you are not feeling good. There are always moments that you are in a high performance state or you just rocked a meeting. You wouldn't be very good at your profession if you didn't have these moments. Lock that feeling in by anchoring it to something – a movement, a song, a smell,... Sounds a bit kumbaya, but your body does this every single day. You smell waffles, what do you think of? You smell freshly mowed grass, what do you think of? You hear a certain love song, what do you think of? You are full of anchors that you have gathered throughout your life – moments where you linked an emotion to something more tangible.

Is your number a seven or lower? That's totally fine. You are just human and not every day is going to be a party. Pinpoint what is causing this and foremost how you can get yourself out of this state, even if it is for the 30 minutes that you will be speaking. Find yourself a way to either anchor a performance state and be able to summon it in the future or get yourself a fixed routine to shake things off, get back in the zone and reignite that high number, even if it is just for the duration of your presentation. I have described my own routine below more extensively in chapter 4, but I cannot decide on your routine, your own anchor. This differs with every person. Start experimenting and discover what works for you. A comedian, singer, actor and speaker also spend a lot of time prepping themselves physically and mentally before you see them in action. It's the rule instead of an odd exception.

My routine for conferences and workshops:

1. Arrive early to avoid unnecessary stress
2. Connect with reception or tech crew
3. Check in with organisation on general feel
4. Set everything up in the room or do stage/tech check with crew
5. Talk to early arrivers to see if I can connect today
6. Quiet down, but do not sit down, keep moving
7. Put phone on flight mode, wash hands with warm water, go to restroom
8. Open the session or speech with a smile and energetic entry

My routine for online meetings:

1. Open the session early to avoid unnecessary stress
2. Do tech check, test camera, lights
3. Move around until organisation or first people pop up

4. Sit down, smile and open the session
5. Connect with certain people, positively call them out (even in online session with hundreds of people)
6. Start the meeting

I have been hammering on about rating one's state before walking in from the moment I started coaching people. And people either embrace it or they stay sceptical and find it too fluffy. But the number you give yourself and walk in with will determine how your speaking will be perceived. No matter how well you prepared your content, people copy behaviour, energy and feel what you feel. Come home from work bringing in a 4/10, have a talk with your partner who doesn't know how to block this, and I guarantee that a heated discussion about nothing will ignite – because somebody didn't bother leaving that 4 at the door. That number will decide your overall energy. That energy will steer your body and voice, which is your movement and intonation while speaking. That movement and intonation will be used by the receiver of your message to rate your intentions (see chapter 9).

If the message was meant with positive intent, but the energy (voice, body) that is used to transfer it is not (4/10), this message will have the opposite effect. This can turn a simple "I don't know what I want for dinner yet", into a trigger for your partner to react, "Well, excuse me, I also had a busy day. Why is it always my responsibility to think about it?" Even if your initial response was with no negative intent, the way you said it made it come across that way. The same applies to your presentations.

However, we are not robots. That means we are susceptible to our environment in moments of weakness. Your presentation comes after five intense meetings; you have caught a bit of the flu; your newborn baby kept you up all night; you just spent three hours in traffic;... All the things we experience in our daily lives have an effect on our state. The level to which you allow your environment to mess with you depends on the state you are already in. This is the reason you can spiral into negativity if you are not conscious about it. Living consciously and in balance with yourself can block most of what the world sends your way, but it's impossible to avoid it completely. Still, you cannot allow it to affect your speaking in moments that matter (workshop, pitch, keynote,...). Your story has the purpose of achieving a certain goal (see chapter 11) and you will need the best version of yourself to deliver that story. Are you a 9/10? Great, walk in and own your stage. Is it a 5/10 and your day isn't going as planned, but you still have to perform? Think about the above and also ask yourself the following question, where your answer will determine the best course of action:

1. CAN I PROCESS THIS? NO.

If you are not feeling great, ask yourself if this is something you can process, something you can temporarily park for the upcoming talk. If you can't – for example, when somebody close to you has passed away – you can decide to postpone the meeting or arrange a replacement. This isn't always easy when it comes to conferences, but in a work context this is perfectly feasible, and people will understand. The point here is that when something in your environment is consuming a lot of energy and is so impactful you know you can't bring your A-game, no matter your anchor or routine, be honest with yourself and give yourself and the audience the opportunity to experience your story at a better time in the future. If you are operating in the right culture, your audience will understand and also prefer it.

2. CAN I PROCESS THIS? YEAH, BUT...

If you are not in a great state, but you do have the feeling you can process it and park it for a minute, you can decide to proceed with your upcoming presentation. You are aware of the impact your one to ten scale has and will use your anchor or routine to get yourself pumped and into the zone. You know this will not solve all your problems, but will at least get you to present yourself with an 8 for the duration of your performance. The audience is your focus during that time. If you notice that despite the 8, you can't completely shut it off, you can opt to be honest and mention it to the audience at the start. No excuse, but a fair mention of the elephant in the room concerning your state. People will understand. When you mention this, it will also lower your nerves (see chapter 4), the audience can frame it and you know that after this mention, you are expected to perform again. That is the condition.

3. CAN I PROCESS THIS? YES.

You have a bit of a cold, got an angry phone call from a client, had serious traffic, an argument with your partner,... All environmental challenges that weigh on you, but are, if you are honest, easy to shake off if you really want to. These types of things could have an impact on your performance state. In this case, you will also go all in, use the anchor, prime yourself with your routine and be 100% present. You don't mention it to the audience and just perform. Luckily, most of the things the majority of people have to deal with in their lives are of this order. It might not seem that way when you are in it, but they are small hiccups that are not hard to process or park if you are living consciously and not like a ball being kicked around in your environment. As Chris Williamson said on his Modern Wisdom podcast:

> ***"Motivation is having a feeling of demotivation and not wanting to deal with certain things, but despite that feeling still doing them."***

I'm in the unique industry of professional speaking. In most cases I have to show up, because workshops, coaching and keynotes are my service. If I don't speak, I don't make money and with conferences that specifically booked me and have me on the agenda, it's not very easy to postpone or cancel. In all the years I have been in this business, I have never cancelled a workshop or presentation. Not for family reasons, sickness or small issues. My philosophy is not, don't be a baby, suck it up or suppress everything. My philosophy is that much in our lives is a choice, a mindset, and that it's okay to take the time to process, be vulnerable, call it out and let it sink in. But if we are honest with ourselves, we tend to use a lot of our daily red lights as an excuse to not perform.

We don't have bad days, we have bad moments and we choose to let them drag down our entire day. I don't want to come across as insensitive and I know, after a heavy burnout of three years, what it means to push a body and mind too far, but self-awareness, resilience and perseverance are also skills that can be taught. Learn them and you will notice that you are able to do more than you think.

Emotion is, in most cases, a choice. You are arguing with your partner, mad at your children for wrecking the house and all of a sudden, a friend rings the doorbell, or you get a call from your client. You immediately switch to a smile, have a lovely chitchat and laugh about something that happened that week. You end the conversation and turn to your spouse or children and continue your rampage. You just chose the emotion that you thought you needed for each interaction. A very easy switch, and the same is possible for your speaking moments. Fake? If it is fake, which it isn't, because it is still you doing it, why does every human being do this every single day without questioning it? But when it concerns speaking in front of an audience, words like introvert, shy, fake,...pop up? Because it scares a lot of people, and they fear possible humiliation, any excuse is a good one to avoid stepping out of their comfort zone and exploring their potential.

What is your physical and mental state when you walk in? What are you giving your audience to copy, even if you aren't happy happy joy joy? Do you choose to ask the attention and time of an audience (their most precious possession), and also make the choice to give them the best possible experience in return? It's about them. You are there to speak and perform and you can only do that if you keep all issues out of the room. Not possible? Ask yourself the process question from earlier to determine your best course of action.

> *Not so long ago, as I was getting off a train, I got a text message from a friend saying another friend had ended his own life. I stopped in shock and had to fight back my tears. I was on my way to deliver a full-day workshop. I could choose to cancel it, hop back on the train or decide to move forward and get myself in the zone, if only for the day. I mentioned it to the group at the beginning of the workshop when I was talking about managing your state. I didn't start with it, because that would be a very cold start for people who weren't expecting news like that on a fun workshop day. I mentioned it and while fighting back some tears themselves, the group was now aware and understood. It was out there, the elephant was mentioned in case they did notice something during the day. I gave them my*

best and the workshop resulted in L&D booking three more workshops for the company. I returned home and focused on family and friends.

In this case, I literally chose a time to mourn and a time to perform. I'm not saying you should be as extreme as me; I'm just illustrating that there is always a choice and that small hiccups during the day should definitely not be an excuse for a speaker to not give it his all. A sexy term for everything we discussed so far is 'managing energy transitions'. In my experience, there is very little focus on this, while it's crucial for you as a professional, spouse or friend with the busy schedules of today.

It even plays a role in processing what comes after a great presentation, the 'presentation high' – something you will certainly experience once you master everything in this book. You will be in a high performance state, with focus and energy, and the audience – whether it is two people or 4,000 – is rewarding you with applause and praise. You will walk out feeling like a million bucks – anchor it and be left wanting more. You go home and after that spike, the drop comes. Like drinking an energy drink, feeling like you have wings and then getting the sugar dip. The more you speak and become good at it, the better you will need to manage the transition from peak to drop. For me this means going on a weekend with Natalie, riding my Harley, playing video games, working out,... Lying on the sofa works for a bit, but it isn't the best remedy. How big these ups and downs become will depend on your journey after reading and applying this book, but they will be there. It's the reason why so many great artists that rise fast crash just as quickly or turn to drugs and alcohol for their continued shot of dopamine and a feeling of bliss, making the peaks and drops only bigger, of course. I guess this goes a bit far for your situation, but if you don't manage your energy after the performance, just as you manage it before the performance, you will soon get exhausted.

I hope you get addicted to the applause and the audience addicted to you. It would mean that you have applied the insights from this book and discovered your full potential. I also hope you will be conscious enough to manage it. If you decide to continue delivering information and flat stories, you can ignore this last part. There will be no peaks, not with you, the audience or in your results.

The number on a scale from one to ten represents your energy, focus, your ability to think clearly, be sharp and in balance with yourself. The higher the number, the more likely you will be able to read the room, adapt to the audience, spot cultural differences in behaviour, speech and humour, interact with people and remember your content. This number is not about having cowabunga energy or becoming a version of yourself that you are not. It's different for everybody.

Put President Obama and President Trump next to each other on their best day and their speaking styles will differ, but their focus, energy and commitment to the content and audience will be 10/10 with both. What number are you bringing to the table, knowing that this number will decide the course of your talk and whether you will be able to put the next chapter into practice? The next chapter deals with a technique that determines 90% of the impact you will have on your audience. If you are not in a performance state, you will fumble it. This is the reason the answer to the question, "How are you doing on a scale from one to ten?" comes first and is of the utmost importance.

Don't tell yourself that the current state you are in at work, at home, and with your friends is the max we are going to get. If you are going to apply for your dream job, introduce me to your favourite hobby or talk about your big passion project, it's guaranteed that I will get that high performance state. That state we need for every one of your next speaking opportunities. We need you to know yourself, trust yourself and in that moment when you are truly living up to who you are and are therefore truly you, your body and voice will know what to do.

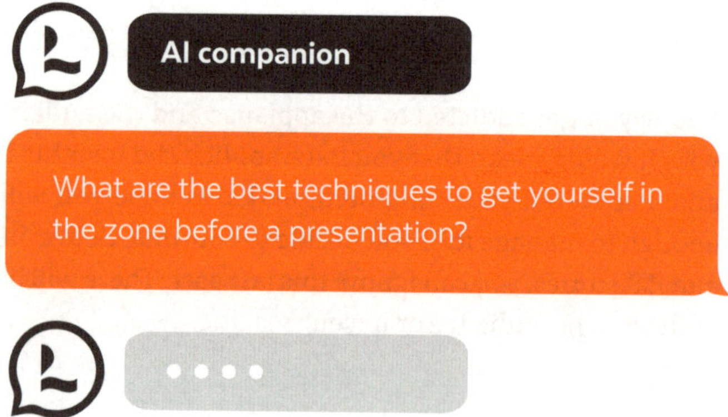

CORE INSIGHTS

- How are you walking in on a scale from one to ten? The answer will decide how successful you will be.
- Manage your energy transitions. Can you shake off your daily challenges, even for a brief moment, or are you bringing your issues into the room?
- Ask yourself: "Can I process this?" The answer to this question will help you determine your next action and how you will deal with your current mental/physical state.
- The energy you give is the energy you will get. People copy behaviour.

9
HOW DO I SPEAK WITH MORE CONFIDENCE AND ENTHUSIASM WITHOUT BEING SEEN AS FAKE?

SHORT ANSWER:
"BE CONFIDENT AND ENTHUSIASTIC; YOUR BODY AND VOICE WILL DO THE REST."

I think you learned, after reading the previous chapter, that I am a big fan of having your own routine before you take the stage. Energy, focus, walking in with at least that eight or nine out of ten. I spend significant time on this during every coaching, presentation or workshop. This is what makes the difference, but is often neglected, because we are globally in love with content and slides. How you present yourself energy wise will determine 90% of your speaking success and how your interactions in general will go. People feel energy, copy behaviour and notice when somebody is focused and fully in balance with himself. Be that person while speaking and you will outperform most speakers at conferences or in your organisation. You will attract the right people, see opportunity and be more resilient in blocking off energy vampires (see chapter 16). Energy, focus, 100% presence – that is what speaking professionals are made of.

Appearing for a presentation in this 'high performing state' has two big advantages. The first one is hopefully clear by now: less nerves, more peace of mind, fun vibe for your audience to copy, easier to connect with. The second reason is that being in that state will grant you the opportunity to 'trust' yourself.

> *The two main reasons for getting yourself in a 'high performance state'.*
>
> 1. *People feed off energy and copy behaviour. What are you giving them to copy?*
>
> 2. *When you are in the zone, you can trust yourself and be truly you. When you are truly you, your voice/body will know what to do.*

If you are a four or five and nervous, stressed, rushed, scared, this will result in the dry mouth, foggy mind, shortness of breath, red spots, blackout, nerve twitches, shaking, lack of eye contact, cracking voice,...All signs of someone who is not in balance with himself. I still have these moments. Luckily, they have become very scarce, but when it happens, I assess my performance and see where I dropped the ball in my routine. If you feel good, you will be able to trust yourself and find peace in the way you speak and move, because your body knows exactly what to do. You just have to allow it.

> **"When you are truly you, your voice and body will know what to do."**

You can do this, because you are in a 'high performance state' and not desperately trying to get your act together. I will rarely tell you how to talk or move in this book, because you already know how to do this, but in uncomfortable moments you are not aware of this ability, or you block it out yourself.

You are pitching, for example, in front of a group of investors; you are a four, rationalising everything, clinging onto your slides and trying to act professionally, which mostly results in a plain grey version of who you are. Afterwards you are discussing the result of that pitch with your friends in a cosy coffee bar, and we get a whole other version of you. You play with intonation, your hands and facial micro movements, you laugh, frown – maybe you stand up to imitate an investor's reaction. You are giving your friends a 'show' about your pitch and supporting that content with everything you've got without thinking about it for a second. You are not aware of it, but you are doing it in your own 'authentic' way, because you trust yourself and feel that your friends allow you to be you. As a result your voice and body know what to do, and your friends love it.

So, who are you? What is your personality truly about? Who is that ultimate version of you? Find it; it probably pops up when with friends. Tweak it to perfection and become a master speaker. The audience will always experience it as authentic; they can't look through it, because they see the true you. It is therefore remarkable to me that people often say that it is all fake when I'm teaching them about this chapter. What is more fake? Putting on an act in front of an audience, because you think this is the professional way to speak and move, while you wouldn't feel inspired by it at all if you were in the audience listening to your own talk? Or is it being who you really are and bringing that coffee bar version to the meeting? What's more fake, the professional grey façade with a slide deck or a genuine you with a great story to tell?

> *"But it's still a professional context. Don't I risk being perceived as a clown?"*

If you are a clown outside the meeting room, then you will indeed be a clown in front of the group, and we will have to downsize the rough edges. I'm assuming you are not a clown, but just a fun human being with ambition and good intent, so you will not be seen as a clown but as a fun ambitious speaker with good intent. I'm exactly the same speaker on a business stage as I am on the comedy stage. No difference. Maybe I clean up my language a bit in the business context, but performance wise you get the same Marnick. Talk to me afterwards, same Marnick. Am I a bit quieter in some moments compared to the energy bomb on stage? Yes, but that is linked to my energy management (introvert – see chapter 2 on page 24) and not me being somebody else.

Maybe you are still a bit unsure about yourself, a bit shy, even when you are with your friends. Then we will amplify the true you and cut that diamond in the rough. Remember the quote from Professor William James, "Most people only use 20% of their ability." We want to get the coffee bar version into the board room and have access to 100% of your ability. I'm confident that that version is already there and that the reason it hasn't revealed itself is due to the misperception that you can't be yourself in a business context, because it is unprofessional. Or that you aren't yet comfortable enough, a bit shy or walking around with a 4/10.

Get yourself in the zone, get yourself pumped and let go. Let's discover who you truly are and can become. Let's amplify or downsize where needed and learn to play the beautiful instrument that is you (voice/body). All the 88 keys to your piano are present; dare to play them all and let's tune the notes that are still a bit false. I like this piano analogy by Australian speaker coach Vinh Giang. He pictures your body and voice as a piano, an instrument you can play and make music with (speaking). Most people see their voice and body as a tool, something you transfer a message with. You speak or move like you are a coffee machine, spitting out the millionth espresso on a drowsy Monday morning. But you are an instrument that can bring joy, inspiration, conviction,...

> ***"Your voice and body are an instrument, not a tool."***

You are that piano with 88 keys to play, but most people play only 12 keys all their life. Those keys are your comfort zone in stress situations. You will add keys when you feel good and comfortable. Imagine what music you will be able to play in front of a group when you have the awareness, mental and physical state and comfort to use all 88 keys? What a performance you will be able to give. How easily you will be able to adapt to your audience. How you will be able to emphasise words. Bring nuance and tie it all together into an inspiring piece that touches the right emotion.

I always loved this analogy, since I play the piano myself and we all know how music, without even having any lyrics (content), can still trigger so much emotion, tell a story and stick with people for life. Your voice and body can do the same, if you allow yourself to be truly you. Being able to do this as a speaker will make you invincible and grant you the power to turn any piece of content into an engaging performance.

> ***"A great presentation isn't just about what you say, it's about how you say it and how it makes people feel."***

> *"I was asked to speak at a major conference for 800 people and got a 30-minute spot in an impressive line-up of professional speakers. I admit to being quite nervous, because I put the pressure on myself that I had to stand my ground amongst these heavy weights. But I was ready, ap-*

plied everything from this book and trusted in myself and my experience. I decided to only make three simple points and use no slides, no flipchart, no nothing. My voice, body and content had to be enough to capture the attention of 800 people for 30 minutes. I did my thing and a week later the organisation told me that they would like to book me a second time (which they rarely did), seeing the survey was full of: "This was amazing, inspiring, great value. Best talk of the conference."

Great to hear, of course, and good for a man's ego, but I'm not sharing this to boast. What this showed me once again was that with all the focus on content, slides, models, fancy terminology,... The right use of energy, voice, body in combination with some very simple points will do the trick. 90% of your speaking impact is energy and how that energy allows you to speak and move. 90% of speakers focus on content and slides. Important, but rarely the differentiator. People make decisions based on emotion and use rational arguments to justify that decision. People forget most content, but remember how they felt about it.

When I translate my client's story back to them with the focus on using voice and body in the right way, they almost always say, "You should do my presentation." Why do they say this? Most of the time I don't understand their profession well enough (e.g. engineering project, financial forecast,...) to really grasp the content, yet they still love hearing me present their own story, despite my content mistakes and poor interpretation. It is because they to get captured by 'how' I translate their story back to them. You can put any professional speaker at a marketing conference, for example, and have him talk about 'a lamp' while mainly focusing on the performance. I guarantee you, that lamp presentation will be voted best talk of the marketing conference. If you think I'm exaggerating, look up the TEDx talk by Will Stephen. He gives an entire talk about absolutely nothing. He admits that he has no message, value to offer and will just talk about nothing, but still you will listen, be engaged, laugh and watch the whole talk as he is actually offering you valuable insights. Or Toastmaster champion Mohammed Qahtani, who tries to light a cigarette on stage, gets a shocked response from the audience and asks them if they would react the same way if he ate a candy bar on stage. He then continues to make the point that it's weird because eating candy is way more dangerous for your health than smoking. After he had made that point, he says he completely made it up, but the audience believed every word, because of the way he said it.

I even have people crying with emotion during some of my keynotes when I translate their story about their family, hobby or life back to them, just by adding the play of my movement and voice. That is the power of this chapter. That is why I call it a 'superpower'. Now combine it with great content, good intent and you will have yourself a cocktail for success. But how can you do this? How can you discover that great speaker you already are and make a difference with your body and voice during future presentations? By understanding what intonation and what movement has what impact on your audience.

The easiest way to explain this is by looking at your behaviour around your pets (e.g. dogs, cats) or a newborn baby. The power of voice and body is just as effective with those who don't understand a word of what you are saying. When you are at the office, you are probably walking around all professional, being important and putting out corporate fires. Maybe you are even dressed up and looking like you own the place. But once you get home and you are in a place where you can be truly you, your behaviour will change – and most drastically with your pets or small children.

You will go from corporate manager to crouching and greeting your dogs in a high pitched cute little voice with lots of facial expression and movement, "Where's a good boy? Did you miss me? Yes, daddy is home, yes, daddy is home. Who's a good boy?" Your dog has no clue what you are saying content wise, but it does understand the facial expressions and mainly the tone of your voice. This high-pitched voice, combined with bigger movement from body and face will signal to the dog, 'My owner is happy, he is engaging me, I need to feel happy, engaged and maybe we are going to play or I will get food'. What happens when you are mad at the dog, or you want him to do something? You automatically lower your voice, give more directives and say, "Go fetch, boy." "Bad dog, stop eating my shoe." "Here boy, sit." The dog doesn't understand the content, but links this to having to be in a state of 'I need to focus', 'This is important, I need to pay attention.' When you frequently use the same words, the dog will also link that specific sound to its name or a certain command. We both know a cat also knows that it has to do something or has done something wrong, but unlike the dog, it chooses to ignore you.

What goes in the animal kingdom also goes for human beings. Nobody walks up to a baby girl and says in a regular voice, "Hey girl, you hungry?" No, everybody around the world will automatically go back to their cute little high-pitched voice and friendly facial expressions, "Hi, hi, yeah, look at that beautiful smile, yes, hiii, who is hungry, who wants yum yum?" Even if you are a two-metre tall, buffed, bearded ex-marine, you will talk exactly like this. Your voice and body know what to do. The baby doesn't understand a word of what you just said, but knows it is play time, feeding time or needs to feel engaged. Talk to a baby in a low voice, with more directives and a stricter face and see the reaction. The baby will be startled, stare back at you and look as if she is thinking, 'What is going on? I need to focus here.' There are plenty of videos online of parents being surprised by their baby's reaction to a change in their tone of voice and facial expressions. What goes for babies and dogs goes for the adults in your next project meeting.

Humans and animals use intonation and movement to determine the intent behind somebody's words. That is why 'how' you say something will have more impact than 'what' you say. You can say to your partner "Honey, what's for dinner?" with a higher pitched voice, lighter tone, open facial expression and positive energy, and your partner will most likely answer in a normal way, "I was thinking fries." "Anything you are in the mood for?" Use the same words, the same content, but say it as more of a directive, in a low voice, with a more questioning facial expression, impatiently or in a demanding way. Your partner will most likely feel attacked and respond with, "Why do I always have to come up with dinner ideas?" The same goes when you were young, and your mother or father called you while you were playing in the garden or in your room. You didn't even have to see them to know by just the tone of their voice whether you were in trouble or not. The way you speak and move can have more impact on people's emotion than just words. If you ever decide to do coaching or NLP certification, this is one of the first things they teach you.

Why is the right use of voice (intonation) and body (face, hands) so important?

- *People use it to determine your intentions. Can they trust you or not?*
- *People use it to judge your intelligence. You can be the smartest person in the room, talk or move funny and they will think less of you. (Tough to hear, but a reality.)*
- *It has the power to steer people's emotions. Get them to feel the right thing at the right time.*

The level at which you perform depends on your awareness of the impact your intonation and movements have on people and on your ability to amplify or downsize these two elements. If you don't know which intonation and what movement is used for what purpose and you are not aware that your voice is too high and your speech is too fast at certain moments, you will do what is expected, but it will have some rough edges. Going back to the diamond in the rough, you are already shiny, valuable and pretty, but your true beauty will reveal itself after being cut and polished. Like a beautiful piece of music that goes up and down, slow and fast, silent and explosive. Like a movie that takes you from a high-speed chase to a romantic moment between lovers. Up and down, grabbing your attention, capturing and mesmerising you. As your voice and body know what to do, the only thing left for you to do to make this performance happen, besides getting yourself into the right state, is to ask yourself a single question:

"What do I want my audience to feel at what point in my story?"

The answer to that question will trigger you to go one of three ways: You will dissociate yourself from your content, you will return to neutral, or you will associate yourself with your content. I call it, 'mapping your story DNA (dissociate, neutral, associate)'. You need all three modes in every talk. There is no right order. There is no right number of times you can use a certain mode. There are only the points you want to make (see chapter 13) so ask yourself for each point, "What emotion do I want my audience to feel here?" The answer will decide the mode and will determine what you as a speaker will need to do.

Before we dive into how this is used by every great speaker around the world, let me show you what I mean with DNA.

STORY DNA

DISSOCIATE

I'm being convinced. I need to realise this is important.

You distance yourself from your content. You are observing the point you are trying to make. You are reflecting, realising something, making a statement. You become more factual, more structured and want to show the audience that what you are saying means something to you, did something for you or is very important for the audience to remember or think about. This can be negative or positive.

What will happen to your voice and body?

Around the world, every person I ask to tell me something, while sticking to the facts or talking about an element that meant something to them or I need to remember, will, without me asking, start to talk in a lower slower voice, give fewer details and more factual and structured content, that is easy to follow, and will use smaller, more directive movements in body and face.

LOWER, SLOWER VOICE
SMALLER MOVEMENTS (FACE/GESTURES)
MORE DIRECT EYE CONTACT WITH THE AUDIENCE
LINKED TO MORE OBSERVANT/REFLECTIVE/FACTUAL CONTENT

Dissociated movement often results in:

- Concise hand gestures in front of the diaphragm
- Making list on fingers
- Concise open hand gestures like you are holding two apples
- Putting thumb and index finger together and moving like a conductor
- Pointing with flat hand
- Bringing hands together
- Standing still
- Expression of determination or conviction or emotion or clarity in face.

What will the effect be on your audience?
People who hear a lower, slower voice, clear-cut content and smaller directive moments will experience this as = I am being convinced, this is important, I need to focus.

Pitfall for people who are too dissociative?
Too long, too slow, too boring.

The advantage?
You will be able to make your points hit harder with your audience. You will talk in a more structured, easy-to-follow way. You will be perceived as more trustworthy and confident. You will automatically build in a pause and some rest for your audience to process the important point you are making. You will automatically talk more slowly and put more emphasis on your words. In piano terms, this is called playing 'staccato'. This means you don't bind your notes together, but play them separately. This makes each note sound more pronounced.

Watch out!

This doesn't mean that dissociative behaviour is without emotion. Dissociation can be 10x more triggering of emotion than associating. When practising, you will tend to see associating more as fun, emotional, and feeling, and dissociating as factual and dry. But as you progress, you will see that being able to dissociate at the right time is where the biggest impact lies. (check the upcoming 'morning' example).

Standout example?

President Barack Obama making a strong point during a speech in his low and slow voice: emphasising his words (staccato) and leaving his famous pauses while looking at the crowd and making a small directive gesture.

NEUTRAL

I'm being led to a new part of the story.

Not everything you say has to be as distinct as dissociating or associating. These content pieces or points will have to be connected at certain places. Those connections or side notes will be made using a neutral way of talking. If you picture your story DNA as a rollercoaster ride, the neutral part will be being pulled up to the top, the dissociative part holding there and realising, this is high and steep, the way down is the association. So, you will automatically insert some neutral speech when going from A to D or the other way around. Not always, but often. Just like the rollercoaster or a piece of music, highs, lows and neutral parts that connect.

ASSOCIATE

I'm being inspired, I'm being engaged.

You link yourself to your story. You are there experiencing that anecdote. You are reliving something or feeling the inspiration or excitement of a project there and then in front of that group. You add colour, details, interpretations and assumptions to your story. You are in your story and engaged with what you are saying. You are feeling and living it, so the audience is feeling and living it. An association can be about something negative or positive. The idea is that you are linked to it.

What will happen to your voice and body?

Without realising it, you will start to talk faster, in a higher pitched voice. You will make bigger movements with your body and face. Maybe you will even start to portray the things you are talking about. You will use more details, a little less structure, but will make up for it in engagement to the words.

HIGHER, FASTER VOICE
BIGGER MOVEMENTS (FACE/GESTURES)
MORE LOOKING AROUND IN FUNCTION OF YOUR ASSOCIATION
LINKED TO MORE DETAILED/COLOURED/INTERPRETED CONTENT

Associated movement often results in:

- big hand gestures
- widespread arms, open body posture
- moving around
- mimicking behaviour or acting out what is being described
- smile wrinkles in face
- dramatic facial expressions – angry, happy, inquiring
- exposed teeth
- moving closer to the audience
- lowering your body towards the audience

What will the effect be on your audience?
People who hear a higher pitched voice, faster speech, bigger movements in face and body, more details and colourful content will experience this as = I'm being engaged, I'm being inspired.

Pitfall of too much association?
Rambling, voice no longer pleasant to listen to, too many details and sidetracks, energy too intense, loss of structure

Advantage?
You will engage your audience more easily and be able to transfer the passion or experience you have; you will get more attention and positive feedback from the audience. You will talk more fluently which gives the audience the feeling that everything is connected and the story is moving forward. In piano terms, they call this playing 'legato'. When you bind your notes together in one smooth play. They will stand out less as separate notes but together will form a whole.

Standout example?
Comedian Sebastian Maniscalco doing a funny bit during a show. Being very engaged, reliving the experience he is talking about, using a high pitched voice, fast talk, big movements, lots going on.

No doubt you have used DNA in your conversations with friends, at the coffee machine at work or at the bar at your local football club. Everybody does this when they are in their comfort zone – some very outspoken, others still scratching the surface of their potential. But you might still lean a bit towards one of the two extremes, dissociative or associative. Due to upbringing, education, work or what you think is expected from your environment. How do you know what your current go-to mode is? Just look at your speaking pitfalls. If you tend to elaborate too much, lose track of your points, talk too fast and have your audience engaged but also a bit lost about what your point is, you are probably more associated and you need to work more on dissociating. When people don't really get excited about your project, you lose their attention or are easily interrupted, you might lean more towards dissociation. It doesn't really matter what you express most at this time, the point is that you always need both and you know now what you need to work on. The DNA of your story is the melody of everything you say, and the points you are making are the beat (see chapter 13 on page 178). Is it too boring, too intense or just right, so that the audience nods, laughs, claps and moves to your tune? As a flock of birds effortlessly sitting on a tree branch that dances in the wind. As a shell moving back and forth over the beach with the movement of the tide.

Now, what does this look like in practice? There are plenty of examples online and in your daily life. As I said before, you even do it yourself without thinking about it when you are in your comfort zone. But to illustrate the above I'll use a simple story about my morning to show you how this can turn any story into something that captures attention. It works for speech, but it also goes for writing. Authors also need to be able to make you feel the right things at the right time, so they apply the same technique in writing. You will literally read faster and slower; the voice in your head will do the associating and dissociating.

Most untrained speakers would present my morning in a neutral voice with little or no supportive movement. Or they make everything too associated or too dissociated.

I woke up this morning after a rough night. I tapped off the alarm and got up with a dull head. Coming down the stairs, I notice that my wife is already up and smell the fresh coffee she has made. I wish her a good morning and take my breakfast and after washing myself, I leave for the train to go to my morning keynote in Brussels.

Let's spice this up, shall we? This is not a bad story, but it is not a morning you would get very excited about if I told you about it. Let's add some DNA to this story. You will automatically start reading it in a different way, but for illustrative purposes I'll signal what is used where, to push you to use the voice in your head in the right way even more.

This morning, I woke up and I felt like I'd been run over by truck. I'd had a rough night, my head was spinning, but I pushed myself out of bed and said, "Come on Marnick, let's do this!", tapped off the alarm with a thud and went downstairs. **= Associated (higher voice, faster talk, bigger movement, more details)**

But as I was taking the stairs down, I noticed my wife was already up and I could smell the fresh coffee she had made. I entered the kitchen, wished her a good morning and as she handed me a cup while smiling... **= Neutral (regular talking)**

... I thought to myself:... "Why am I so grumpy?... How lucky am I to wake up to a beautiful woman like this every morning.... I am one lucky man." **= Dissociated (lower voice, slow voice, observing, making a point, smaller movement, more pause)**

That boosted my morale, I drank the hot coffee, threw water in my face and with newfound energy I made my way to the train station, ready to rock my morning keynote in Brussels. **= Associated (higher voice, faster talk, bigger movement, more details)**

Now read this story again but read it out loud or at least in a whisper if you are in a public place. Really picture yourself being that person getting up and rushing to the train in the associated parts and slowing down on the stairs and realising you have a great partner. Read it out loud, get into it and you will notice that your body will automatically start to support your reading. If you have really trusted yourself, let go and committed to this little story, you will now have caught yourself acting out this story, talking with intonation and gesturing at your book. If you are reading this on the train, you will probably have some people looking at you, wondering what you are doing.

I mentioned before that there is no right order or number of times you can use DNA. It's just "What do you want your audience to feel at what time?" So, we can easily turn this story around if you didn't agree with the DNA that I gave it. This first DNA was...

A I want to engage you with that rough morning, make you relate to those mornings.
N I wanted you to feel me slowing down on the stairs and coming out of my grumpiness a bit after smelling the coffee.
D I wanted you to realise how I appreciate my wife and that you should appreciate your partner and realise this from time to time.
A I wanted you to feel my newfound energy and run with me to the train in excitement for my keynote.

What happens if we switch it up?

D I want you to realise I hate mornings, I'm not that kind of person.
N I want you to feel my slow pace downstairs, still sleepy, but waking up a bit due to the coffee smell.
A I want you to feel my excitement about having coffee ready, seeing my wife, feeling new energy.
D I want you to know that it is important to stop and realise what you have in your life, which you sometimes forget in the rush of things.

This would turn the story into the following:

...I hate mornings... Never been good at getting up and never will be.
= Dissociated

But I got up, tapped off the alarm and made my way downstairs, when all of a sudden I heard a noise and noticed the smell of fresh made coffee. **= Neutral**

I love it when my wife wakes up before me. So, I jump the last couple of stairs, walk into the kitchen, greet my wife with a big kiss and the hot cup of wake-me-up she hands me. I quickly eat something, do some dance moves in the shower and with newfound energy I rush out the door to catch my train for my morning keynote in Brussels. **= Associated**

And as I plump down in my train seat,...looking at the landscape starting to move past as the train leaves,...I think to myself,... "How am I not a morning person,...when I can wake up to a beautiful and sweet woman like her." **= Dissociated**

Notice the difference? We could switch up this story many more times, even add A, D, N's to make it even more entertaining or touching. If you actually tried to read this a couple of times in the way it is supposed to be read, I hope you feel that you can hear, see and most of all, feel the difference. Same story, minor tweaks to the content, in function of the DNA and big play in voice and movement. This is a simple example of my morning; now imagine this to be your next boardroom pitch or conference talk. Imagine yourself taking people along in what this project would mean for the ambitions of the company, then slowing down and making the point that these big ambitions have a great advantage, which is that they require only a small budget. Then go back up to how you would execute it and go back down to emphasise the role the board will play in this, and go back up... You get the idea, and more examples will follow as we move into the coming chapters around building up your content. For now, I am a happy man, if you have realised the following:

- The state you are in will determine whether you are able to play with voice and body.
- 90% of your speaking impact is determined by your voice and body.
- The difference between associating, neutral talking and dissociating, and their purpose linked to emotion.
- That there is no right number or order; there is only what you want people to feel, and at what point.

- You only have to link and unlink yourself with your content; your voice and body will automatically jump in to support in the right way.
- Yes, there will be minor tweaks in content. 90% is voice/body, but it can't be separated from the content so this part will also be affected as you switch up your story DNA.

"90% of the impact is how you say something. Is content then unimportant?"

Scan the qr-code to watch the video:

Content is very important. which is why I will spend lots of time on it in the next chapters. The right words in the right order can make up a nice quote. The right words in the right order can make up a funny joke. Words do matter, but the 'impact' they have isn't as big as the way they are conveyed. Think back to the "Honey, what's for dinner?" example. Words become memorable through 'how' they are said. Let me give you the example of Gerard Butler in the movie 300. He did the scene where he kicks the Persian messenger into the pit, saying, "This is Sparta," dozens of times. But he and the crew didn't really feel the scene was working. It had no impact, and they wanted to call it a day and maybe cut the scene entirely. But Gerard pushed the crew to give him one more attempt at nailing it, as he wanted to change the delivery of this sentence completely. He kicked the Persian messenger and yelled as hard as he could, supporting the words with his entire body and face, "This... is...Sparta!!!!!". The crew was shocked, surprised, laughed a bit, but also thought, 'Hey, this could work.' They left it in the movie like this and now so many years later, every fan of the 300 movies remembers this quote as if it was yesterday. They would have probably forgotten it if the words were said in a different tone, with a different expression. Would the words "I'll be back" be famous if Arnold Schwarzenegger hadn't said them in his unique way? Would the words "You can't handle the truth!" be top of mind to this day, if Jack Nicholson hadn't delivered them in that tone of voice and with that facial expression? Would "I have a dream" be so iconic if Dr Martin Luther King hadn't said them in that exact intonation? We can debate it, but I know from my experience in speaking and comedy that words matter, and how you say those words matters more.

You lead, the audience follows. You want them to feel engaged and relive an experience or feeling that you had, so be engaged and relive that experience on stage. You want them to focus, observe or reflect with you, so do the reflecting, observing or focusing on stage. Coming back to the title of this chapter, if you can't be enthusiastic about something and bring that enthusiasm to your audience, they won't feel it, they won't believe it. And instead of listening to people telling you, move your hands like this, walk like that, talk like this, which will result in you becoming a bad actor, a puppet and a cringe B version of yourself, listen to yourself. Feel good, trust yourself, link or unlink yourself to your content and your voice and body will do the rest. It knows what to do, just like you know what to do when talking to a baby, your dog or sharing your last holiday experience. It will result in authentic speech, and movement, and no nervous tics or shaking or not knowing what to do with your hands.

You will be an instrument, playing the beautiful song that is your story. Yes, will you need to practise, discover those extra piano keys, downsize or amplify certain threats, of course; every diamond needs to be cut and polished to shine its brightest. But the core, the foundation is present in each of us.

If you are not in the zone, if you are too nervous and revert to that grey default-mode, you are literally saying, "I don't trust myself." Dear voice and body, I don't need you right now, you will only make me look nervous or weird. While they are saying, "Let go, be who you are and can be, we got this, let us cook." Will this take some effort? Yes. Will this feel awkward, fake, forced in the beginning? Probably, but it is not fake, as this version already exists to some degree in your coffee bar conversation with friends. The difference is that you are now consciously going to work with it, because you now know the impact it has and how that impact can be enlarged. You have already done it in the video exercise I gave you. Practise and the awkwardness will quickly disappear. Not because it will become your second nature, but because it is in essence your nature, who you are. After a while you will no longer think about it and it will feel like riding a bike.

A young man in one of my workshops for a large IT company was looking very sceptical when I was discussing this chapter with the group. I asked him for his input and he said, "Honestly, I think this is a load of bullshit. Very fake. We don't all have to be very dynamic speakers like you." I told him that this was far from the goal and asked him to stand up for a second and experience what I mean by this chapter. Reluctantly, he stood up. I asked him to tell the group about his morning, but dissociating everything. This went smoothly because this was his default mode at work. Factual, observing, reflecting, structured, low and slow. Then I asked him to tell the same story, but only associating. He answered by telling the story again in a very dissociated way.

I asked him to do it again and to really go for it even if it felt fake and he would never talk like that again after this workshop. Just to do me a favour. Irritated that he was still standing there and being pushed by me, he went for it with an attitude of 'Here you have it, stupid trainer, you will see this is completely ridiculous.' I knew it would work out – since anger, irritation are associations, he could put that in his story. He went for it and looked at me afterwards with a face that said, 'Is this what you wanted?' I stayed quiet and asked the group, "Be honest, how did you experience this?" The group immediately said, "Wow, why don't we see this version of you in meetings? This is how you should speak at our next town hall. This was really good." With big eyes he looked at his colleagues and said, "Are you serious?!" He couldn't believe what he was hearing. He had just discovered a side of himself that he hadn't consciously known. Even though I was certain I would get this version if we went out for some drinks in a more comfortable setting. We worked on this a bit more during the workshop and combined these insights with the actual presentation that he had to give and mapped out the story DNA. This young man became a big fan, and nothing binds people more than when you help them discover that they are capable of more than they let themselves believe.

We base so much of our communication on the sounds and movements we hear and see. Only a handful of speakers use the insight of this chapter during presentations. They hope to inspire and convince people with just their content, slides and professional façade. They count on achieving 100% success, while they ignore 90% of what will determine this result. We are all just human beings and for as long as we have existed, we have been fans of great stories, told in such a way that they spark emotion. It is who we are, but we often forget that our audience is human when we are speaking to them. We see the group as a scary judging monster and ourselves as a tool instead of an instrument. An instrument that can play the most captivating song, even if you think you have the most boring topic in the world. Learning to map your story DNA and mastering the play of voice and body, true to who you are and can be, will be one of the most rewarding parts of your speaking journey.

> *A banker decided to practise this chapter by using his famous recipe for béarnaise sauce. He was literally going to guide the group through his recipe. He had mapped his story DNA and put Ds, As and Ns next to each point he wanted to make. He presented his recipe in about five minutes and the group ate it up completely. How you needed to stir the pot, the right stove temperature,... Simple things, but due to his story DNA and trusting himself completely with the right energy, he brought his recipe to life through voice and body. The group felt joy, realisation, surprise and was even touched by a certain part of his story – emotions they had never expected to feel when hearing a recipe for béarnaise sauce. That is the power of voice and body and knowing how to play the instrument that is you. This banker's way of speaking, his confidence in front of a group changed completely after that workshop. He is now a frequently requested host of internal events for his bank.*

Lamps, mornings and béarnaise sauce recipes are all fun, but this technique becomes even more powerful when you can combine it with actual content you will use professionally. That's why story DNA mapping will come up again in the bonus chapter. For now, start observing yourself and others, start experimenting, step out of your comfort zone like that young sceptical ITer. Trust yourself, because you are capable of way more than you think.

How to get started:

- **OBSERVE:** Watch great speakers at conferences, at work or online and focus specifically on how they speak, when they speed up, slow down, move a lot and compose themselves. Be aware of how it makes you feel and what it does to the audience and the vibe in the room.

- **EXPERIMENT:** Try to associate and dissociate a bit more in everyday conversations. A colleague asked you how your weekend was. Give him a bit more association in some parts and see how he responds. Or try to dissociate and focus on what is important when you notice your partner is losing himself in his association about something that went wrong at work.

- **MIRROR:** Is somebody associating about the new game that has just been released? Associate with them. They will love it. Is somebody sharing a deep feeling? Dissociate with it and slow down to show you know this is important for them. They will appreciate it.

- **FILM YOURSELF:** You don't like hearing your own voice, or watching your own movements on camera? How can you expect the audience to listen and pay attention if you can't even listen to yourself? It's awkward for a lot of people, because we hear and see ourselves differently than the people around us. That is normal due the sound bouncing around in the chambers of your skull etc. Get used to it, watch yourself on video a million times until you recognise the person that you see on that screen. Once you are used to watching and hearing yourself, you can start experimenting in front of the camera (see chapter 19) and fine-tune what needs fine-tuning.

Remember, you are a diamond in the rough; now you know, and you can start cutting and polishing. It's the reason body builders watch themselves so much in the mirror. Many people think it is because they are vain. Some could be, but they mainly spend so much time in front of the mirror posing and flexing to see how the jury and the audience will see them on stage during competition. Which muscles are overdeveloped, and which ones are underdeveloped, so they know what needs work.

Never underestimate the power of flexing. The same goes for learning to play with voice and body: watch yourself on video until people around you think you are vain. Then watch yourself some more. Make videos at home, post them online to test people's response. If they suck, no worries, the algorithm and your audience will ignore or forget them. If they are good, you can remember what made them so good and replicate it.

Film yourself at a conference or meeting. Ask to record an online call for educational purposes. You have so many opportunities to get video footage, to test and learn, so take advantage of today's technology and reach. You will know exponential growth.

EXERCISE

- *Take a recent presentation you made. Write D, N or A next to each point or slide that you have. Perform that presentation again in front of a friend or camera and analyse how the emotion changed due to paying attention to your story DNA. Switch the DNA and see how the same content gets a whole different feel.*
- *Observe, experiment, mirror, film yourself.*

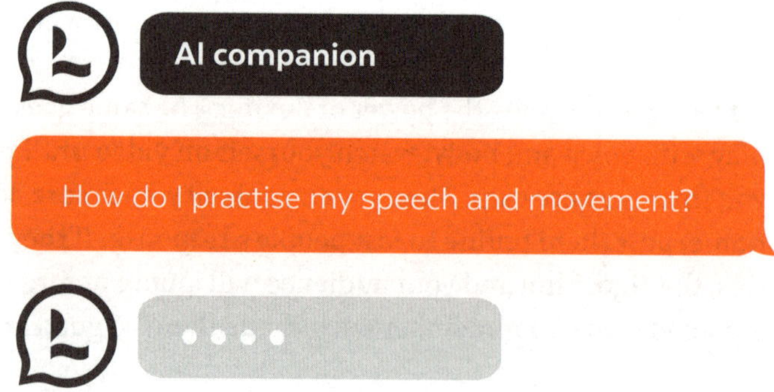

CORE INSIGHTS

- Being in a performance state will allow you to trust yourself. If you are truly you, your voice and body will know what to do.

- You are probably using only a small percentage of your true speaking ability = default mode. Master consciously playing with associating and dissociating and add those keys to your piano.

- Dissociative/Associative speaking goes for animals and humans. No matter the age, nationality or culture.

- Don't ever let anybody tell you how to speak or move. It will result in forced, cringey behaviour. The DNA impact is the same for everybody, but how your voice and body will express this will differ and determine your speaking style.

- Film yourself, listen to yourself and get to know the person the audience sees and hears and what needs amplifying and what needs downsizing.

- Watch professional speakers, be aware of how they apply this chapter and go experiment yourself. Awareness - practise - mastery.

CONTENT
TURNING INFORMATION INTO IMPACTFUL STORIES

10

HOW CAN I CAPTURE THE AUDIENCE'S ATTENTION?

SHORT ANSWER:
"MAKE IT RECOGNISABLE, SIMPLE, TANGIBLE."

Why do you love certain presentations and others don't seem to capture your interest? We are all perfectly capable of deciding if something is attention worthy or not, but defining it isn't as easy. It's like you know you are drinking a great wine, you can say something basic about the taste or colour, but miss the expertise to really identify what makes this wine so much better than others. The same goes for the stories we hear. We know what we like and dislike, but can't quite put our finger on it. After this chapter you will be able to. There are six core elements to any great story when it comes to content. Six key elements that capture people's attention and make your message stick, no matter whether you are talking to somebody at a coffee machine, pitching your product in a meeting or speaking on the big stage. Incorporate these elements, combine them with the structure and way of speaking covered in this book and you will have everything you need for an engaging experience.

I divide these elements into two groups, with three elements per group.

- How people CAPTURE your story = recognition, simplicity, tangibility
- How people REMEMBER your story = narrative, place, emotion

They serve not as a structure or technique, but as a guide to understanding what makes great stories so captivating and, at the same time, as a checklist to see if you have ticked all the boxes with your story. Later in this book, I will offer you the tools to realise these elements yourself, through structure, linking and creative sauce. See these elements as the flavours you eventually want your audience to taste, where your preparation is the collecting of ingredients that facilitate these flavours and your structure, the recipe to follow. So, let us cook. The first step in mastering these elements is knowing them, what they represent and being able to detect them in other presentations. That you are able, like a sommelier with wine, to listen to a talk and define why it is working so well with the audience.

How people ***CAPTURE*** *your story:*

RECOGNITION
"I know it"

SIMPLICITY
"I understand it"

TANGIBILITY
"I see it"

RECOGNITION - I KNOW IT

> ***"The goal of storytelling is not to tell your story, but to tell your story in such a way that the audience recognises their own story in yours."***

From this moment on, this quote will become your speaking mantra. It will become one of the most important elements to master in your speaking journey. For that reason, 'recognition' is the first key element for any great presentation. People love things they know, what they know, they trust and what they trust, they want to give attention to. Recognition is the foundation of the strongest political speeches, what makes your favourite joke and the foundation of most successful online videos and ads, "Mate, check this video, this is so us."

The more recognition you can create in your story, the more probable it is that the audience will feel connected to what you are saying and open up to your core ideas. Recognition shows the audience that you know and understand their world, without literally saying this; see chapter 12. I call it getting 'the nod'. People listening to you and unconsciously confirming that they are relating to what you are saying nod their head. The more you get 'the nod' the more people are inclined to give you attention and trust what you are saying. They are priming themselves to agree with you and say 'yes' to your ideas. Note that in certain situations like e.g. a negotiation, getting a 'no' is just as powerful, but that is not the focus of this book. Or you are getting a 'no' that is actually the audience also saying 'yes, I agree.' E.g. We don't want more work, do we? No (shaking head), we don't. = confirmation they agree to that statement = is also getting the nod.

Recognition is a key factor and is the first thing that comes back from my coachees when I ask them for an evaluation of their most recent presentation. Which parts do you feel were the most powerful or gave you the most audience feedback? It is most often the parts where we really worked on creating that recognition. If you do your preparation (see chapter 11) right, creating recognition isn't that complex. Without the proper preparation however, you will quickly start talking from your own world view, your own experience and forget to take the time to understand the context of your audience. This is the reason so many people zone out when a politician tries to relate to the public in a clumsy way. The public will react with, "You don't know what it's like." "It's easy for you to say." Experienced political speakers do their prep, know how to speak and get the nod, applause and cheers, "Yeah, you tell 'em." "Preach, that's exactly what is happening." Remember, speaking is not about you, it's always about the audience.

SIMPLICITY - I UNDERSTAND IT

Simplicity leads to understanding – certainly when you are speaking to people who aren't in your business or share your expertise. Keeping it simple for your audience might sound logical, but it is hard to do. We are all so into our projects, jobs, hobbies,... that it's hard to still see what is simple for us and not so simple for somebody who is hearing or seeing it for the first time, like an engineer talking to a marketing director about a machine. (= nerd-language, You know how smart I am in Spanish = chapter 1) I frequently catch myself forgetting this and quickly moving through a topic during a workshop, not realising my audience is hearing this for the first time, while I do this every day and have told the story a million times before. That is why an observer or sounding board is always handy; in this case my wife Natalie regularly reminds me to be aware of what is not so obvious for the audience.

Our brain likes simple things, no matter if you have a PhD in quantum physics. We prefer content that we understand and speakers who can explain things in a very easy way. We like it because the speaker has already done the processing work for us. Simplicity gives the brain the confidence to make a well thought through decision or opinion based on the presented information. And it increases the re-tell value of your story – how easily people can re-share your story after they hear it. The simpler the story, the easier this becomes. Add the fact that people need to hear something three to five times before it sticks and your simple points repeated multiple times throughout your talk will nest themselves into the speech of your audience. Your points will become theirs.

Your language will become theirs. It's your job as a speaker to facilitate this. But what is simple for one audience can still be too hard for another. Or if a simple story is too simple for an audience that shares your expertise, then dive deeper into more complex ideas, but simplify those complex ideas for this audience.

It's a constant adaptation in service of your target group. If you think that simplifying is not always a good idea and can lead to a dent in your credibility, remember the quote below, from Jeff Bezos, who is famous for his shareholder letters – letters written to a very educated and highly experienced audience, but in such a way that a seven-year-old kid could understand them. Even though they were written so simply, his investors loved it.

> **"Simplifying doesn't mean dumbing down your content. It means outsmarting your competition."**

> *Hi, I'm X, founder of Y. In short, we make smart sensor networks for industries, so they can use their sensor data for structural health monitoring. We do this in two different ways. We develop custom setups for clients with a specific need and we create our own products and market them. Strain gauges are our sensors of choice, but we work with multiple types of sensors. Collecting data might not come across as innovative, but us detecting anomalies, warning our clients and immediately pinpointing the problem with our algorithm can make a big difference for the lifespan of their materials.*
>
> *Hi, I'm X, founder of Y and this is an elastic band. You know when you stretch this elastic band, pressure will arise. Stretch it too far or when the elastic is too old, it will snap. Nothing special, just take a new one. But imagine that elastic band being the band around your waist when you are about to bungee jump off a bridge, the cable of a ski lift or the rail of a rollercoaster. In those cases, you want to know when the material is about to break or needs replacement. That is what we do with our sensors; we measure the movement of materials and can precisely predict when something is about to rip, snap or break due to movement, heat, cold, pressure or age.*

I am responsible for the availability of the safe and effective use of health products globally. I make sure the company meets all legal requirements. I work together with federal and local governments and advise on matters of climate that can influence the planned products and activities.

Do you ever struggle with folding the piece of paper that is in your medication packaging? You can't fold it the way it was and fail to put it back into the box? Well, the small print on that piece of paper is what tells you about side effects, what is safe and not safe to do. That information is what I go over. Information I check with the responsible authorities. I'm not responsible for the paper and the design, I struggle with it just as much. Also, the reason I'm playing a role in the broader adoption of e-prescription and more sustainable packaging. In short, let's say it's my job to be the ethical compass of the company. Where product and marketing decide what we are going to do, I'm the one who can decide what we can't do.

Building Information Modelling (BIM) is a process that allows the construction sector to create a virtual project-model that can be analysed and adapted before the physical execution of the project. This leads to more accurate budget and material estimations and creates less surprises during construction and an overall better end result.

A BIM-model is like the instruction sheet of an IKEA closet with documentation of all the materials, the assembly instructions, the screws and the amount of everything, including the reference codes if you need to order extra. It's the same in construction, only digital, on a larger scale and with a little bit more screws.

I am responsible for the analysis of mortgage loans based on the sociodemographic data that is made available by the government and financial institutions

I predict based on data if you will be able to pay back your mortgage.

They say, "If you can't explain it to a seven-year-old, you don't understand it yourself." I agree with what this quote is trying to say, but I notice that in reality the better we understand something, the more we get lost in the translation to others. We got so used to seeing the sun set into the ocean that we can' t remember what it was like seeing it for the first time. Step into the mind of your audience, determine what is too simple and too hard for them, adapt your content and master the art of simplicity.

TANGIBILITY – I SEE IT

When a message is recognisable and simple it will automatically become tangible for the audience. Tangible means that what you say isn't just abstract or hollow words, but words supported by exactly the right information for your audience so they get the feeling that this idea is something they can use, apply, think about, re-share,... I feel, hear and see that what you are saying applies to me and my context. I now know what to do with this information. The simplest way of doing this is by adding an example to what you are saying, but as the following example of tangibility illustrates, that isn't always necessary. An easy way to make your content tangible without adding an example is by asking and repeating the well-known management question: "What does this mean?" I have asked this question many times before to great frustration of some of my coachees, to push them to make their ideas more tangible. Here is a small example of one of those conversations:

> ***Coachee:*** We need to start working with more 'lifetime focus' as a marketing team. This year that will be the most important pillar for our team. Diving deeper into the spending pattern of our clients and realising more revenue as a result.
>
> ***Marnick:*** Okay great, and what does that mean?
>
> ***Coachee:*** Well, that we are going to look at what our clients spend in their time with us instead of just the conversion rate per purchase. Seeing that conversation rate metric is often a snapshot and depends on a lot of external factors that we can't control.
>
> ***Marnick:*** Sounds good, but what does that mean?
>
> ***Coachee:*** Well, what I just said. That the conversion rate is not a good metric to determine success as a marketeer. Our low converting clients spend more in the long term and offer us the highest margin.

Marnick: Aha, so it's better for me as a marketeer to focus less on the conversion rate and more on the total spend and margin of my clients, because less converting clients spend more. This way I can determine if my marketing activities are successful, instead of losing myself in the conversion rate and panicking if it is too low.

Coachee: Yes.

Marnick: Why didn't you say so?

Something recognisable is something you know. Something simple is something you understand. Something tangible is something you see yourself applying. Recognition, simplicity and tangibility are liquid. This means that what works for one audience completely falls flat with another. Ketchup on fries is relatable in the US, but we Belgians like our mayonnaise. The simplified technical explanation will be just right for investors, but too simple for engineers. The advantages of conference calling will be very tangible for HR professionals, but factory workers will have no clue how this applies to them. The board is excited about the new strategy and the matrix it is based on, while the employees have no idea how this will work in practice and mean for their job. These elements only capture the hearts and minds of your audience when they are designed in function of your audience. For how to accomplish that, see chapter 11.

How people
***REMEMBER** your story*

NARRATIVE
"I linked it"

PLACE
"I experienced it"

EMOTION
"I felt it"

NARRATIVE - I LINKED IT

We love connections. Good connection between our family, friends, colleagues and the content that we hear. Most presentations are a sequence of pieces of information, because the speaker thinks the links are clear to him so they must be clear for the audience, or there just aren't any links present. These presentations can work, they must, since there are so many of them in today's business, but they hope for results instead of leading the audience by the hand to the desired outcome. Every piece of content should be in its rightful place, being a cause or effect for their neighbouring part, serving a specific purpose in the story. All these pieces together will lead the audience to a pre-determined outcome.

People love when things are linked to each other, when stories come full circle. It makes the story easier to understand, follow and re-tell. The best known examples are songs, connected by melody, and words that rhyme and are very easy to remember. Movies where different characters and scenes cross each other's paths all come together at the end. We love it! Watch a couple of Guy Ritchie films and you will know what I mean. But also, in the corporate and political landscape a narrative red thread is appreciated by audiences. When I host events, survey results compliment the fact that I linked all the speakers and their stories together to one big whole (see chapter 13). Campaigns like 'Yes we can' and 'Make America Great Again' are more than just slogans. They are carefully crafted narratives that bundle all political stand points together. The easier and more connected they are, the bigger the chance they will stick and be passed on. The ability to link content is such an important part of your speaking journey that I will dedicate a whole chapter to it on page 178.

PLACE - I EXPERIENCED IT

Place might seem the odd one out in this list of six, but it does play an important role. Place comes down to: "Where were you when the Twin Towers were hit on 9/11?" "Where were you when the first Covid lockdown was announced?" You probably remember the time and place when you got the news and something changed in your emotional state.

Maybe you even know who was with you at the time and what you were doing. It might get blurry over time and your brain might alter some stuff, but you do still have an idea of that moment. Just as we like to link content, we are also programmed to store a sense of time and place with the experiences we have for better memorisation.

How does this effect your future presentations? By not only focusing on your story, but also on 'how' that story is delivered, in performance and where that performance is delivered. You control the online/offline room as a speaker. Influence the experience as much as possible. Do you stand while speaking in a small meeting? Do you have slides, a flip chart? Is the room a boring white cubicle or a unique location that stimulates the mind? Can people interact in different ways during your webinar? What are you doing to enhance the experience and anchor it in the memory of your audience? I'm not saying you should turn every day-to-day meeting at work into a Cirque du Soleil show, but if you have any opportunity to influence the place in which people experience your talk, do it. It can be as simple as using your voice and body, standing up or changing the room setup from classroom or theatre to a circle without any tables. One of the trainings I do almost every year for one of my long-term clients is in an open zoo. The training room has big top to bottom windows all around and animals (rhinos, giraffes,...) walk around the room. The other day it was a castle looking over a beautiful lake. Again, extreme examples, but I share them to show you what I mean by place. Where people are, what is happening and how their surroundings influence their experience and emotional states matters. Go to Disneyland Paris and you will see what it means to spend a crazy amount of time and effort on the 'place' element.

The second aspect of 'place' is a bit more abstract. It links to the tangibility element. Can your audience picture themselves applying what you are saying in their own context and are you helping them picture that context in their mind while you are talking? Help shape the film that is playing in their minds; can they picture themselves acting out what you are saying? Great, then it is tangible enough. Can you help shape the place where they are acting this scene? Nice, you just gave them a place to link it to. Well written novels do this very well. They write a scene in such a way that you feel you are one of the characters fighting in an elven war, for example, on a battlefield described in just enough detail that you can imagine it at the border of a dark forest, surrounded by misty mountains, yet there's room for you to fantasise and interpret how it looks. Can you help me picture the place I would execute your idea, vision, strategy? What would this look like? How would the work floor change if we implemented your employee experience plan? The more I can link what you are saying to a physical or mental place that triggers emotion, the more it will stick.

EMOTION - I FELT IT

Not to ruin the mood, but even if you checked all the previous elements with your content, people only remember 10% of what you say, if you are lucky. Maybe a bit more if they bother to write it down. The only thing that will engrave itself into their memory for weeks, days, months, years is the emotion you made them feel with your talk. And yet emotion is the thing that is completely cut out of most business-oriented presentations, while social media platforms, advertisers, movie makers spend billions on getting you to feel something and therefor wanting more of it. We doom-scroll our phone for hours, because the algorithm is designed to do just that (dopamine). Why does it then feel like an odd thing to do, when somebody asks to design your next presentation-algorithm (= your story/performance) in the same way? People don't have to cry, jump scare or roll on the floor in laughter, but they do need to feel convinced of your project proposal, inspired by your company vision, appreciated by your end-year keynote and want more of it.

Emotion will stick and push your audience towards acting on your ideas. People take decisions based on emotion and use rational elements to justify that decision. As a speaker you need to trigger the right emotion and offer the data, facts, examples,...so the audience can justify following you in your ideas.

> ***"People take decisions based on emotion and use rational elements to justify that decision."***

I have given speeches at conferences years ago that still generate new requests to this day. They have very little recollection of what I said 10 years ago, but they remember how I made them feel as if it was yesterday.

In case you are thinking that I'm making this up, or that these three elements can't possibly have such an impact on how people remember your story, just think about how you recollect experiences. I'll use my own speaking examples to show you that it is always a combination of these three elements, and the same will go for your recollection of your last ski trip, a bar night with your friends or crucial moment in your team's last match. People who saw me speak at a conference, workshop or internal meeting will come up to me weeks, months or years later and always say the same thing:

"Marnick, you probably don't remember me, but you spoke for our team in that old train museum (place) and told us about Pikachu playing a vital role in change projects (narrative). I felt really inspired by your talk (emotion)."

It can even be a combination of positive and negative, just to show you how our brain combines these elements to create a memory.

"Marnick, I saw you at the last kick-off event of our network organisation, you remember, it was that super-hot room where we were all sweating and hungry (negative place). You really turned that situation into a very entertaining evening (positive emotion). I don't remember much, but I do remember you made a lot of sense in your view on storytelling within sales (narrative). I would like my sales team to get trained by you."

When your story is recognisable, easy to understand and tangible for your audience, the information is linked, the experience, memorable and everything combined calls up a certain emotion, you have yourself a very influential presentation. One for the books and one that will not only open the current door you are knocking on, but also future ones. Like in music, you have then created an earworm. What makes an earworm? A song that is instantly recognisable, with a simple and repetitive melody and words that speak to your emotional state. So, a busy brain that has a little time to wander off or is tired will quickly start humming a song like this, as all these elements speak to the memory part of our mind. It captures you and doesn't let go. If artists aim and succeed to make their song earworms, you can do the same for the song that is your presentation.

> **"Does your story have the potential to become an earworm?"**

Now, all these six elements seem obvious on paper, because you know that making things relatable, simple, tangible, linking them by a red thread, and giving the right context and emotion will do the trick. But knowing does not equal doing. I don't know how experienced you are as a speaker, but even though the world is aware of the above, of every ten speakers I see at conferences or internal events, one, maybe two at best really know how to incorporate these elements in their talk. All the rest lose themselves in complexity, nerd-language, their own world view, vague terminology and buzz words and trigger little to no emotion. Being able to work with these elements is, in my eyes, as I said before, a superpower. Speakers who master them will have people eating out of their hand.

All big claims, but now the question remains: "How can we make the previous more tangible for you?" How are you going to collect all the necessary content to insert these elements into your next presentation? As with everything, it all starts with solid preparation.

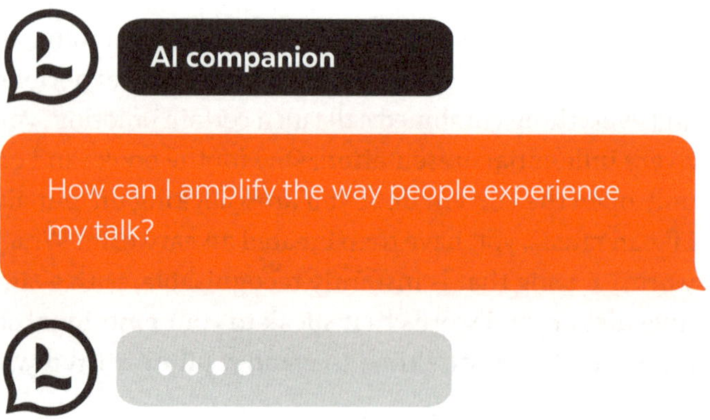

CORE INSIGHTS:

- You capture people's attention with recognisable, simple and tangible content.
- You make your content stick with a narrative, place and emotion.
- Increase the re-tell value of your story by making it simple and repeating your key points multiple times.
- Mastering these six elements is like having a superpower.
- The first step to mastery is consciously being able to recognise these elements in other presentations.
- What is the re-tell factor of your story? Does it have the characteristics of an earworm?

11
HOW DO I PREPARE MY PRESEN-TATION?

SHORT ANSWER:
"DOING A GOAL-AUDIENCE-VALUE EXERCISE."

A marketer who wants to run an online ad will always get the following questions from the related platform: One, what is the goal you are trying to achieve, e.g. clicks, app downloads, views,...? Two, what can you tell us about your audience, e.g. demographic, interest, behaviour,... ? Three, what do you have to offer (value) in visual, video, text that speaks to this audience? Goal, Audience, Value is what every marketer thinks about in function of every campaign. I assume it is also what you think about when coming up with a new project, product, service. It's also known as, 'coming up with a strategy'. I assume you spend weeks, maybe even months getting it right. Focus groups, market research, test runs and dozens of meetings. But how much time do you spend on the most important moment of your whole project,...presenting it? Or in other words, "Do you have a story strategy?"

I don't know you, but this is the time in most workshops when people start smiling with eyes that say, 'you got me'. Most people spend an immense amount of time in preparing their project, but when it comes down to the internal or external pitch of that project, the pitch that will decide whether it is a go or no-go, they slap a slide deck together the night before and hope that it will be enough to inspire and convince their audience. I'm not saying winging* it like that won't work, but you are still 'hoping' for action, while we aim to 'lead' the audience to a guaranteed action. Preparation is key in everything in life, but often neglected when it comes to presenting ideas. Either out of fear of speaking and dreading it (procrastination), not knowing how (skill), or having no more time and energy for this last part, because everything was spent on what came before. Stephen Covey was right when he wrote,

> ***"If they give me 6 hours to cut down a tree, I'll spend 4 hours sharpening the saw."***

Even if people prepare, it is mostly prepared from their own perspective. Preparation like that could still result in a talk that doesn't hit its mark, because it is not recognisable, tangible, simple, linked and emotion triggering (see previous chapter).

**Winging it: Speakers who say they wing it and are successful don't wing it, but have a filled backpack with a lot of insight, experience and practice they can tap into. Speakers who say they wing it, without that backpack, will fail 9 times out of 10.*

So, how do you prepare yourself for any meeting, conference talk, or webinar and inject all these necessary elements? How do you lay the foundation for a strong story and an equally strong performance? Very simply by doing your GOAL AUDIENCE VALUE preparation and filling your backpack with insights. A backpack that will, even without a slide deck or structured story, provide you with more confidence, credibility and arguments if challenged. I'm not going to lie, this preparation takes a lot of time in the beginning, because it triggers you to think differently. During workshops, participants take a piece of paper with the idea that they will quickly fill this in, only to realise as a group that this isn't as simple as they thought it would be. GAV is a very simple concept, but the strain sets in:

- *Letting go of your own world view and thinking like your audience.*
- *Being able to crystallize the ideas that are in your head and writing them down. From mental to physical creation.*
- *Being strict with yourself and courageous enough to make a choice in what your 'goal' is, since there can only be one.*

We all have many ideas in our head and know our business cold, but expressing that knowledge in a simple and tangible way for others to understand is difficult. It's like writing a book. You know what you want to write about, what you want to share with your audience, but then a publisher/editor comes and says, "Great idea, now put it in actual writing." Afterwards, "Nice writing, now re-write it so it actually makes sense for the reader." The struggle of writing a book is crystallizing your ideas, thinking about your points, structuring it and constantly asking yourself if what you are writing will also make sense to somebody else, who isn't an expert, doesn't know you and will not have you around to offer extra information when needed.

Your next presentation equals writing a book. Less intense and a lesser time investment, but the idea stays the same. That is where the first step, GAV, comes in. We are not yet building a story, we are brainstorming, sound boarding, picking brains and collecting all the elements we could possibly need, and more. The story building itself will then go 10x smoother.

The good news is, most speakers already know a lot about their audience, they just have never taken the time to think it through and challenge themselves to dig deeper into their knowledge and experience. GAV can be compared to 'rubber ducking' in the programming (coding, IT, development) world. When you can't find the solution to your problem (code), because you are too close to the project and get tunnel vision, a great way to fix those blind spots and get the necessary insight is to start rubber ducking. It's talking to an object, like a rubber duck, and running through the code and all the steps taken. What will happen is that even though the duck won't say anything back, by saying it or even writing it down, the mental to physical creation will open your eyes and make you see the solution.

For you as a speaker, rubber ducking can be writing it down and sound boarding with friends or colleagues. Run them and yourself through what your audience challenges you on, what you think is necessary for success and you will notice that by just going through this process, you will uncover insights you wouldn't have thought of if you just started building a story or slide deck. It happens in every single coaching and workshop. People are stuck in their own world view, not digging deeper, but just by running through GAV alone, or with me or colleagues and saying everything out loud, writing it on a wall or flip chart reveals the golden nuggets for the eventual story. A coachee once said, "Marnick, you have a special job, you just listen and repeat back to me what I said and still you are worth every penny." In coaching, I am that rubber duck. When I'm not around, the GAV will be your yellow quacky friend.

To illustrate how the GAV works, I'll use an example from one of my clients and take this example along in the next chapters. This way you can see how every step will gradually turn a list of information into a compelling story. If you would like to start immediately and join me, take a piece of paper or your laptop and write the following:

GOAL

What do you want to achieve with your story? What is your specific call to action for this story? When are you successful?

AUDIENCE

What do you know about your audience in function of your goal and in function of this specific meeting/conference/webinar?

VALUE

What does your audience want/need/crave? What will nudge this audience towards your goal?

I'm first going to explain a bit more in depth what each element of the GAV preparation means, to then follow it up with example questions you can ask yourself with each element to get you going and an actual real life example from one of my clients. As I said before, don't get discouraged if it is hard in the beginning or takes some time to fill in. You are probably not used to thinking about your stories like this. I guarantee you, do this a couple of times and you will be like one of my coachees a few years back. It took him two hours and a lot of curse words to fill the GAV in for his keynote, even with my help. After a few sessions of practising, he now does this whole exercise in his head. He says it only takes him 20 minutes to get it right for any new presentation. I have seen him do it and I was proud and impressed. And remember, if you think you don't have the time to prepare like this due to work or private life, there is no such thing as no time, there is only priority and not a priority. If a certain presentation is not a priority, don't expect the audience to treat your story and call to action as one. It might seem like an investment at first, but needing five meetings to achieve success with your story takes longer than preparing it right and getting buy-in first time. There are also no wrong answers, this is a brainstorm. Write everything down that could be relevant, and use friends and colleagues as sounding boards. You will probably not use every point in your eventual story, but you will have allowed yourself to fill that backpack and walk into that on- or offline room with a massive amount of arguments, value, knowledge about your audience,... You will already have become unshaken, and we aren't even building a story.

GOAL

Here is where you write down what you want to achieve with your story. This goal is not your department goal, your overall project goal, your life goal,... This is what you want to get out of this specific meeting, conference, webinar,... with this specific audience. It tells you when your story was successful. It gives you and the audience direction and a destination to work towards. When I ask people what the goal of their presentation is, they often answer, to inform, to entertain, to teach or to inspire. That is not a goal as every great story informs people, entertains, teaches something and is inspirational. Those things are your ticket to play. What will your audience do when you have informed, entertained, inspired them? What action do they have to take? What do 'you' need out of this interaction with them? How are you going to measure success?

There is also only one goal. If you are convinced that you have multiple goals, you need to map out a stakeholder journey. Look at how many meetings you need, with what audience and the specific goal of each encounter. It is hard enough for a speaker to work towards one goal with their story and it is hard enough for an audience to follow that speaker to that one goal. Don't confuse or mix things up by adding multiple goals, risking having to take multiple paths and leaving the audience unsure of what it is you want them to do.

Even if you say that besides getting a budget approved, the extra goal is to gather insight from your audience on their priorities for the project, then I would say that the budget is your goal. You walk in with the confidence, the preparation and the story that will lead this audience to the approval of that budget. Will you gather insight and get feedback along the way? Certainly, if you listen carefully and are in a focused performance state, but that is a bonus, not your goal. If you say that getting the budget is too soon and you first need input, that's okay, but then your goal for this meeting is not the budget, the goal is getting as much input as possible. Totally different setup of the meeting, totally different story.

Let me compare it to sales, to make this last part extra clear. When I ask sales professionals "What is your goal?" they mostly say, "Closing the deal". Great, that could indeed be the goal of your story. Then I will question that goal, just to be sure. "Will it be possible for the client to sign the deal in the meeting or right after?" "Do you have the right person in the room to make that decision?" When the sales person confirms that he can make that sale there and then, great, that is the goal. But when he answers, "Indeed we don't have the right people in the room for this deal," then your goal is to secure a new meeting – getting these people to invite the right people. If you don't have the decision maker in the room or if this person is very well shielded by other managers, make it your goal to help these managers tell your story so well that they secure your deal for you. Closing; new meeting; and helping to pitch internally are three different goals depending on the context and the stakeholder journey you are in. Three different goals, three different GAVs, three different stories. Which one is it?

What is your goal? Such a simple question, but in workshops, frequently the hardest to answer. You need a goal, a call to action. You need something to work towards, an underlying red thread. You need to be so convinced of this goal that you align everything towards it. That it's already 99% sure that this goal will be achieved by you and your story, before you take the stage. People who walk into a room without a clear goal will talk a lot, but say little. They will guide the audience, but with uncertainty, leaving room for strong characters in the audience to highjack the meeting, secure their agenda or grill the speaker.

Those presenters walk out frustrated, lose credibility and get the feeling that they are getting punished for leaving room for feedback, input and questions. There is nothing wrong with feedback, input and questions, but they need to be in line with your goal. You have probably heard the saying, "If you stand for nothing, you will fall for everything." The same goes for the goal of your story. What is your big idea, the red thread, your story destination, the thing you need, the thing you want and the thing nobody can distract you from? You lead, the audience follows, but you have to make sure that you know exactly where you are leading them, or there will be mutiny on your ship.

Your goal will determine everything else in this and the next chapters, so getting this right is crucial for success. Most people will be speaking in a corporate context, presenting their product, service or project. If you need to speak at a conference, your audience will be big, diverse and no event likes speakers selling on stage, certainly when you have a paid booking. Here the inform, teach, entertain, inspire factor needs to be very big, but there still needs to be a goal. What is that big idea that you will lead your audience towards and that will glue the whole story together? What is the big shift you want people to make after they have heard your talk? What are you so convinced of that they need to agree with at the end of your session? It will be harder to check if you rocked it, but looking at survey results afterwards, book sales, social media posts, and people reaching out to say that they implemented exactly what you said will be the indicators that you reached your goal. If you are a mindset coach and your goal was to convince people that yoga will change their stressful lives, you had better have people tagging you online afterwards, saying they just bought some yoga pants and are on their way to their first class.

If you are struggling with determining or deciding on your goal, a little 'goal' finding hack is to write down the goal that you currently think is the one that needs to be achieved – the thing you see as story success, and you want or need within your context. Then go to the next part – 'audience' – and start writing down everything you know about your audience in function of this goal. Once you have a substantial list, go back to your goal and ask yourself, "Now that I know this about my audience and reflected on it, is this still the right goal?" I had a gentleman in coaching who said with conviction, "My goal is to convince the board of this project and get approval." After talking about the board and what he knew about this audience, linked to this goal, he said, "Now that I see this information, I'm doubting my goal, because I just said myself that the board is already on-board with this project. They actually want to know what I need from them to make it happen."

If he had walked in with a story to convince the board of the project, he would have been stopped halfway and somebody would have said, "Yeah, that is all great, we already believe in this project, but what do you need from us to make it happen?" Uhm... Here you see that the goal you have might not be the right goal for this moment and this audience. Is what you want already a given, granted or no longer relevant? Is the audience expecting your goal or do they have a different view on the purpose of the meeting? There are still too many professionals starting presentations with either no goal, multiple goals, the wrong goal for them or the wrong goal in function of the audience. As rapper Eminem said in 2002, "You only get one shot; do not miss your chance to blow." Meaning, if colleagues, investors or a conference audience grant you their time, make sure you walk in with a crystal-clear purpose.

AUDIENCE

Once you have determined your goal for this specific presentation, you can start brainstorming about your audience. Remember, if you are unsure about your goal, you can revisit it after this 'audience' phase. In this part you are going to write down what you know about your audience and the world they live in, linked to the goal you have. Write down everything. This is not your story but your preparation. Do research, use colleagues or friends as a sounding board, get in touch with the meeting organiser or event team. Do whatever you have to do to get as much information about your audience as you can – who they are, the world they live in and what they will challenge you on. The more you know, the more elements you have to choose from when building your story in the next chapter. Plus, a backpack full of interesting information that you might not use in your story could come in handy when being challenged.

In chapter 10, we discussed the importance of recognition, tangibility, simplicity, place and emotion. All these elements are linked to the characteristics, thoughts, challenges and overall context of your audience. You need to map out what the world of your audience looks like before you can tap into it. Just like a marketer needs to know everything about the target audience to create an advertisement that sticks. You will be tempted to start with the low hanging fruit. Low hanging fruit is writing down who is in the room, how many people, what their function is, what their personality is like, how they relate in decision-power to the others,...

That is very interesting information to have in your backpack and should certainly be on this list, but please don't stop there, as that information is hard to incorporate in your story. It is more a field guide to understanding individuals and knowing who has the most influence in the room, which comes in handy when dealing with challengers; see chapter 16. Go further than the low hanging fruit. Use the questions in the next part to dig a bit deeper into what these people are bumping into, what is happening in their world, what they will challenge you on, what they have tried before, what is going well,... Low hanging fruit is who they are – easy to answer if you are prepping an internal meeting, a bit harder for a big conference audience. What their world is like, is where the magic happens.

VALUE

You have a whole list of information about your audience. Now that you have intel about their world and what you want, you can start to map out what it is that this specific audience wants, needs and will trigger them to follow up on your call to action (goal). Everybody wants something, is in search of certain things and it isn't always time or money. It could also be respect, security, control, insight, competence, autonomy (freedom), connection,... There is so much that people know they want or aren't aware of until somebody mentions it. As a speaker you will have to find those buttons to push. Value isn't about the value that you think your project, idea, product, service offers, but the value this specific audience is looking for. As Dale Carnegie said:

> ***"You have to bait the hook to suit the fish."***

It's like convincing your partner who loves sunny beach holidays to go skiing instead. What value do you have that links to this audience, your partner? Is it that you can get a tan quicker due to the reflection of the sun on the snow? Is it the après ski that is even crazier than the Ibiza clubs? Is the not-feeling-guilty about eating delicious food, because you burn the calories during the day? Depending on your audience, these are strong value offerings, but they could also fall flat, because they are not what your audience is looking for.

What does your audience want, need, crave so their world (audience) will change for the better and they will grant you your goal? It is the answer to the well known question: "What's in it for them?" The answer is not what you 'think' it is, looking from your world view. The answer is what you 'know' it is, looking from the perspective of your audience. Goal is a tough cookie in the GAV preparation, and value can be equally challenging. A value-hack is to try to turn the challenges your audience has into positives. A coachee of mine was struggling with the value list.

"I don't know the value my client is looking for."
– "Who is your client and what do you know about him? Give me one element from your audience list."

"Well, he is an insurance broker who runs a family business. The insurance broker is being cut out too much from the process when there is a damage case. It's almost entirely automated."
– "Great, what does your tool have to offer that plays to this insight?"

"Well, it gives him more contact points with his clients, because they can follow up where the client is in the automated process and where it is stuck or clarification is needed and it offers the NPS-score the client gives to the entire handling of the claim."
– "So, you offer a return to the connection insurance brokers used to have with their clients and due to the insight in NPS you give the broker the tools to *start a conversation with their client*, seeing insurance is about *trust and not just growth*; the *core of any family business* = how they like to deal with their clients."

"That is indeed what this man wants, is frustrated about and is looking for."
– "Great, now let's find some more value we can offer this man."

Later he also found out that his broker contact wanted to stop alienating his older clients who weren't digital savvy, and also still give them the opportunity (autonomy) to easily handle their claims. The brokers were losing their local brand awareness, as it was all about the mother brand or the brand of the service provider in current tooling. He offered personalised branding for the broker during the entire process (visibility). A fellow participant responded to this GAV discussion and said, "But isn't this a value you can use for any insurance broker?" I asked him what his 'audience' list said about his audience. He replied by saying that his contact was a man who wanted to grow his agency as quickly as possible and even said that the less he talked to his clients, the more money he would make, as it was fee for no work. I asked him if this man would be persuaded by the same value offering as his colleague had just described. He shook his head and acknowledged that this broker wouldn't care about that.

My coachee got a whole list of values he could offer this broker. Will they also work with other brokers? Maybe, but as illustrated, not every broker is looking for this. Some might want to automate even more, only target young people or feel that less contact with clients is easy money. Value is always linked to your specific audience. Will the value you come up with be world shocking or unique? Probably not. They will often link to time, money, the ABC of needs (autonomy, belonging, competence) or any of the elements in the Bain & Company value pyramid. The way you link these elements to your audience is where you will make the difference. The broker might crave more autonomy, but what does that mean for this specific broker? That is what you need to find out in this part of the GAV.

Aren't we missing something?

We are talking about GOAL – AUDIENCE – VALUE, but where do we actually talk about the solution we are bringing, e.g. your roadmap, 5-step-plan, tool, strategy model,...? The reason I don't incorporate this in the GAV is because that is what you will easily talk about. If I ask workshop participants, "What is it that you want to explain to your audience?" (see next chapter), I get an avalanche of words showing me what they want to do, how the tool works, what roadmap will lead the company to the promised land,... Your solution is important, but it's something you know very well, because this is what you have been working on, thinking about and preparing for ages. If I asked the coachee in my previous insurance example, "Besides the GAV, tell me, what is it that you want to explain to this broker?" He would say "That we have a great tool that makes it possible for insurance brokers to do X Y & Z, that takes clients through three phases to get their claim registered. The first phase... and so on." That is the explanation of your solution, that is top of mind for you and is easy to talk about. The key here is to link this to your audience and value, but that is for the next chapter. Let's first start filling that backpack – come up with our story strategy by mapping out our GAV. The following series of questions and example will help you get started.

PLACE

When are you going to tell this story?
Where are you going to tell this story?
How long do you have?
Conversation or presentation?

SOLUTION

What do you want to explain?

GOAL

What do you want to achieve?

AUDIENCE (example questions)

What does the current world of my audience look like? What are they being confronted with?
What is going well? What is going not so well?
Who are they and what is my relationship with them? Who calls the shots?
What have they tried before in function of my goal?
What could they have against my goal?
What are possible positive or negative assumptions my audience might have? What would the most positive/negative person in the room ask me?
....

VALUE (example questions)

What challenges from my audience's world can I turn into a positive for them?
What specifically is my audience looking for in function of my goal?
What will my audience gain personally or professionally from what I am saying?
What things have made my life/business better, easier, more successful after I applied what I am saying to another client, department, my own life,...?
What does my audience really need right now?
...

Example

I will use the example of a client of mine who needed to speak to a group of students. I picked this example for three reasons, though I have hundreds in my backpack.

One, it's about networking. This book doesn't focus on networking, but by using this example I can also share some insights on networking with you, on the side, since that is also a form of speaking and telling your story.

Two, because I don't know what business you are in. So this example will speak to everybody – students, CEOs, IT managers, HR managers,... everybody needs a strong network. This way you can hopefully also relate to this example.

Three, if you can capture the attention of a group of students, you have mastered this book. A business audience will be polite and grant you attention, because they feel it is the right thing to do, even if you are boring as hell. Students either like you or they don't, and they will make sure you know and feel it. Keep them engaged with their very short attention span and you know you did a great job. It is therefore no surprise that the woman who built this story rocked her presentation and was later asked to teach as a guest lecturer at the school.

PLACE

When are you going to tell this story? *Tuesday next week at 9am.*
Where are you going to tell this story? *At the student entrepreneurship day at the local university for economics and trade sciences.*
How long do you have? *I have a speaking slot of 30 minutes + 10 minutes* Q&A
Conversation or presentation? *Presentation*

SOLUTION

What do you want to explain? *My 5-step approach to networking which includes preparation; coming in early and alone; energy; walking the eight; connecting online.*

GOAL

What do you want to achieve? *I want to convince the students of the importance of networking while still in school to kickstart their career – so they will connect with the speakers and the business owners that are present at the event.*

AUDIENCE

- Motivated students
- 100 participants
- Partners of the school are present (= business owners)
- 18–23 years of age
- *Alumni are present*
- They are studying towards their Masters in trade sciences and economics
- *Ambitious people*
- Dutch speaking

  = This list is what I called 'low hanging fruit' earlier.

- Students *don't* think they *need networking* in their current context
- This entrepreneur day is boring, obligatory and just older people preaching
- Still *live at home*; only person they need is mom/dad
- They think they have *no time* to network
- *I'm an alumni* of the school myself, I sat in the same classrooms
- They *don't* expect to *need* it in their future job
- They don't realise the *importance of internship* and their first job is still far away
- *Some have no idea* what you mean by networking
- There are *already students networking* on Linkedin who added speakers to their network
- *A lot of social media usage*, but just to look at funny videos or take pictures of their food
- Perception that *degree* and knowledge is *enough* to make it in business
- Networking and promoting yourself is *only for slick people*, it's hard to do, they don't want to

- How to start, *out of the comfort zone, scary*
- I don't want to do it alone, always *awkward*, often take friends or colleagues along

  = This list can be even longer, but for the purpose of illustration on how the GAV works, I think this gives you a good idea. Will some things in your audience list be assumptions? Could be, check upfront or even during the talk, to see where your audience stands on this. Remember, you know more about your audience than you think, so don't doubt yourself too much.

  The bigger the audience, the more common denominators you will have to come up with. They are always present. You can't talk to everybody specifically. In a small meeting you can narrow it down more, as you probably know the audience and their context (colleagues, board, clients,...) on a more personal level and the group is smaller.

VALUE

- Some students already added speakers on Linkedin before the event. They already know me now and every person is only 4–6 steps away from another (6 steps of separation). They are one step closer to their dream job. = *being connected and closer to someone they admire or a job they really want*
- You are already using your phone, social media. The world is at your fingertips without having to create an extra habit. = *simplicity, no extra work needed*
- You will score an internship, kickstart your career and won't have to risk bringing coffee or sorting documents. = *not having to fear the thing no student wants during their internship*
- Your university degree is just your ticket to play, who you know and who knows you is your differentiator = the alumni present will vouch for this. = *confirmation from successful peers*
- People like to talk about themselves. You can move around and you are a young energetic person – the only ingredients you need for successful networking. = *the competence to execute the networking tips*

- Linkedin SSI (social selling index), how strong are you online in networking? = *competition and comparison, you don't want to be the one with the lowest score*

  = The value that is listed above is very simple, but taps into the world, challenges and fears of this specific audience. Students like things easy, things that include the internet, want to be somebody and be linked to people or brands they admire or adore.

You now know where you want your story to lead in order to be successful. You are aware of how your audience is looking at you, the world and your solution, in function of the goal you want to achieve. You established the different value offerings you can make to this specific audience, so they will want to take action on your goal. Your backpack is now filled with insights and elements you can use to start building your story. It's time to put these elements in the right order and show you the universal story structure every successful speaker uses.

AI companion

How do I know if I'm saying what my audience wants to hear?

CORE INSIGHTS

- Your presentation securing your project, budget or sale is just as important as your project itself. Prepare with the same intensity.
- A GAV takes time at first. Having to do five meetings to get what you want, because of bad preparation, takes longer.
- Determine what you want to achieve with your story, how your audience is thinking, feeling and behaving and what they want deep down.
- Your goal is what you want, your call to action. Your measure for success for the story you tell. It's the red thread linking everything together.
- Look at the world through the eyes of your audience, step out of your bubble and let go of your truth. Rubber duck those blind spots away.

12
HOW DO I STRUCTURE MY PRESENTATION?

SHORT ANSWER:
"USING THE UNIVERSAL 4-STEP-STRUCTURE."

How to structure a story is one of the most frequently asked questions. When people think about story structure they often think about beginning, middle, end; hero journeys and transformation moments. They think about starting with your main idea, adding an anecdote and closing with a final thought. The internet is packed with models on how to build the perfect story. The good news is they pretty much all say the same thing, because there is a universal story structure* that everybody uses. They might name the elements differently, but they are saying the same thing. Once you know and master this structure, no story you tell in a meeting, at an event or at the coffee machine will ever be the same. This structure allows me to have audiences throw different elements, ideas and challenges at me while I'm on stage and I present this content back to them as a powerful story or business pitch, on the spot, right there on stage. What takes inexperienced speakers a couple of hours to come up with takes me a couple of seconds due to having this structure in the back of my mind when I'm listening to the audience. Artificial intelligence is fast, but with this structure along with your GAV preparation, you will be faster and more impactful.

**I'm talking about structuring business content. The structure for movies is also universal, but different. Every great movie in history is built up in the same way. The hero is living a dull, normal life. There is a rise of evil, a big event. A hero is called for, but our potential hero denies being the one who is being called to step up. The hero gets pushed on an adventure and reluctantly picks up the mantle. There is a transformation through which the hero starts to realise he has a calling, a purpose and is the hero. He changes, defeats evil and everything goes back to normal. Only the hero has changed and can't go back to normal. He must move on to a different life, world, planet,...If you don't believe me, watch The Matrix, Alice in Wonderland, Lord of The Rings, Star Wars, Harry Potter and basically any other very well known movie – it's this structure. That is movie structure. I will be talking about presentation structure.*

Scan the qr-code to watch the video:

The structure I will present to you consists of 4 steps and I'll start with the step most speakers start with. Step number 3, which I like to call 'explain'. We love to explain things as human beings. We love to talk about our product, service, what we did on holiday, give advice to friends. Which is great, but only when the audience is willing to listen and accept this explanation. If there is a wall, a lack of trust or the audience doesn't have the feeling there is value for them, they will check out. This is why many start ups and scale ups lose pitches – they are so invested in their product or service they can talk about it for hours, how it works, how great it is, what all the features are, to only get a 'no' from the investors, because they don't really care and share the enthusiasm. It's the same as complaining about something to a friend.

While you only want to complain and get things off your chest, your friend, with the best intentions, will start giving you advice and explaining what you should do or what they did in a similar situation. If you are open to it, all the better, but chances are you are not and didn't want advice, just a listening ear. We are drilled in school, in our upbringing to have a solution (explanation) for everything, but that doesn't mean that our audience is ready to hear it, yet. As German political and story campaigning expert Julius van de Laar says,

"Wer erklärt, verliert." (Who explains, loses.)

That's why we start with step 1 in our structure and that is 'relate'. Here we create a connection with the audience, find rapport in coaching terms and convince the audience that we are worth their attention and trust. In this phase you want to show the audience that you know and understand their world – without literally saying "I know what you think and feel" – as this could cause push back. See chapter 16 (for example, a top manager from HQ saying, "I know what you have been through, I know what you feel," while speaking to a group of factory workers that just went through one of the most challenging projects in the history of the company. You don't.) You understand their context, challenges, wins, thoughts, feelings linked to the topic you are talking about. This phase can be a minute or 15 minutes; there is no fixed time frame. There is just how much rapport you have with the audience and how much you need to show you understand their world. You describe their world to them, what you have seen, noticed, experienced, heard and you are letting the audience decide if they recognise themselves and their world in what you are saying. If you did your GAV right, you know this will be the case. As a reward you will get the 'nod' (see chapter 10 on page 128). The nod (which can also be a shake of head) is the physical confirmation of an audience agreeing with what you are saying and confirming their attention and trust. You lowered potential walls and have earned more time and attention through this. Like a comedian opening with a great joke and buying more time and attention through the laughter. The audience is literally saying, you have earned my attention, you seem to know what I'm all about and so I am open to hearing what you have to say. Speakers who nail this part of the story have secured a solid foundation to build on.

You just acquired the attention and trust of the audience, they are ready to listen and feel that this story is about them. Now you can go to step 2: 'offer'. In this step, you are not going to talk about 'their' world (audience world), you are going to talk about 'your' world (speaker world). Their world is full of challenges and things they want to change or struggle with, they just confirmed this. Your world is full of value and somewhere they want to go, because it is packed with value that they want, need, crave. Where I call the 'relate' phase the 'nodding-phase', I call the 'offer-phase' the 'drooling phase'. You literally make them drool over the value you offer. They are thinking, 'I want that, I need that, why am I not living in your world?'

For storytellers who want transformation in their story, well, here you show them how their world could potentially change for the better if they decide to step into your world. If you execute this step right, the logical question popping up in your audience's mind is, "How?" "How do I step into your world and change mine for the better? How do I acquire all this value?"

Very simple, by following my roadmap, my 5-step plan, through this tool, this project approach, this new IT infrastructure implementation,... By listening to my solution to your problem, by letting me 'explain' my product, service, idea, project a bit further. Welcome to the third step, the step a lot of speakers start with. If you do and you have the feeling a lot of your stories fall flat, it's probably because you skipped steps 1 and 2. The audience doesn't feel like you understand their world, they don't recognise themselves, and therefore don't feel that the value you offer is really something for them and will shut the door to any advice or solution you have. You can skip steps 1 and 2, even if in most cases I don't recommend it, when you know the person in front of you trusts you completely, is on board with everything and just wants to hear the how and what you need to get this done. In that case you can dive into the explanation and go straight to step 4: 'achieve'.

The achieve phase is the logical next step to the explanation, because now they trust you and know you understand their world. You have a better world filled with value they want, they now know there is a way to get it and are now wondering, and hopefully already know what action to take to make all of this a reality. They only have to give you what you want, as a speaker e.g. budget approval, buy the book, approval for a new hire, new meeting with the decision maker,... You wrap it all up and ask for your specific action to achieve the goal that you determined in your GAV. And if you did your job right, the audience will have already spotted this red thread and will know what you want.

Interesting fact: if you do a really good GAV preparation and get good at filling in this structure, you will notice that for most stories you only need steps 1 and 2 to achieve your goal. Those 2 phases are where an audience decides if they will follow you all the way or not. If you still have to close the deal at the end, you have to reassess your story. Steps 1 and 2 capture an audience; the rest is filler and in extreme cases won't even be necessary. If you are speaking at a conference, then I recommend you tell the entire story on stage, but in a regular meeting, wrapping it up earlier is a plus for everybody. I'll give you an example of what I mean in this last part.

> *I had a meeting with a German HR director of a large pharmaceutical company. I had never met her before, but she got my name from a colleague that said she would check if I would be a good storytelling partner for her upcoming HR transformation project. Her assistant scheduled a*

video call. The call started with a good afternoon, a short introduction of who she was and what her request was, immediately followed by the question, "What can you do for us?" Germans don't waste time. A lot of people would answer this directness and question with a word cloud of explanation, "Well, we are this type of company, we can do this, that, and so... We are very much invested in... we also have books,..." A whole lot of mumbo jumbo, which would raise her walls and make her decide that I was just another partner trying to get the project. Too much explanation even when she asked, what can you do for us? I started with step 1 and answered her question by saying, "What I see with other clients is that HR has a seat at the table, but is often still seen as a cost, where sales and marketing are seen as strategic partners and vital for the growth of the company. But with a high-pressured job market, burnout and the rise of AI gunning for people's job, HR is more at the forefront than ever, but is not always seen that way. (Note that she had started to nod and lean into the screen.) We help our clients to be heard and seen by the board as that strategic partner through influential storytelling, in the form of coaching and workshops." She replied, "Great, you are coming to our kickoff next month. I'll have my assistant send you the details, so you can make me a price offer. Looking forward, see you soon." She cut the call that roughly took 10 minutes. I didn't go into my explanation about our services, or how we work, what projects we had done or what our great philosophy is. No, I just talked about her world, she started to nod, talked about what she secretly wanted (seeing I know a lot of HR departments crave this strategic position and perception = common denominator). She decided that I knew her world, knew what she wanted and that if I knew those things, my services would be equally on point. I'm not saying all my calls go like this, but I am saying that in my 15 years on stage, I have noticed that every audience decides on granting you your goal during steps 1 and 2. Some speakers skip these steps or don't bother doing a GAV preparation and prepare steps 1 and 2 from their own world view.

So, what does this universal structure look like in short?

1. **RELATE**
   The world of your audience, their world.
   Nodding phase – ***AUDIENCE*** *insights*

2. **OFFER**
   The world of the speaker, your world.
   Drooling phase – ***VALUE*** *offering*

3. **EXPLAIN**
   The answer to the question 'How?'
   Your ***SOLUTION****.*

4. **ACHIEVE**
   What you as a speaker want.
   Your ***GOAL****.*

Notice that I have already incorporated the GAV in this structure. If you paid close attention, they were already blending during the previous chapter. You will need the insights from your AUDIENCE to RELATE. You will need your VALUE offering to show your audience you have something they want in OFFER. You will elaborate on your SOLUTION in the EXPLAIN phase and then end it with ACHIEVING your GOAL in step 4. The GAV is your preparation, the 4-step structure is your storyline.

"But why do I need to do a GAV preparation if I can just fill in this structure?" You can indeed just fill in this structure. That is what I do when I translate people's content elements back to them on stage.

> *What are they bumping into? = RELATE*
> *What do they want/need? = OFFER*
> *How can they get it? = EXPLAIN*
> *What do I want them to do? = ACHIEVE*

It's the reason I can quickly craft stories on the spot, because I thought myself to fill in this structure at a rapid pace. You can too. The reason I hammer on the use of GAV in this book and in my workshops is that filling in this structure is building a story. It will trigger you to get to the point immediately and will make you stick to what you know on the surface. The GAV is a brainstorm, the rubber duck for speakers. This preparation will force you to dive deeper into the world of your audience, what you want and what the audience is looking for – to see if you are stuck in your own world, with your own beliefs. Do the GAV first and your eventual story will become way more recognisable, tangible, simple and emotion triggering, plus, as said before, you will also have the elements you aren't using in your story stored in your backpack. So, in the case of a question or challenge by the audience about something you didn't use, you will remain calm, credible and unshaken, because this popped up in your GAV and you knew this could be put on the table and you have an answer ready. That's why I love GAV. Most workshop participants struggle with the exercise and wonder what the point is, only to come back to the workshop room after some brainstorm work to say, "This is so incredibly valuable. I never thought about my content this way."

I'm assuming you understand the idea of this structure by now and I challenge you to go online and look at great speakers. You will see them running you through this structure every single time, resulting in you nodding, wanting, learning, acting. Will elements in the different steps be blending? Yes. Will some OFFER elements already be connected to parts of the EXPLAIN phase? Yes. Will some speakers already mention their goal/red thread in the beginning? Yes. I chop this structure up into 4 clear steps for your understanding, but as you start to master them, you will start to play with them. As long as you respect the psychological order that your audience needs to go through, attention/trust, value, how, next step.

Besides the Networking example from the previous chapter, which I'm taking along as promised, I will also show you some bad examples to illustrate how this structure is generally used. They are bad examples, not because they respect the structure, but because they are too slick, too in your face. But as we discussed in chapter 7, enlarging points we are making can help with the understanding of that point. If you are on social media, I assume one of these influencer ads has crossed your path. These so-called business gurus selling you the dream life or fitness coaches selling you a ripped body in no time. You might not click them and think that they are cringe, but a lot of people do click, because they go through this structure.

Let's say you are an engineer and one of these business ads pops up. It will go a bit like this.

> **RELATE:** *Have you also been studying for years, gotten yourself in debt and wasted your student years on books and pulling all nighters? To only realise you are now working 80 hours a week, in a windowless office, having to ask a less qualified person for a raise or some time off? = You nodding that this is you.*
>
> **OFFER:** *I was like you and got stuck in thinking this was normal life and the way it is if you want to live and provide for your family. But I decided to step away from this rat race and now I'm talking to you from my yacht in Ibiza. I work 2 hours a week and make 50,000 euros a month. = You craving this lifestyle.*

> **EXPLAIN:** *How did I make this drastic change for a better life? Simple, I applied my guaranteed success 5-step plan. Names step 1, 2, 3, 4 and 5. = You writing down the steps.*
>
> **ACHIEVE:** *The only thing you have to do to get a life like this is register for my upcoming free webinar. = You registering for the webinar.*

Let's do the same with the fitness influencer:

> **RELATE:** *You like to eat, go to nice restaurants and enjoy great food, but why does it always come with that sense of guilt? You want to enjoy food, but also live a healthy lifestyle, without having to live off carrots and soup all year.*
>
> **OFFER:** *I used to struggle with this as well, but I changed my training programme and went from a belly to a six pack. I eat pie every day and still I look like an athlete.*
>
> **EXPLAIN:** *How you can eat pie everyday and still be ripped? Just follow this easy food and training programme that changed my life.*
>
> **ACHIEVE:** *Want to take that step towards a healthier body and still be able to enjoy all the delicious treats the world has to offer? You want to get rid of that guilt with every bite. Download my fitness app, subscribe and get your first monthly customised programme for free.*

This structure doesn't just pop up in advertising, but also in politics. Who better to take as an enlarged example than Donald Trump?*

> **RELATE:** *There are too many immigrants crossing the border, making our streets unsafe and taking our jobs. Jobs we no longer have, since everything is made in China – things we can no longer afford as we can't make any money for our families. = Yeah, preach, you know it!*
>
> **OFFER:** *We want to walk the streets again knowing our children are safe to play and walk to school. We want Americans making American products to be in control of our economy instead of trade deals and climate restrictions. = That's what we want!*

EXPLAIN: *That's why we are going to build a wall and pull out of all treaties and start making our product in America again. = Sounds like a plan!*

ACHIEVE: *The only thing you have to do is vote. I'm Donald Trump and I will Make America Great Again. = We will! Let's Make America Great Again!*

**No matter which politician I chose for this example, this book carries no political meaning. This example is purely focused on the application of the structure, not the ideas you may or may not agree with. Just like I will not advise you on eating pie every day or not. It's about the structure.*

These examples are intended to enlarge my point that everybody applies this structure and how it is built up. Start looking at other great speakers and you will see they apply the same flow, only a little more subtly. We did our GAV, we know the structure, time to fill it in with our networking example. Remember:

RELATE = your audience *insights*
OFFER = your value *offering*
EXPLAIN = your how/solution
ACHIEVE = your goal, *call to action*

Example

Notice that I keep all the information in bullet form. I will start fine-tuning the content, as you will notice during your read-through, but I will not start writing long sentences and creating paragraphs. It's important that the points remain and do not blur into too much text.

RELATE

- *I'm an alumni* of the school myself
- This entrepreneur day is boring, obligatory and just older people preaching
- *No idea* what you mean by networking
- Students *don't* think they *need* it in their current context
- Still *live at home*; only person they need is mom/dad
- They think they have *no time/no need/no idea* to network
- Don't realise importance of internship and first job is still far away

OFFER

- You are already using your phone, social media. The world is at your fingertips without having to create an extra habit.
- Some students already added speakers on Linkedin before the event. They now know me and are one step closer to their dream job. (6 steps of separation)
- You will score an internship, kickstart your career and won't have to risk bringing coffee or sorting documents.
- Your university degree is just your ticket to play; who you know and who knows you is your differentiator
- Linkedin SSI (social selling index), how strong are you online in networking?

EXPLAIN

- How do you start?
  1. Connect online
  2. Walk eights
  3. Prepare
  4. Get in and out early
  5. Energy

ACHIEVE

Realise the importance of networking while still in school, connect with the speakers and the business owners that are present at the event and kickstart your career.

Reading through this structure you will already get some feeling of it becoming a story. As discussed, you could just fill in this structure to come up with a story fast, as I do during my live performances working with what the audience throws my way, but filling it in after doing a proper GAV is the way to go. Why do I say, 'becoming a story'? Because it is not a story yet and I deliberately kept it in its rough form by mainly copying the GAV information into the structure. Once you get the hang of it, you can combine this chapter with the next chapter and speed things up. For now it's just valuable information put in the right structure, but not yet in the right order and not yet linked together for it to take the audience by the hand and become an actual story. Linking content is where true storytellers arise.

The next step for a lot of people would be to get super excited about having this structure and to now start building a slide deck and writing it all out in full sentences over several A4s. That's not what we are going to do. We now have what we need to build the story, we have it placed in the universal structure; now we are going to link it for it to become the backbone of our story.

We are even going to cut some content before we add more content. It sounds counterintuitive, but will make perfect sense after reading the next chapter.

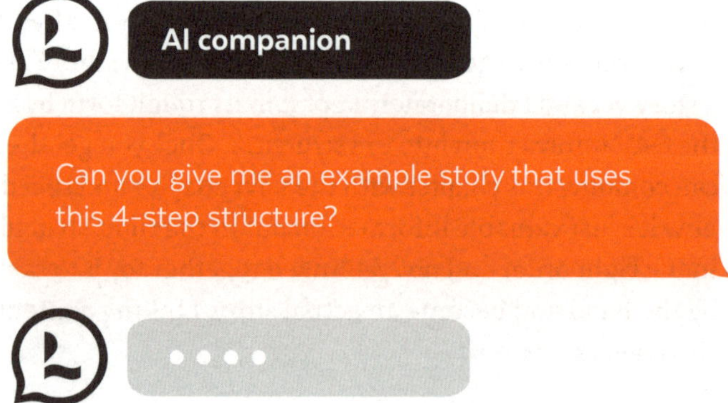

CORE INSIGHTS

- Start by doing a GAV preparation to step out of your own bubble. The more we are expert in our trade, the more we get tunnel vision.
- What is valuable for you is not necessarily valuable for the other person. How are they looking at the world, what do they need?
- There is a universal structure for any presentation: RELATE - OFFER - EXPLAIN - ACHIEVE.
- The 4 steps in this chapter give you the blueprint to structure your information: it's not a story yet.
- Linking information is what will create the backbone of your story.

13
HOW DO I TURN MY MESSAGE INTO A STORY?

SHORT ANSWER:
"BY LINKING IT THROUGH CAUSE AND EFFECT."

We were all very proud of the jokes we wrote during one of the first comedy masterclasses we did – rookie comedians taking our first steps to becoming funny, even though we thought we already were. We got the assignment to write down a couple of jokes. Most – including myself – came back with pages full of text, thinking it was the funniest thing ever written. I presented my text to the professional comedian who was leading the workshop. He looked at it and said, "Great, now downsize it to 140 characters without losing the joke." My reaction was that putting this entire joke with its genius build up into 140-characters while still being funny would be impossible to do. But that was the assignment. We all thought it wouldn't be possible, until we got the hang of it and were asked to produce five to ten of these 140 character jokes a week. Once we had these downsized versions, the lead comedian said, "Now you have the backbone of your joke, the core. Now you can start adding extras to fluff it up."

That is the assignment I also give to my clients. Not to downsize their presentations to 140 characters, but to first go to the core, before they start fluffing it up. The way you do this is by using a popular technique within storytelling. It starts from the idea that every point in your story has to have a reason for being there and needs to link to the previous and following point. It's a constant play of 'cause' and 'consequence or effect'. Most people create 'and then' stories. It's the way most of us wrote papers in our school years, and then this happened, and then this happened. Most presentations in business are 'and then' stories. You want to tell an actual story where every point has purpose and a specific cause and effect.

How can you do this? Just read through your structured content from the previous chapter and put 'because', 'that's the reason why', 'therefore' or 'but' between your different points. If that is possible and you can read through it while every point makes perfect sense and feels like it's in the right order, you have the backbone of your story. Trey Parker and Matt Stone, the creators of the successful South Park cartoon series, said it best, when they told a group of aspiring writers the following.

"We used to write our scripts in the 'and then' way. And then this happened and then that happened. The scripts and eventual shows were good, but not great and we noticed this in audience viewership and response.

We started changing the scripts and seeing if we could put words like 'because' 'that's why'... between the different scenes to see how they were linked to each other. If not, we switched the order or we deleted scenes. When we started doing this, our shows became more attention grabbing, viewership increased and got better responses from the audience."

That is what we are also going to do. Take the structured content from the previous chapter and put the above words in between the points to see if it makes sense. You will probably cut some content, reshuffle some points (without losing the RELATE OFFER EXPLAIN ACHIEVE structure). I'm not saying you should use these words (because, that's why, the reason why,...) in your final presentation or talk, but they now serve as a test to see if every point makes sense and plays its part. If we quickly apply the above to the speaker notes points I shared in chapter 6 then this would be the result:

1. Cybercrime has evolved from password guessing and dodgy mails to deep fake video calls and complete ransomware lockdowns.
   THAT'S WHY
2. It's no surprise – the no. 1 concern for entrepreneurs is cyber security according to recent research.
   BECAUSE
3. Any company can become the victim of a type of cybercrime.
   BUT
4. Ransomware is the most common in our country.
   BECAUSE
5. One wrong click on a maleficent link about a package you ordered, and the hackers are in.
   THAT'S WHY
6. More than 100.000,00 euros in ransoms have already been paid in recent years.
   BUT
7. There is one foolproof way to protect yourself, Cyber Security Insurance.

We can even do this with random unrelated objects and turn them into a story.

As I'm writing this part, I currently have a cup of coffee, a water bottle, a pen and a laptop in front of me. What could this become?

1. I always write my books on a laptop
   BUT
2. I keep a pen close by
   BECAUSE
3. I can only spot flaws and add ideas when I physically write them down
   THEREFORE
4. I drink coffee to make sure I have enough energy to stay sharp
   BUT
5. Coffee on its own will sit too heavily on my stomach
   THAT'S WHY
6. I have a bottle of water to stay hydrated and level the coffee out

I also took our networking structure from the previous chapter and applied this linking technique, which presents us with the following. Notice how the rough information from the previous chapter now not only sits in the right structure, but makes sense and feels like a story due to it now also being in the right order within this structure and linked together using the method we just discussed:

> **EXAMPLE**
>
> - *I'm an alumni of the school myself.*
>
>   **THEREFORE**
> - *I thought back to this entrepreneur day, which was boring and just older people preaching about my future.*
>
>   **THAT'S WHY**
> - *I can imagine some of you having the same feeling about my speech today, networking.*
>
>   **BECAUSE**
> - *A lot of students that I talk to have no idea what networking means or how it will benefit their student life.*

BECAUSE

- *Students don't think they need it in their current school context or don't have the time or skill.*

THEREFORE

- *They don't realise the importance of networking for their internship and first job.*

THAT'S BECAUSE

- *The power of today's technology at your fingertips is not leveraged. Luckily some already do.*

THAT IS THE REASON

- *A couple of students already added me and other speakers on Linkedin before the event and increase their SSI.*

THAT'S WHY

- *These students are one step closer to their dream job (6 steps of separation) and will score an internship, kickstart their career and won't have to risk bringing coffee or sorting documents.*

BECAUSE

- *Your university degree is just your ticket to play, who you know and knows you is your differentiator. Just ask the alumni present here today.*

BUT

- *How do you start? – By applying the following 5 simple techniques:*

1. *Energy BECAUSE people are attracted by positivity*
2. *Prepare for target BECAUSE you can't talk to everybody*
3. *Walk eights BECAUSE you need as many people to see you*
4. *Get in and out early BECAUSE the best happens in the beginning*
5. *Connect online BECAUSE you want to stay top of mind*

- *Combine these simple techniques and you will create so much opportunity for yourself.*

BECAUSE

- *Your degree is your ticket to play; who you know and who knows you will make the difference.*

THAT'S WHY

- *Networking while still in school is so important and I urge you to connect with the speakers and the business owners that are present here today, offline and online, and kickstart your career.*

EXERCISE

- *Take 5 objects that are currently in front of you. Think about how they are linked together and connect them using 'but' 'because' 'therefore' 'that's the reason why' as shown in the above example. When done right, you just turned 5 random objects into a story in just a few minutes.*
- *Now do the same for your story. Crystallize and reshuffle your points in the 4-step structure and link them together. Circle the word that best facilitates the link.*

RELATE

....

but / therefore / and that's the reason why / because

....

but / therefore / and that's the reason why / because

....

but / therefore / and that's the reason why / because

OFFER

....

but / therefore / and that's the reason why / because

....

but / therefore / and that's the reason why / because

....

but / therefore / and that's the reason why / because

EXPLAIN

....

but / therefore / and that's the reason why / because

....

but / therefore / and that's the reason why / because

....

but / therefore / and that's the reason why / because

ACHIEVE

....

I deleted content and re-ordered content and combined some points versus the content in the previous chapter. What we now have is the backbone, the skeleton of our story. We used the GAV to open our eyes and gather as much insight as possible. We used the ROEA to pick the most relevant points from the GAV and put them into the universal structure, while we use the technique above to link it all together and see if everything plays its part. No matter whether you have written pages full of text or have already tried the previous chapters, during a coaching or workshop, I will always ask you to bring all the content back to this 10–15 point backbone. The '140 character' version of your talk. The core of your story.

If you have a presentation, a keynote a workshop and you can't tell me the entire story in 1 minute, you don't know your story. This linking technique allows you to run through all the important parts of your story and remember them more easily, because they are connected. When I tell their story back to them, clients often ask me how it is possible for me to remember the entire presentation while only having it heard once. That's because I don't try to remember everything when listening to your presentation; I try to remember the points you make or tried to make and how it links to the next point. I'm building this backbone in my head, so I can easily go through it afterwards. It's the same technique people use to learn large amounts of information by heart. Don't remember everything, just the points and how they are linked to each other. This is how your child can easily remember their entire history book before an exam and how you can easily remember your entire presentation for a meeting. (Remember, narrative (linking it) = one of the elements of how people remember things (see chapter 10).

"If you can't tell your story in 1 minute, you don't know your story well enough."

I urge my clients to not start practising their entire story before a talk, but to only go through this 1 minute structure. In the car, on the train,... constantly going from point to point, linking it by cause and effect. When I'm building a new keynote, this is the thing I do in front of my wife. I stand in front of her and ask her to listen to my 1 minute version. I then ask her to comment on the flow. Are the links clear and logical or are there hesitations as I talk? Are the right points made at the right time? Only when she says, this is easy to follow and makes perfect sense, will I continue to applying the next chapter. This structure needs to be drilled in. Once you've got it, you can start practising the fluffed up version of your story in the next chapter. Not before. Do this and I will guarantee you will hardly forget anything during your talk, you will never black out, no matter how nervous you are, and you will be able to take your audience by the hand, guiding them from point to point. Making their life easier, since you clearly know the points you want to make. They don't have to filter them out themselves and you give them the feeling it's all connected and that is what our brain loves.

Of course this skeleton needs some meat on the bone, but without the bones to cling on to, the meat will drop to a bloody pile that no audience wants to sort through. If you find this a bit macabre, just think back to the music analogy we made earlier in this book and see the result of this chapter as the beat of your story emphasising every point you want to make and the melody that connects them all together. Now you just need to write some more lyrics to it to make it more recognisable, tangible and emotion triggering.

Can you now tell me your story in 1 minute, making each point on the snap of your fingers like a ticking metronome and having clear cause and effect between these points? Nice, then you are ready to expand your story. If not, go back to the drawing board. Notice that one of the shortest chapters in this book is one of the most important ones in my opinion. This is where true storytellers differentiate themselves.

ADVANTAGES OF DEFINING YOUR POINTS AND LINKING THEM:

- You have a clear 1 minute version of your story that you can expand to 5 minutes or 60 minutes when needed, but the core of your story is always present and understandable for your audience.
- No matter how nervous, you will hardly forget anything and will never black out, because your points and links are engrained in your mind.
- Your audience will love your story more as they don't have to discover your points in a word cloud and are taken by the hand from point to point.
- If you have your speaker notes, this is what will help you keep track on stage, not the full text.
- You have the foundation for your AI prompt if you want to generate slides.

> *A coaching client of mine needed to prepare for her first ever conference speech – a great step up from the regular internal presentations. The only problem was that this first ever speech was on a huge stage for almost 2.000 people. I'm convinced of the steps I shared for you to take for controlling your nerves in chapter 4 and I'm a big fan of stepping out of the comfort zone. But I wouldn't recommend this step up from 5 colleagues in a meeting to 2.000 attendees. There was no way back, the speech had to be given. We did a GAV, we put it in the structure and brought it back to 10 well linked points. I drilled her on this, "What is your one minute story?" "Make your points." "Don't forget your links." "Too much fluff, back to the core." The next session I asked her the same. The next session, the same question until she said, "Yes, yes, yes, I know, make my points, link it*

together." It became an annoying mantra, but one I knew would save her in the end. The day of the conference came and they moved her up to being the opening talk. She was not nervous, she was out of this world nervous. Big stage, huge screen, close to 2.000 people.

I went to sit in the audience and had my fingers crossed, "Come on, you can do this!" She walked on and even though you could clearly see that she was ready to explode and shocked by the view of the crowd (due to the nerves she ignored my tip to stand on stage beforehand to acquaint herself with it and that view), she started talking and made every point, every link, didn't black out and gave her first big stage performance. I was so proud, because this was one hell of a first time, but she stood her ground, probably lost 5 years of her life, but did what she came to do. Why didn't her body and mind shut down? The backbone of her story was engrained in her mind. A couple of weeks later I saw another person giving their first big conference speech. She had lots of text in front of her on the monitors and had clearly practised remembering every word of her story. Two minutes in, the nerves took over, she blacked out and walked off stage.

AI companion

Why is linking the points in my presentation so important?

CORE INSIGHTS

- Information in order is not a story. Clear points that have cause and effect and are therefore linked to each other is.
- Put words like 'because', 'that's the reason why', 'but' and 'therefore' between your points to help you discover the right position for each point and help you remember the links.
- You first need the backbone, the skeleton of your story, before you can put meat on the bone.
- If you can't tell your story in 1 minute, you don't know your story well enough.
- Mastering this chapter is what will separate people who just present information from actual storytellers.

14
HOW DO I INTERACT WITH MY AUDIENCE AND POSE GOOD QUESTIONS?

SHORT ANSWER:
"DO EVERYTHING FOR A REASON."

"Are there any questions? No questions? Then my story must have been clear. In case you still have any, I will be around for the rest of the day."

This is something I hear at every conference or internal corporate event. I understand where it comes from; you want to trigger a response, share your expertise, get some feedback from the audience, but an audience not posing any questions doesn't necessarily mean your story wasn't interesting. It could just be that people don't have questions or they are still in awe of your performance. Most of the time, the lack of questions is due to one of these causes:

- The distance between you and the audience is still too big. The audience doesn't feel confident enough due to the room size, the screen (webinar), the size of the audience or the nature of the subject to talk themselves. Remember, people fear public humiliation and speaking up in a big room, risking asking a dumb question,... all add to the fear of interacting.
  Solution = Downsize the physical and figurative distance between you and the audience by moving closer to the audience, asking specific people for their input on the topic or facilitating a Q&A through an app, chat or host. The smaller the distance, the lower the effort, the safer and more anonymous the interaction is for the audience, the more likely they are to engage with you, online and offline.

- The company or country culture plays a role. You will notice that in some companies or countries interaction will come more naturally. I know that in the Netherlands, they will challenge many points, while in Denmark I am happy to get a nod. After the presentation, the Dutch will congratulate you, the Danish will ask their questions. Belgians, Germans, Danes,... like to interact afterwards, Americans, Dutch,...will challenge you on the spot.
  Solution = Lower the physical or figurative distance between you and the audience. Pose strong questions to the audience during your

talk. Show them that interaction with you is an added value and safe. Facilitate a Q&A or give people the possibility to interact with you in their preferred way – a Q&A corner afterwards, a QR-code, answering online direct messages,...

- You just don't have a compelling story. Your story is very straightforward, not very thought-provoking or surprising. There are few elements in your story that your audience hasn't thought about or bumped into during their life or work. Everybody just agrees, has no strong opinion or didn't get the feeling that you really understand their world and its challenges.
  Solution = Read this book again and make your story more recognisable, tangible, simple and trigger that emotion.

- The audience is tired of interacting with you. You have been asking weird, pointless questions throughout your presentation and the audience doesn't feel that interacting with you is an added value for them.
  Solution = Continue reading this chapter.

I rarely open the floor for questions after one of my talks, unless it's for a project presentation or collaboration proposal. But in the latter cases, the goal and flow of the meeting is in function of that feedback, as we discussed in chapter 11. I will also make time for it if the organisation of the event facilitates a Q&A through a host, app or webinar chat and the audience is urged throughout to ask questions in a safe, easy and almost anonymous way. In all other cases, I use the time that I have been given for my story, the experience and interact with the audience during the speech and in service of what I want them to do, learn or experience. Other questions can always be asked afterwards, via mail or direct message. I am more than willing to reply.

Regardless of the cultural aspect or not having a strong enough story, the distance between you and the audience and the lack of value in the interaction between you and the audience is where you can gain the most. If you have applied chapter 12 and chapter 13, then you are currently looking at a tight 4-step-structure story of ten to fifteen points, linked together and based on solid preparation. The foundation of your house is ready, the backbone of your story is set. Now, you want to start building and putting meat on the bone and making all your points even more recognisable, simple and tangible. One of the elements to do just that is interaction, valuable interaction. I say 'one' of the elements, because even though this chapter is titled, "How to interact with your audience", there are four more elements that you probably already use, have heard of, but don't entirely know what they represent and when they are best applied. Those other elements are: anecdote, data, analogy, surprise.

Together with interaction, they form what I like to call 'the creative sauce'. Strategic, well thought out add-ons to your point-based structure. Considering the title of this chapter, I will continue to dive deeper into the correct use of interaction, but I will take the liberty of further expanding this chapter by discussing all the 'creative sauce' elements. These five elements are the most used techniques by top speakers to upgrade their stories. I'm confident that you have used all five of them in your previous presentations, because they are far from a secret. What is unknown to most is their function, the purpose they serve. Just as with our entire story, if it doesn't serve a specific goal, it goes nowhere and adds no value. Most speakers use an anecdote in their story because they think it will turn their message into an actual story. The anecdote goes nowhere, it's too long, serves no purpose and the audience is wondering why this is being shared with them. A speaker poses a question because he learned that a question is good for audience engagement, but the question itself is pointless and only annoys the audience. If these elements aren't used for the right reasons the following will happen:

- **INTERACTION:** Questions without value or purpose are confusing for the audience and will make them less likely to engage with you.

- **ANECDOTE:** People like to listen to stories, not long anecdotes about your life without a clear point or added value for them. I don't care about your last holiday, unless there is a golden nugget in there for me.

- **DATA:** We love data, but too much data without filter or story will bore the audience, confuse them or make the numbers dance in front of their eyes.

- **ANALOGY/METAPHOR:** I can no longer count the amount of corporate presentations where there is talk of passing the baton like a relay team, a seed becoming a tree or a caterpillar turning into a butterfly. Beautiful messages, but they can quickly become cringey.

- **SURPRISE/CONTRAST:** People have a very short attention span and want to make as little effort as possible to get something. With a lack of highs and lows in your story, the audience will quickly get bored and lose interest.

What are they used for then?

- **INTERACTION:** Getting value out of the audience as a speaker to uplift your story or to let the audience experience/think about the point you are trying to make on the spot.

- **ANECDOTE:** To show the audience that you have experienced the point you are making before. That it's not something you thought of or believe, but have actually done or seen before.

- **DATA:** To prove a point and make it undeniable. You can say something is the way it is, or you can turn it into a fact by showing the data.

- **ANALOGY/METAPHOR:** To make a difficult concept simple. Instead of trying to explain something at length, it's easier to just use the right analogy or metaphor.

- **SURPRISE/CONTRAST:** To keep attention, enlarge a point so that it becomes overly obvious or shock the audience a bit to emphasise that point.

THE CREATIVE SAUCE

Interaction

A good presentation doesn't need interaction. It helps to involve the audience in your story and make them part of it. Plus, it will lower your nerves as we talked about in chapter 4. But interaction is no guarantee of a strong and engaging performance. Interaction is an aid that you can use to emphasise a point. How do you know if it is wise and useful to interact? By asking yourself the following two questions. If the answer to one of these questions is 'yes', it could be useful. If the answer is 'no', maybe it's sufficient to just make the point or a different element from the creative sauce list is more relevant.

1. Do I as a speaker want to get value out of my interaction, and can I use the answer in my story?

For example, you are talking about food and are going to make a point about the health benefits of eating nuts. It's of value to you to know if there are any people with nut allergies.

If there aren't, you can go full on in promoting it; if there are, you can take that into account and show a replacement fruit or vegetable for the allergic people that has the same effect as nuts. If you have prepared well, this is also something you can figure out about your audience up-front. But the point here is that if you need information from the audience and that information can and will be used to upgrade your already great story, then interaction is the way to go. These can be open questions, yes/no questions or just a raise of hands, as long as the answer delivers value to you and the story.

The audience will love to answer the question, and they also immediately learn something about each other (I didn't know you were allergic to nuts?) and you can use and play with this information in your talk. This will give the audience the feeling that your questions are useful, in function of a clear goal and their answers aren't wasted, but used to enhance the story.

Let's say you ask the following question to a group of basketball players, "Who here knows Michael Jordan?" That is a stupid question. Chances are the whole room knows who MJ is. Their answer will not add any value to you, or your talk and the audience will be less inclined to answer future questions, because the interaction with the speaker is pointless. If this example seems a bit dull, I can't count the number of times I have seen speakers asking these types of questions. Recently a speaker at an ecommerce conference started his talk by asking who in the audience had ever ordered something online. Don't ask a question just for the sake of asking a question.

2. Does my question make the audience think about or experience the point I am trying to make on the spot?

These are the most fun questions for the audience. They increase the engagement, are often fun and a bit confronting. Result, a point that becomes very tangible, as they are thinking about or experiencing it on the spot. The easiest example of these types of questions comes from speakers who talk about neuro-marketing, change management or relationships. They ask the audience questions or have little interactions where the audience is confronted with themselves, their limits, biases, ways of communicating,... For example, "Have you ever switched sides of the bed with your partner?" Some people might have, but most people will answer no. I have my side of the bed. Even in hotel rooms, I sleep on my side. This is a great interaction to let people think about how they are creatures of habit and resist change.

Or when you are talking about the key elements of trust and ask the audience to hand their phone to the person next to them for the remaining duration of the talk. People become extremely nervous, hesitate or refuse. Why is that? Why is it such a stretch to hand over your phone to a stranger, colleague or your manager sitting next to you? This is a great way to let people experience the need for certain elements to be present before there is trust and a platform to share something as personal as a person's phone.

You can do this with any topic and these types of questions don't always require a response. Sometimes it is enough to just give people a second to contemplate what you have asked them. For example, "What is your response when you are low on cash in your business? Would you hold on to your old stock and find other solutions or would you be willing to sell it at 50% less?" You will answer the question yourself as a speaker, but you will let the audience think about it for a second. You know most people will not want to sell at half price, and your point is that this proves to be a great method to restore cash flow, but everybody avoids it. I'm not great in finance, so don't ask me how, I just learned this from one of my clients.

So, if the answer is yes to one of these two questions, your interaction could prove to be very relevant for you and the audience. Is it a must to use interaction? Not at all. When you do decide to pursue an interaction, besides the two questions above, keep in mind that the following guidelines will increase your chances of a response and engagement success:

- Make the distance literally as small as possible between you and the audience. For example, move closer, to the front of the stage, walk around in the meeting room, remove barriers like tables,...
- Make the figurative distance as small as possible. For example, start with easier questions first, gaining trust and showing that there is value in answering.
- Make answering as easy and risk free as possible via throw mic, chat, host, app,...
- You pose your questions with conviction, clarity and simplicity. People need to understand the question, feel that you want an answer and that this interaction is a valuable part of the story. Hesitation in posing the question will cause hesitation in answering it.
- You repeat the answers the audience gives you for everybody, certainly when they don't have a mic. It will give you some time to think and the rest of the audience feels involved in the conversation and knows what is going on. Thank the person for the interaction, make them feel good, seen and appreciated. Make them an ally.
- Pick out a person (online/offline) and talk directly to them or call out their name if you know it. If the group is still somewhat reluctant to participate, single out a person and ask directly. Most of the time that person will answer and if it is a great interaction, the group will follow later.
- Embrace the silence and give people time to think and answer. Also, dare to take a moment to answer a question from the crowd.
- You come prepared and have already thought of most possible answers you can get to your interactions. Avoid being surprised, because then pivoting your story on the spot can become difficult. If you do get a lot of answers you didn't see coming, take them along for the future and go back to your preparation, because there is something missing in your audience analysis.

Execute all of the above well and the audience will love to chitchat with you and play a part in the story. The chances for questions after your talk will have also increased, as the audience has become acquainted with interacting with you and the diffidence is gone. If you are getting questions you don't like or are a bit trolling, read chapter 16 on how to deal with those. The good news is that if you did your preparation right and your story is built in the right way for the audience, chances of trolling are very low.

Note: You can ask very easy no value questions when you are super nervous. We talked about this in chapter 4. Then the purpose is just to make you more comfortable. Still, try to make them as useful as possible, but if asking, "How was lunch?", helps you to relax more, do it.

Note: Interaction, asking questions goes further than what is discussed here. You ask questions in feedback conversations, coaching, negotiations,... I don't go over questions in that context in this book. The focus here is speaking, telling a good story in front of a group, big or small. If you want more insights on the conversation part, how to read people, probe for their intentions,... best to check my previous book Stand Up to Stand Out: Expressing yourself in the most powerful way, follow an NLP course or read books, like 'Never split the difference' 'Crucial conversations' etc.

Anecdote

A common mistake is thinking that adding an anecdote to a presentation will turn it into a story. Yes, an anecdote can be a little story in itself, but adding an anecdote to a boring message does not magically transform it into an impactful story. Add to that a more associated person (see chapter 9), no preparation, no clear point and the anecdote will quickly turn into a too detailed, too long, unstructured word cloud that will end like a bad joke, "Aah, you should have been there."

The purpose of using an anecdote to emphasise a point is to show the audience you have seen or experienced the point you are trying to make before. For example, I use anecdotes a lot during sales pitches, when the potential client frames his challenges and context and I have worked with a similar company on a similar challenge and resolved it. This shows the prospect that I don't just claim to know how to deal with these challenges,

I have seen these exact challenges before and have dealt with them. When I am talking to a bigger audience, I talk about how I fumbled in my early boardroom presentations and got eaten alive, but found a way to change that. An anecdote about that can create a sense of recognition in the audience. This speaker knows our corporate world and knows how we get eaten by our board members, but he figured it out. I must hear this.

Two questions you need to ask yourself to tell an impactful anecdote:

- *What is the exact point I am trying to make?*
- *When does this point happen, or when do I see, experience this in the anecdote?*

Answering these two simple questions allows you to tell only the part of the anecdote where this point pops up. You can leave out the rest, because the audience doesn't care. It lowers the time spent on telling this anecdote, and it is less distracting for the audience, because the point and its value are clearly present. For example, you want to make the point that taking a backpack on an airplane is better than taking a trolley to avoid stress when there is no more cabin space. Inexperienced speakers start by saying they went on holiday last month, the family wanted to go to Spain, you needed to pack a lot, getting through security was a hassle, they feared it would rain that week, your plane was delayed, etc. = The audience doesn't care, it's too long, too distracting.

It's similar to showing your holiday pictures; nobody likes to see them all, we weren't there, just give us some highlights. Experienced speakers ask themselves, where does the point happen, the learning? When you were boarding. Okay, then start the anecdote there.

"Last month we flew to Spain. A couple of minutes after boarding, the crew announced that the cabin was full. We asked the crew why we always had to hand over our bag when, for example, the person in front of us didn't. It is so frustrating. The cabin crew replied that they only take trolleys and never backpacks as they are easily stored under the seat. From then on, I switched my trolley for a backpack and I never have to worry about cabin space again. I recommend you do the same."

The purpose of an anecdote is to show the audience that you have seen or experienced your point before. It will increase credibility, make a point more tangible and recognisable and if you gather enough of them, you will have a backpack full that you can chose from and pop out when relevant. Very handy when preparing a speech, but also in day-to-day meetings where people are sharing their challenges or when they ask you why you are the best person for the job.

Analogy/Metaphor

We like things simple, but some points or concepts are harder to explain to an audience that isn't entirely familiar with your topic, or you just don't have the time to go into much detail. The easiest way to solve this problem, to respect the time and still get your point across in an understandable way is by using an analogy or metaphor.

What is the difference?

Analogy: Making a comparison to a known image to come to a logical conclusion or explanation. For example, searching for that type of candidate is like searching for a needle in a haystack. Life is like a box of chocolates; you never know what you are going to get.

Metaphor: Using certain known imagery to evoke an emotion or feeling. For example, life is a journey. It was a rollercoaster of emotions.

When people listen to your talk, they aren't asking themselves "What is the speaker talking about?" They ask themselves the question, "What is this like?" Because if I already know it, I understand it and what I recognise and understand, I want to give attention to. That is what we strive for in every story and an analogy or metaphor has the power to make that happen really quickly. An analogy is literally comparing one thing to a more known other thing. If you have paid attention while reading or revisiting this book, you would have noticed that I use a ton of analogies.

If you master this particular creative sauce element, you will have a very powerful tool at your disposal as a speaker. The world's best communicators master this and take great pride in finding great metaphors and analogies in their speeches. As I have mentioned many times before and will throughout this book, people like simplicity, people like what they know, and this element taps into exactly that. For this reason, this point will also be made again in the following part about using data.

Data

Certainly in a business context, data is a preferred element from the creative sauce list. Data is very powerful, because it makes your points more factual, more concrete. When an audience is confronted with data instead of just your beliefs or ideas as a speaker, they are more tempted to believe what you are saying and accept it as true. Data also offers some more concrete insight into your point and helps the audience analyse and conclude things for themselves. Adding data to your story isn't hard; marketing, finance, IT, business lead,... almost any profession or topic is sitting on a pile of data. The trick is to being able to select and show the right data in the right way. Too much data, unstructured data, badly visualised data,...can cause the audience to be overwhelmed or distracted. As Carmine Gallo says,

> ***"Data never sleeps, your audience does."***

How can you present your data in an impactful way?

- **SHARE THE STORY BEHIND THE DATA:** Don't just show and talk about the data, focus on the story behind the data. The audience doesn't really care about the data, but about the story behind the data. Our brain is lazy, I don't want to do the work as the audience. You are the speaker; I expect you to have interpreted the data beforehand, reached some conclusions and share the insights with me. What does this data mean and what point is it proving? As a speaker you are not saying, "Look at all these numbers." You are saying, "I looked at these numbers beforehand and this is what you need to know and remember."

- **ONLY SHOW THE RELEVANT DATA:** Building further on the previous point, when you know the story behind the data and the point you want to prove with it, you can pick the exact data you want and need to show. Never show entire data sheets, graphs,...only show what is relevant. Maybe 1–3 numbers or percentages; leave out everything that can distract me. If you are obliged to show a graph or entire data dump, at least highlight the relevant numbers, use arrows and guide my eyes to what is important. Again, our brain is lazy, I as the audience don't want to do the work. Plus, too many distractions and newfound conclusions will make you lose the audience's attention; they start reading, analysing, coming to their own conclusions and you lose control over their attention and your story – most certainly, when they are also experts on the topic you are presenting.

- **MAKE THE DATA TANGIBLE:** As mentioned before, people don't ask themselves during your presentation, "What is this point he is talking about?" They ask themselves, "What is this point he is talking about like? What can I compare it to?" Our brain is constantly trying to make sense of the things we hear and see by linking it to something we already know. That's why analogies and metaphors are so powerful in making difficult concepts simple to understand. The same goes for data. If your audience isn't an expert in your topic, you need to help them answer the question, "What is this like?"

  To give you a concrete example, in a business meeting, if I said that our data centres are under pressure because they have to process 1 petabyte of data every day, this would mean something to an IT manager, but very little to the board of directors. If I then compared it to you having to listen to almost 300.000,000 mp3 songs every single day, that would make sense to the board. It isn't possible; if you tried, your brain would explode. Our data infrastructure is built for 200.000,000 mp3 songs, but we are processing 300 million and continue to grow. We need new investment, so our company's data brain doesn't explode. This is very easy for any non-tech person to understand.

Using data to make points more powerful is definitely an option. But I hope you now see how data is often misused in presentations; it distracts or confuses the audience rather than helping them to understand and see the importance of your point.

Surprise/Contrast

When we read about becoming funnier in chapter 7, we mentioned the use of surprise/contrast to trigger a smile or laughter without really making a joke. It is not the sole purpose of this creative sauce element, but just as with recognisable content, it often makes people laugh. This is a nice bonus, because we like to be entertained.

We aren't very fond of change, we like things we know and want to have a sense of control, but deep down we also crave change, discovery, are curious and want to let go. A story needs to deliver both. It needs to connect, feel familiar and tangible, but it can't be too predictable and flat, or we lose interest. Just as with comedy, we want to be surprised, shocked, taken on new paths. When we want to do that and enlarge certain points, make them stand out or make them more extreme so the audience can't miss the point, surprise and contrast comes into play. The best known and most often used surprise is 'naming the elephant in the room'. It's in people's heads, and once you mention it, depending on the elephant, it will shock, surprise, lower tension and re-ignite attention. But the surprise and contrast can also come from talking about A and instead of going to B, you take them to C. In the same way, a great movie has plot twists, things that stand out, haha and omg moments.

It can't be a predictable flat line of content. To illustrate the use of surprise/contrast and how different creative sauce elements can even be combined to make a point, I'll share a great example of a successful Belgian speaker on the topic of customer experience, Steven Van Belleghem. Combining analogy/metaphor with surprise/contrast.

> *He was giving a talk about customer experience to a very large audience of CEOs, CX leaders and marketers. The point he wanted to make was that customer experience and service is about two parties (client and supplier) adding value to each other at the right time and leaving each other alone when no interaction is needed. Now, instead of explaining this and boring the audience with models and graphs, he showed the audience a picture of a rhino and a bird sitting on top of this rhino. He said, "This is the rhino and the oxpecker." The rhino is minding its own business, grazing the savannah. But sometimes the rhino gets parasites on its thick skin. The oxpecker likes to eat these parasites and comes to sit on the rhino and*

> *removes the parasites and also acts as an alarm for sneaky poachers. This is also great for the bird, as it is also protected from predators while it is on the rhino's back. No more parasites, no more bird, until new parasites come. This is what great customer service is: a partnership with value for both parties and the client (rhino) not getting bothered or spammed when no interaction is needed. People in the audience felt almost touched by this story and understood what Steven was saying. He then said, "But what is customer service like in most companies?" He showed a picture of a cow and a big dirty fly. There is no partnership, there is just the cow being harassed by the buzzing, itchy fly that is around 24/7, not adding any value, but constantly asking for something. The whole crowd laughed and nodded in recognition that indeed most companies worked like this.*

I hope you can spot all the elements used and that, with this chapter, you can start fluffing up your 10–15 point story structure from chapter 13. Make it more recognisable, tangible, simple and emotionally triggering. As with everything in this book, if you haven't yet mastered it, you can now at least recognise the use of these elements and techniques in the presentations you listen to yourself. We all use these elements; the difference between poor speakers and really good speakers is that the latter are aware of the purpose of each element and therefore use it at the right time. Now you can too.

How does this chapter apply to the 'networking-example' we have been taking along since chapter 11? We have our preparation from that chapter, we have our structure from chapter 12, our backbone story from chapter 13 and now we can add the fluff, or what I like to call 'the creative sauce'. Time to uplift our points that are carefully linked, to make them more recognisable, simple, tangible and emotionally triggering. Let's put some meat on the bone, write the lyrics to our song or start cooking with the ingredients and recipe we prepared.

> *The first step is taking your 1-minute skeleton story and defining where you want to use which element of the creative sauce. There is no right or wrong, or how many times you can use something, you don't have to use every element and there aren't combinations you can't make; there is only what you think is needed and the best element to use to make sure your point comes across. Not every point needs creative sauce; sometimes it's*

sufficient to just make the point. I left out the linking words (because, therefore,...) from the previous chapter, as you know the links.

- I'm an alumni of the school myself.
- I thought back then that this entrepreneur day was boring and just older people preaching about my future.

= ANECDOTE – I have experienced this before.

- I can imagine that some of you have the same feeling about my speech today, networking.
- A lot of students that I talk to have no idea what networking means or how it will benefit their student life.
- Students don't think they need it in their current school context or don't have the time or skill.

= SURPRISE – Name the elephant in the room

- They don't realise the importance of networking for their internship and first job.

= INTERACTION – Make them think about it on the spot

- The power of today's technology at your fingertips is not leveraged. Luckily some already do.

= SURPRISE – Name the elephant in the room

- A couple of students already added me and other speakers on Linkedin before the event, increasing their Linkedin SSI.

= DATA + INTERACTION = Prove it + Make them experience/think about it on the spot

- These students are one step closer to their dream job (6 steps of separation) and will score an internship, kickstart their career and won't have to risk bringing coffee or sorting documents.

= ANECDOTE + DATA – I have experienced this before and I can prove the importance
= INTERACTION = Make them experience/think about it on the spot

- Your university degree is just your ticket to play, who you know and who knows you is your differentiator. Just ask the alumni present here today.

  = INTERACTION + DATA – Make them experience it on the spot and prove it

- How do you start? – By applying the following 5 simple techniques:
  1. Energy = DATA + INTERACTION
  2. Prepare for target = ANECDOTE
  3. Get in and out early
  4. Walk eights = ANECDOTE
  5. Connect online = INTERACTION

- Combine these simple techniques and you will create so much opportunity for yourself.

- Your degree is your ticket to play, who you know and who knows you will make the difference.

- Networking while still in school is so important and I urge you to connect with the speakers and the business owners who are present here today and kickstart your career.

Step two takes some experience and creativity, which is the reason I call it the creative sauce. If you live like a true storyteller, you will have a notebook full of possible quotes, data, anecdotes,... that you can draw from. The more you fill your backpack overtime, the easier it will be to find the right creative sauce to amplify a point. Like a comedian that has many shows under his belt and knows exactly what will get a laugh and what not. Start filling your backpack. You can of course always ask an AI agent to help you come up with creative ideas when you are just getting started.

Let's look at the story when I add the elements that I chose + some extra content to go from points to text without losing the point I'm making. This is to show you how the backbone story can expand using the creative sauce elements. I have highlighted the creative sauce elements by making them bold.

- **Hi, I'm X and not so long ago I sat on the chairs where you are sitting right now. We also had these entrepreneur days and to be honest, I always thought they were boring and a waste of time, because you had to listen to older people talking about your future. I was like, "You sound like my parents, what do you know?!"**

- Now I'm standing here myself, as I've been asked to talk to you about the importance of networking. I'm not saying this goes for everybody, but I can imagine some of you are now thinking, **"Yup, just get on with it, we don't care."** (first laugh, students changing posture from 'bored' to sitting more upright, while smiling and showing interest)

- Which is perfectly normal since a lot of students that I talk to aren't overly excited about networking and the added value for their student life.

- Why would you be? You are still in school. **Let's be honest, the most important people you need in your network are your parents and your friends. The first for money and laundry, the second to party up that money in those fresh clothes.** (second laugh) You also have so much homework and projects that you don't have the time (nodding) and your priority is not connecting with a bunch of professionals you don't know.

- But you shouldn't underestimate the power of networking as a student. It is key for any student to start with it while still in school, certainly in economics and trade, **because what is it that none of you want to do during your internship that is coming up?** (students shouting, boring internship, just sorting documents,...) Exactly, you want a cool internship place; you don't want to bring coffee to the boss all day and print or scan documents for 8 hours straight. (third laugh) The power of your network will determine where you will end up, for your internship and for your job.

- And while networking can seem time consuming and awkward, it has never been as easy as it is today. You have the world at your fingertips through your phone, social media. **But what is it used for? Taking pictures of food, doing cutes dances and taking selfies on holiday.** (fourth laugh) Nothing wrong with that, but with more power in that phone than in the rocket that put people on the moon, it could be used differently. Imagine using that power to expand your network. Luckily some of you have already done this.

- A couple of students have already added me and other speakers on Linkedin before the event. They have already boosted their network and chances of an awesome internship and solid first job by a couple of simple clicks. **I have 7.000 connections. These student boosted their network and increased their Linkedin SSI. Because how strong are you at the moment? You should be between 80 and 100 points. Let's check your current Linkedin SSI. Scan the QR code and see who is already building a network.**

- **The students with a good SSI and that added me are now already one step closer to a potential person they need in the future, because every person in the world is only 6 steps away from anybody they want to get in touch with.** They say social media downsized these 6 steps of separation to only 4 steps. Imagine a brand you want to work for, a famous artist you want to get to know,... **Who are you a fan of? (Taylor Swift) Let's see how many steps your are removed from that person?** You are basically only 4 to 6 steps away from any person, if you have a network. **This was me** (*shows student picture*) **in my last year of university (just like you) I looked up to the following people** (shows pictures of well known entrepreneurs and artists in the country), **their achievements, company and brands. I got to work and started connecting with people via the school, online,... and now...**(*shows pictures of selfies with all these people*) **they have giv-**

en me my first job, they have become friends, mentors and even clients. They seemed unreachable, but they are all so close once you start connecting with people.

- Your network is the key to a great internship, a great first job and basically kickstarting your career. Some think they can just finish school and then start, some think they don't need it in their job because they aren't in sales and others still believe that their university degree will do the work for them. Your degree is just your ticket to play, who you know and who knows you is what makes the difference. **X% of employers in this country state that they value the online presence, attitude and network of a person more than the degree they have.** If you don't believe me, **who here is also alumni like me?** (alumni raise hands) Great. Who here landed a great internship or first job, because they waved their degree around? (nobody raised their hand). Who here landed it because they knew the right people? (all raised their hand). Can you elaborate at bit (*alumni tells short anecdote of how he landed his internship and it kickstarted his career*).

- Knowing it's important and seeing the value doesn't mean it has become less awkward or difficult for some to connect with others. It's normal to feel some hesitation; even people who have been working for quite some time still find it hard to network. So, how do you start, how can you already connect with people here today? By applying my 5 simple techniques, now and in the future.
  1. Energy – **How did you feel about me when I walked into this room?** (students shout nice positive things and great first impressions) Nice to hear, thank you for the compliment. Why was that? I walked in with a smile, open posture, said good morning, interacted and brought a 10/10 in energy and focus. People pick this up and are attracted to it, they want to be a part of it. Do this in any room with people you don't know and people will flock to you.
  2. Prepare a target when you go to a networking event or somewhere where you believe interesting people for your goals and ambitions will present. Prepare yourself upfront. Try to get hold of the list of participants or find those who have already flagged online that they will be attending this event. See who you want

or need to connect with. Research those people, so you will have easy conversation hooks to connect with them at the event. At a recent event, **I knew a potential client was going to be present, so I looked him up and found out that he had done an interesting podcast on the future of sales a little while ago. I listened to it and when I saw him at the event, I walked up with a positive attitude and said, "Hi, I'm X, I just listed to your podcast this week about the future of sales. I really liked your view on things." It kickstarted the conversation and before I knew it, I was talking to my potential client that I wanted to connect with.** If I hadn't prepared, I wouldn't have known that somebody interesting would be there and it would be harder to find an entry point. And most certainly when you are not yet experienced and are stepping out of your comfort zone.

3. Get in and out early. You also want to get in early at these types of events, so you can talk to people when it's still easy going. By the time people start getting drunk or it gets too crowded, you have spoken to most of your targets. Arrive early and leave early once you have talked to the people you came for.
4. Walk eights. You can't talk to everybody and sometimes you miss out on certain conversations. Not to worry, just make sure you are seen. When I'm at an event, I will always walk eights in between my conversations. This will ensure that I have covered the whole floor and everybody had the potential to spot me. **I had an event just last week, where I didn't talk to everyone I wanted to talk to, but after the event I got a DM from one of these people saying, (shows screenshot), "Hey X, we didn't get a chance to talk, but I saw you at that event. Was was your experience of it? Maybe we should get some coffee."**
5. Connect online. You will be able to use the internet to research and prepare, but also afterwards. The days of business cards are over; connect with people online so you stay top of mind. Connect and share valuable content, so you keep popping up in their feed, so the moment they have an opportunity, they immediately think of you, the person they met at that one event and connected with later online. By making that person a part of your network, you just got one or more steps closer to the person you really need or want to connect with.

- Now combine these simple techniques and you will create a world of opportunity for yourself. Don't start when you need the internship or that first job, start beforehand, start now.
- Remember, your degree is just your ticket to play, who you know and who knows you will make the difference.

- Networking while still in school is the key to kickstarting your career and getting all the opportunity you want. Look at my story, look at the stories of the alumni here today. Follow in their footsteps and take one or more steps closer to getting what you want, by connecting on Linkedin with all the speakers here today, the alumni and using these simple techniques at this event and others in the future. Your career starts today. I'm X, thank you!

EXERCISE

- *Choose one element (in your actual story, you can of course combine multiple elements) and fill in that element next to the point you are trying to make in your core structure that you now have. Do you want to make your point more simple, tangible, emotional or recognisable? When you just want to make your point, no element is needed and it can be left blank. After this step you can also try to write your story a bit more in full as I did in my own example.*

RELATE

.... *CREATIVE ELEMENT =* ....

.... *CREATIVE ELEMENT =* ....

.... *CREATIVE ELEMENT =* ....

OFFER

.... *CREATIVE ELEMENT =* ....

.... *CREATIVE ELEMENT =* ....

.... *CREATIVE ELEMENT =* ....

EXPLAIN

.... *CREATIVE ELEMENT =* ....

.... *CREATIVE ELEMENT =* ....

.... *CREATIVE ELEMENT =* ....

ACHIEVE

.... *CREATIVE ELEMENT =* ....

.... *CREATIVE ELEMENT =* ....

.... *CREATIVE ELEMENT =* ....

AI companion

Why don't people interact with me during or after my presentation?

CORE INSIGHTS:

- A powerful story doesn't necessarily need interaction.
- Interaction can make the audience feel part of the story, add value and make your points more tangible.
- There are multiple reasons for people not asking questions after your presentation. It's your job as a speaker to always make interacting with you easy, safe, fun and rewarding.
- Interaction is just one of five frequently used elements to emphasise points in a story and make them more tangible, recognisable, simple and emotionally triggering.
- The five creative sauce elements are: interaction, anecdote, analogy/metaphor, data, surprise/contrast.
- Not every point needs a creative sauce element. Some points are just good as they are and just need to be mentioned. Afterwards, move on to the next point.

15
HOW DO I BUILD A POWERFUL SLIDE DECK?

SHORT ANSWER:
"EXECUTE THE PREVIOUS CHAPTERS FIRST."

A great presentation doesn't need any slides, because you as a speaker are enough. You are the instrument that can keep people's attention with the movement of your body and the play of your voice. Combined with your well-structured content that you turned into a compelling story, you can trigger emotion and inject your audience with dopamine, like the drug dealer you have now become as we discussed in the first part of this book.

In my opinion, your aim should be to become so good at speaking that you don't need any slides or visual aids to tell your story. It will also release you from all the technical worries and save you a lot of time in slide deck building, even if you ask AI to assist. I'm used to it from my comedy years: there is only you, the mic and the audience and I have been speaking professionally without slides for some years now. But you are probably still on your learning journey and speaking without slides can be very scary, because you have nothing but yourself to hold on to. There are even very seasoned speakers who have shared with me they are only now taking their first steps in speaking without slides. So, if it is still a big step for them, I can understand that a slide deck is still something you want to bring to your meeting or conference talk.

The good news is that if you ticked off the previous chapters, making a slide deck will not consume a lot of time. In the overview following this chapter, you will see that making slides is only step 5 in the 6-step process we went through, while most speakers consider building a slide deck as step 1. In this case, you will either come up with a crappy deck, information instead of a story and will have to pull an all nighter to get it done. When it's step 5 it will take you 30–60 minutes, maybe even less. I'm assuming you have some notion of your preferred slide building tool. I'm not going to give a detailed description of how to build a slide deck; there are plenty of 'how to' books for that, but I am going to give you 10 things to keep account of that will make your slide deck stand out and support your story, without becoming the story (you are the main attraction) and how the previous chapters set you up for a quick build of the deck.

1. VISUALISE THE POINT YOU ARE TRYING TO MAKE

Let's take our 'networking example' that we have been taking along for the last couple of chapters. Below is what we have after we added the creative sauce. If you now want to build a slide deck for this story, you just need to ask yourself at every part, "What point, part of my point or feeling do I want to emphasise or highlight? What needs to be remembered or should stand out?" The answer to that question is what you put on a slide. I'll illustrate it by writing next to each part what was put on a slide by my client to serve this story.

- Hi, I'm X and not so long ago I sat on the chairs where you are sitting right now. We also had these entrepreneur days and to be honest, I always thought they were boring and a waste of time, because you had to listen to older people talking about your future. I was like, "You sound like my parents, what do you know?!"

  SLIDE = PICTURE OF MY CLIENT IN HER STUDENT YEARS

- Now I'm standing here myself, because I was asked to talk to you about the importance of networking. I'm not saying this goes for everybody, but I can imagine some of you are now thinking, "Yup, just get on with it, we don't care."

  SLIDE = PICTURE OF BORED STUDENT HAND RESTING IN FACE

- Which is perfectly normal as a lot of students that I talk to aren't overly excited about networking and the added value for their student life.

- Why would you be? You are still in school. Let's be honest, the most important people you need in your network are your parents and your friends. The first for money and laundry, the second to party up that money in those fresh clothes. You also have so much homework and projects that you don't have the time (nodding) and your priority is not connecting with a bunch of professionals you don't know.

  SLIDE = PARENT DOING LAUNDRY

SLIDE = FRIENDS PARTYING

- But you shouldn't underestimate the power of networking as a student. It is key for any student to start with it while still in school, certainly in economics and trade, because what is it that none of you want to do during your upcoming internship? (students shouting, boring internship, just sorting documents,...) Exactly, you want a cool internship place; you don't want to bring coffee to the boss all day and print or scan documents for 8 hours straight. The power of your network will determine where you will end up, for your internship and for your job.

SLIDE = QUESTION "WHAT DON'T YOU WANT FOR YOUR INTERNSHIP?" BIG ON SLIDE

- And while networking can seem time consuming and awkward, it has never been as easy as it is today. You have the world at your fingertips through your phone, social media. But what is it used for? Taking pictures of food, doing cutes dances and taking selfies on holiday. (fourth laugh) Nothing wrong with that, but with more pow er in that phone than in the rocket that put people on the moon, it could be used differently. Imagine using that power to expand your network. Luckily some of you have already done this.

SLIDE = VISUAL OF SMARTPHONE IN HANDS
SLIDE = COLLECTION OF PICTURES OF SELFIES, FOOD, DANCES

- A couple of students added me and other speakers on Linkedin before the event. They have already boosted their network and chances of an awesome internship and solid first job by a couple of simple clicks.

SLIDE = LINKEDIN SCREENSHOT OF NEW CONNECTIONS

- I have 7.000 connections. So, the students who added me are one step closer to a potential person they need in the future.
SLIDE = "7.000 PEOPLE" BIG ON SLIDE

- Every person in the world is only 6 steps away from anybody they want to get in touch with. They say social media has downsized these 6 steps of separation to only 4 steps. Imagine a brand you want to work for, a famous artist you want to get to know,... you are only 4 to 6 steps away from that person, if you have a network.

  SLIDE = PICTURE OF FAMOUS PERSON
  SLIDE = "6 STEPS OF SEPARATION" BIG ON SLIDE
  SLIDE = MY CLIENT'S SOCIAL SELLING INDEX WITH QR CODE FOR STUDENTS TO TEST THEIRS ON THE SPOT

- This was me in my last year of university (just like you). I looked up to the following people, their achievements, company and brands. I got to work and started connecting with people via the school, online,... and now they have given me my first job, they have become friends, mentors and even clients. They seemed unreachable, but they are all so close once you start connecting with people.

  SLIDE = ORIGINAL PICTURE OF MY CLIENT IN HER STUDENT YEARS
  SLIDE = PICTURES OF PEOPLE MY CLIENT LOOKED UP TO
  SLIDE = PICTURES OF MY CLIENT POSING WITH THESE PEOPLE

- Your network is the key to a great internship, a great first job and basically kickstarting your career. Some think they can just finish school and then start, some think they don't need it in their job since they aren't in sales and others still believe that their university degree will do the work for them.

  SLIDE = "YOUR NETWORK IS THE KEY" BIG ON SLIDE

- Your degree is just your ticket to play, who you know and who knows you is what makes the difference.

  SLIDE = "YOUR DEGREE IS JUST YOUR TICKET TO PLAY" BIG ON SLIDE

- X% of employers in this country state that they value the online presence, attitude and network of a person more than the degree they have.

SLIDE = "X% OF EMPLOYERS VALUE YOUR NETWORK OVER YOUR DEGREE" BIG ON SLIDE

- Who here is also alumni like me? Great. Who here landed a great internship or first job because they waved their degree around? Who here landed it because they knew the right people? Can you elaborate a bit?

- Knowing it's important and seeing the value doesn't mean it has become less awkward or difficult for some to connect with others. It's normal to feel hesitation. Even people who have been working for quite some time still find it hard to network.

SLIDE = PICTURE OF SOMEBODY FEELING AWKWARD

- So, how do you start? How can you connect with people here today? By applying my 5 simple techniques, now and in the future.

SLIDE = "5 SIMPLE NETWORKING TECHNIQUES" BIG ON SLIDE

1. Energy. How did you feel about me when I walked into this room? (students shout nice positive things and great first impressions) Nice to hear, thank you for the compliment. Why was that? I walked in with a smile, open posture, said good morning, interacted and brought 10/10 in energy and focus. People pick this up and are attracted to it; they want to be a part of it. Do this in any room with people you don't know and people will flock to you.

SLIDE = PICTURE OF VERY OPEN POSITIVE PERSON WITH THE WORD "ENERGY" WRITTEN OVER IT IN BIG LETTERS

2. Prepare for target. When you go to a networking event or somewhere where you believe interesting people for your goals and ambitions will present, prepare yourself upfront. Try to get hold of the list of participants or find those who have already flagged online that they will be attending this event. See who you want or need to connect with. Research those people, so you will have easy conversation hooks to connect with them at the event. At a recent event, I knew a potential client was going to be present, so I

looked him up and found out that he had just done a cool podcast on the future of sales. I listened to it and when I saw him at the event, I walked up with a positive attitude and said, "Hi, I'm X, I just listened to your podcast this week about the future of sales. I really liked your view on things." It kickstarted the conversation and before I knew it, I was talking to the potential client that I had wanted to connect with. If I hadn't prepared, I wouldn't have known that somebody interesting would be there and it would be harder to find an entry point – most certainly when you are not yet experienced and are stepping out of the comfort zone.

SLIDE = PICTURE OF SOMEBODY DOING RESEARCH WITH "PREPARE FOR TARGET" WRITTEN OVER IT IN BIG LETTERS

OPTIONAL SLIDE = SCREENSHOT OF THE PODCAST AND OTHER INFORMATION YOU FOUND

3. Get in and out early. You also want to get in early at these types of events so you can talk to people when it's still easy going. By the time people start getting drunk or it gets too crowded, you have spoken to most of your targets. Arrive early and leave early once you have talked to the people you came for.

SLIDE = PICTURE OF PERSON GETTING OUT OF BED OR PERSON THAT IS DRUNK WITH "GET IN AND OUT EARLY" WRITTEN OVER IT IN BIG LETTERS

4. Walk eights. You can't talk to everybody and sometimes you miss out on certain conversations. Not to worry; just make sure you are seen. When I'm at an event, I always walk eights in between my conversations. This will ensure that I have covered the whole floor and everybody had the potential to spot me.

SLIDE = PICTURE OF SOMEBODY WALKING WITH "WALK EIGHTS" WRITTEN OVER IT IN BIG LETTERS

SLIDE = FICTIONAL FLOOR PLAN OF NETWORKING ROOM WITH A FIGURE OF EIGHT PATH DRAWN OVER IT

Just last week I had an event where I didn't talk to everyone I wanted to talk to, but after the event I got a DM from one of these people saying, "Hey X, we didn't get a chance to talk, but I saw you at that event. What was your experience of it? Maybe we should get some coffee."

SLIDE = SCREENSHOT OF DM OF THIS PERSON

5. Connect online. Use the internet to research and prepare, but also afterwards. The days of business cards are over; connect with people online so you stay top of mind. Connect and share valuable content, so you keep popping up in their feed, so the moment they have an opportunity they immediately think of you, the person they met at that one event and connected with later online. By making that person a part of your network, you just got one or more steps closer to the person you really need or want to connect with.

SLIDE = SCREENSHOT OF CLIENT'S LINKEDIN PROFILE

- Now combine these simple techniques and you will create a world of opportunity for yourself. Don't start when you need the internship or that first job, start beforehand, start now.

SLIDE = OVERVIEW OF ALL 5 TECHNIQUES

- Remember, your degree is just your ticket to play, who you know and who knows you will make the difference.

SLIDE = "WHO YOU KNOW AND WHO KNOWS YOU" BIG ON SLIDE

- Networking while still in school is the key to kickstarting your career and getting all the opportunity you want. Look at my story, look at the stories of the alumni here today.

SLIDE = "START NOW" BIG ON SLIDE

- Follow in their footsteps and take one or more steps closer to getting what you want, by connecting on Linkedin with all the speakers here today, the alumni and using these simple techniques at this event and others in the future. Your career starts today. I'm X, thank you!

SLIDE = ALL THE WAYS STUDENTS CAN CONNECT WITH THE SPEAKER

EXERCISE

Take your points and creative sauce elements from the previous chapter and try to make a slide for each point with the insights from this chapter. Or use AI to do it for you with the same information. Witness the creation speed and the quality of your deck.

The only thing we did was go through this structure and highlight the most important points, numbers or feeling that we wanted to get across. It takes some creativity to come up with the creative sauce from the previous chapter and you need to spend some time coming up with the best visual or prompt for an AI agent, but I hope you notice that the process of going through this story and making a slide for every part will take you a very limited amount of time versus starting from scratch and trying to build your story by making a slide deck. Now you can go through the story and say, "Oh point = 7.000 people, big network. Nice, I'll put that big on the slide and just tell the rest. Cool, next slide." The pace of creation is crazy. Now imagine using your 1-minute backbone story or the version where the creative sauce is already added, give this as a prompt to your AI agent and you will get a solid slide deck without you having to tweak it too much. The AI will know exactly what it needs to visualise, and where. People used to say to me that they were going to pour themselves a glass of wine in the evening and start building a slide deck. Do it this way and you will have a deck before you have a chance to take the first sip.

2. MAKE EVERYTHING BIG AND BOLD

You will already have noticed it in the previous point: make everything BIG. Steve Jobs once said that if you can't put it on a slide in 190 font size, you have too much text. I think that is a bit extreme, but I agree with the idea behind it. Your slides are for support, to emphasise and highlight your points, not to tell the story. The focus should be on you. The moment people need to start reading text or are getting confused by all the info on the slide, you have lost the attention of your audience. Everything needs to be big – titles, numbers, quotes, visuals,... This will ensure that what the audience needs to focus on is clear and easy to remember and it will stop you from putting too much on one slide. I still see so many slide decks at conferences and during meetings that are packed with small print, complex graphs and 700 bullet points.

3. SLIDES ARE FREE

The reaction I then get to the previous point when I'm helping a client is, "Yeah, but this information is important and I do think I need to put this number, quote or statement on a slide." If you are really convinced it has added value if it is visualised, then remember this third point: slides are free! Put one point big on a slide, then use a new slide to put the other point big on a slide. It is free, it only takes one click and it will give your audience another attention-injection, because the screen changed. It's like scrolling through your social media feed: watching one visual or clip for a couple of minutes will get boring, but flipping through the ever changing content is what keeps you locked in. The same goes for slide decks. That's why I don't understand companies saying that you need to limit your deck to 20 slides to make sure people come up with crisp presentations. No, they just jam everything onto 20 slides and the visualisation goes all over the place. Back when I used slides for my presentations, I had 85 slides for a 45-minute talk. If every slide is a word, a sentence or a big number, people will like the change and won't mind the clicking. It will also give you room to build up a model or flow, instead of having everything jammed onto one frame. You could also use animations for that. If you go too far and bring 175 slides for 45 minutes, you have to click so fast that it will become a film. That is a bridge too far.

4. FILL THE SLIDE

If you are using a picture, make that picture fill the whole slide. If the quality isn't good enough for that size, use a different picture. Everything needs to be big and visuals need to fill the space. This becomes even more important if you are speaking at bigger conferences where the screens are huge. You need to leverage those screens. Like a movie in the theatre, every visual needs to fill the screen and grab the audience. It looks very novice when you have a white slide with a small picture in the middle.

5. GUIDE MY EYES

As a speaker, attention is what you want and you want the attention on the right elements. When you make things big, divide it over multiple slides. When you fill the slides, you have significantly downsized the chance of the audience getting distracted. But there could be moments when you have to show a graph, a model or set of numbers that can't be separated. In this case, you need to make sure people focus on what you want them to focus on. Highlight the number that is the most important, put a circle around it, use an arrow to point out the main element (As sales expert Michael Humblet says, "We are trained from childhood to follow arrows.") Use one arrow, not multiple, because only one thing can be the most important. If the information is dense and can't be separated or simplified (in most cases it can), you need to guide the eyes of the audience to what is important – circle, arrow, bold letter, highlight, different colour. If you don't, people will start reading, searching for other stuff, get confused or start challenging you on things that are beside your point – you didn't guide them, so they decided to go rogue.

6. MAKE IT POP

Building further on the previous point, making it stand out is a red thread through great slide decks. Besides guiding the eyes of the audience, filling visuals to slide size and sizing everything as big as possible, making it readable and attention-grabbing by the use of font and colour will add to the experience. Make it pop is what I often say to clients. White letters on a darker background will be much easier to read and will grab attention. Switching up darker or white slides with slides of bright colour will surprise the audience and regain their attention. Using clean sans serif fonts will be much easier to read than curly fonts with a lot of distractions. Visuals of people who have nice expressions on their faces will get more attention than stock pictures of plain people without character. Font, colour, visuals – everything needs to pop. Switch things up and surprise the audience or make it so easy to digest that it keeps their attention. Again, see it like a movie and consider the lengths directors and visual effects artists go to, to make sure that the sound, colour and imagery is of the highest quality, to keep your eyes wide open, getting impulse after impulse. That movie is your slide deck. If your corporate brand team says you need to respect the brand colours, I agree. When they limit your creative freedom in making your slide deck pop due to plain and boring corporate identity templates, I disagree. It's not about the template, it's about the audience and how they experience the story.

A nice side effect of great slides that pop, are pretty, highlight value and really trigger the audience in wanting to remember the point on the slide is when they start taking pictures. How picture worthy are your slides? The reason a lot of speakers put their credentials under these slides is that they know they will be photographed. People looking back at them see the valuable content and immediately get reminded of the speaker who shared the insight.

7. EVERYTHING HAS TO HAVE A REASON

"So, it's okay if I put a Minion in my finance presentation?" is a question I recently got from a banking client. He wanted to put it in his slides to make the topic more fun and to surprise the audience. I like Minions, but with every idea you have for spicing up your slides, I recommend you ask one question, "Does it add value to my story?" I asked the banker the same question, "Why do you want to put this Minion in? Does it add value to your story or the point you are trying to make?" He answered no and that it was purely to make a boring presentation more fun. If you are reading the book in chronological order, you will now know that this man needed to go back to the drawing board and actually build a story instead of trying to save a Titanic of a presentation. I like Minions,

I like funny cartoons, I am the GIF master in my friend group, but that doesn't mean they need to be in your slide deck. That is not making it pop. Every element on your slides, from visuals, cartoons, characters, quotes, numbers, and statements to graphs needs to have a purpose. It needs to add value – not distract – and support what you are saying. If there is doubt – it's just an extra, I thought it would be funny or whatever other answer you have – take it out.

It has no business being in your slides. Perhaps you are making a point about teamwork and how you can reach the moon with your organisation if you just put your mind to it. Even if everybody has different personalities and wants to have some fun on the work floor, if the vision is there, the moonshot is achievable in the long term. If that is your point, I can imagine putting a visual of a bunch of Minions on a slide (full size). If your audience watched the first Minion movie, as most people have, they will get the reference. If they haven't seen the movie, use something else or incorporate the reference as a metaphor for your point. If the banker used his Minion in this way, I would see the added value. But if it's a case of "I just want to add something funny", it's a no go.

8. STRUCTURE YES, AGENDA NO

Not everybody thinks about or views the world in the same way. I like a story that just takes me along for the ride. I don't need slides in between parts that give me an overview; I'll do that in my mind while you are talking. I'm more focused on the experience, the value and how you capture my attention. Other people like structure and they need to hear and see that structure. They want to know where we are in your 5-step plan, they want to get a regular overview of where you are in the presentation. Nothing wrong with that; know your audience. I didn't want a table of contents in my first book or to add these core insight summaries, but I got a lot of positive responses from people who absolutely loved this. Everybody views the world in their own way. That's why I'm all for adding slides where you give an overview or landmark to let your audience know where you are in your steps, plan or roadmap. I don't use them a lot, but I do acknowledge their value. What I don't recommend is an agenda slide. A table of contents in a book, yes, because people need to know where they can find what topic in the book and some use it to decide if they want to buy a book. In a presentation, I wouldn't do it. All surprise is gone, you are using the beginning of your talk to go over an agenda, you have already lost all anticipation and attention in the first minutes. I can support an agenda, when you are giving an 8-hour workshop, a little overview of the day, but in a 30-minute presentation, just start. Just start and make sure you keep a clear structure and add some landmark slides in between.

Lose the agenda. Just like losing the slide where you introduce yourself and your company in the beginning of your talk. If your introduction has no added value to your story (see previous point), don't talk about it, you are wasting time. At a conference, the host will have introduced you, so get on with it – unless we need to know something about you that will add to the story you are about to tell. For example, nobody cares about the fact that I have two cats when I'm talking about storytelling within change management. But if I'm doing a talk in which I explain that cats don't have the ability to self-reflect and change behaviour, the intro slide about me being a cat person has added value.

9. EMBED VIDEO AND AUDIO

A piece of music, a podcast clip or a video that doesn't play. If I got a euro for every time that happened in a meeting or at an event, I would be on a yacht in Ibiza right now. Making sure you can move smoothly through slides that include audio or video is very simple. Embed everything you want to play. Put the video or audio offline and insert it into your presentation and set the animation to auto-play when the slide pops up. This way the video is linked to your presentation and you don't have to click, it will start the moment you switch to that slide. This will also allow the tech crew at an event to jump in and start the video for you if something still goes wrong. The moment you rely on a link to the internet or you need to do extra clicks to play it, it will freeze, not play, start to render or say there isn't a stable internet connection. You will get nervous, lose credibility and your whole story will be interrupted. I have just returned from a big conference in Amsterdam and one in Brussels as I'm writing this page and there also, most videos didn't play or had to be started by the tech crew, because they weren't properly embedded.

10. YOU ARE THE STORY

Building a nice slide deck isn't that hard when you know your points and creative sauce. You don't need to be a presentation-building wizard who knows all the ins and outs of the tool you are using. The best slide decks of professional speakers are just clean backgrounds with big white letters or stand-out visuals. You can go further and get creative with animation, AI, branding, but just make sure it adds value and isn't a distraction. As I said at the start of this chapter, you are the story. People come for you, want to listen to you. It's not a competition, but I have seen speakers with fancy pants 3D animated slides get blown away by speakers with no slides. The story will always win if the speaker knows how to tell it. Slide decks you find online or that speakers send afterwards on the request of the audience are useless without the speaker if they are built correctly (see chapter 18). Yes, you get the main points, numbers or quote, but everything else was told by the speaker. You are the story, your slides are just there for support. You need to be able to tell your story in such a way that if your slide deck fails due to a technical hiccup, your videos don't play and you are left with yourself and the microphone, the story and the experience will remain the same for the audience. Many beginner speakers spend 90% of their time on building slides, making sure all the content is in the slide deck and lose themselves in the minor details of where each bullet needs to go. They spend the remaining 10% on understanding the audience, getting their story structure right and practising the use of body and voice. Their slides became the star of the show, but will not have the power to sweep the audience off their feet. Turn it around and spend 90% on understanding your audience, structuring and linking your points, practising your story DNA and 10% on building slides. You will blow people away.

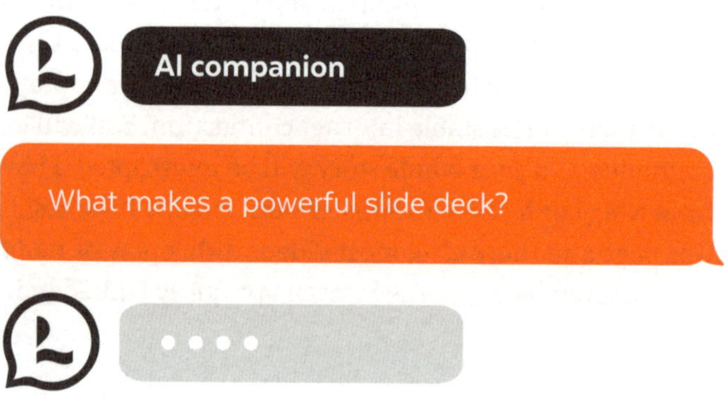

CORE INSIGHTS

- You are the story, your slides are just there for support.
- You will have reached the highest speaker level if you are able to take people along in your story without any slides.
- Building slides is a quick and fairly easy process if you know what points you want to make and what creative sauce you have linked to them.
- Most people start with building slides and spend 90% of their time on them. It's their first step. Great speakers spend 0–10% of their time on slides and realise it's one of the last steps.
- Everything needs to add value. If it offers no value or is distracting, leave it out.

BONUS CHAPTER
COMING FULL CIRCLE

This chapter is not in the table of contents and is not an extra question. This chapter is you as a speaker wrapping up your 6 steps to building any great story and linking it back to your performance. We started in chapter 11 with filling our backpack, we then structured it, linked it, added creative sauce and visualised it with slides. Time to determine how we are going to deliver all this content and trigger the right emotion with our body and voice at the right time. We talked about our story DNA in chapter 9 and will now be able to apply it to our networking example we have been taking along in the previous chapters.

We now have our content in a logical structure, we have clear points, they are linked together, and we can now easily decide where we want the audience to feel engagement or importance. Applying chapter 9 will look like the following example. Remember, there is no right order, there is just what you want your audience to feel, and when. It could be that you disagree with my DNA and would approach it differently. That is okay, as long as you grasp the concept and the technique for all your future stories. If you aren't reading this book in order, I recommend you read this last mentioned chapter before continuing.

You know the story flow by now; this chapter is just to illustrate how you can run through that story and pinpoint for yourself where you want to do what and practise it this way. Will all these As and Ds seem awkward in the beginning – forced and confusing? They could. The goal is not to have you stick to this DNA like a clumsy robot. The goal is to make you think upfront about your performance and be very conscious in practising where you need a switch in movement and intonation, and why you are doing this switch = audience emotion. When I do this exercise with clients, it feels very weird at first, but once they allow themselves to be bad at it and push through the awkwardness, they start to feel, hear and see the difference, certainly when I film every version and play it back to them. As with the GAV (chapter 11), and the linking (chapter 13), this DNA practice will take effort in the beginning, but once you master it, you will start doing this automatically. I no longer write As, Ds and Ns next to my story. I'm trained to feel what is needed on the spot, just as

I can build your story in seconds, live on stage using the 4-step-structure (chapter 12). I have referenced playing the piano many times in this book, but again, it's the same thing. I challenged my teacher on why I need to do these stupid, repetitive scale exercises all the time. I just want to play the piano. She answered: "You want to play the piano? Or do you really want to master the piano? I can spot a self taught piano player from miles away; they can play, but lack the technique to be truly great." The same goes for this part of building your presentation. Adding and practising DNA seems weird and dull in the beginning, but stick with it and you will not become a good speaker, you will became a great speaker. The choice is yours.

Below is what the story DNA will look like for our networking presentation. I added D, N or A where I would switch my intonation and movement and I removed the slide comments from the previous chapter, because in real life this would be your actual presentation. Also, I will not do the entire story – just enough for you to get the idea and to be able to apply it to your own story. Read through it a couple of times in the way the A, D or N suggests you read it. Do it out loud for maximum effect and notice how this story will come to life and points will be made.

STORY DNA - NETWORKING PRESENTATION

D - Hi I'm X...and not so long ago I sat on the chairs where you are sitting right now....

N - We also had these entrepreneur days and to be honest, I always thought they were boring and a waste of time, because you had to listen to older people talking about your future.

A - I was like, "You sound like my parents, what do you know?!"

N - Now I'm standing here myself, being asked to talk to you about the importance of networking. I'm not saying this goes for everybody, but I can imagine some of you are now thinking,

D - "Yup, just get on with it, we don't care."

N - Which is perfectly normal as a lot of students that I talk to aren't overly excited about networking and the added value for their student life.

A - Why would you be? ...You are still in school. The most important people you need in your network are your parents and your friends. The first for money and laundry, the second, to party up that money in those fresh clothes. You also have so much homework and projects that you don't have the time and your priority is not connecting with a bunch of professionals you don't know.

N - But you shouldn't underestimate the power of networking as a student. It is key for any student to start with it while still in school, certainly in economics and trade,

D - because what is it...that none of you want to do during your upcoming internship...?

A - Exactly, you want a cool internship place, you don't want to bring coffee to the boss all day and print or scan documents for 8 hours straight.

D - The power of your network will determine where you will end up..., for your internship and for your job...

A - And while networking can seem time consuming and awkward, it has never been as easy as it is today. You have the world at your fingertips through your phone and social media.

N - But what is it used for?

A - Taking pictures of food, doing cute dances and taking selfies on holiday. Nothing wrong with that, but with more power in that phone than in the rocket that put people on the moon, it could be used differently.

D - Imagine using that power to expand your network...

N - Luckily some of you have already done this. A couple of students added me and other speakers on Linkedin before the event. They have already boosted their network and chances of an awesome internship and solid first job by a couple of simple clicks.

D - I have 7.000 connections...

A - So the students that added me are one step closer to a potential person they need in the future. Every person in the world is only 6 steps away from anybody they want to get in touch with.

N - They say social media has downsized these 6 steps of separation to only 4 steps.

A - Imagine a brand you want to work for, a famous artist you want to get to know. You are only 4 to 6 steps away from that person, if you have a network.

D - This was me (shows student picture) in my last year of university (just like you)... I looked up to the following people (shows pictures of well known entrepreneurs and artists in the country), their achievements, company and brands. I got to work and started connecting with people via the school, online,... and now...(shows pictures of selfies with all these people)

A - they have given me my first job..., they have become friends..., mentors and even clients. They seemed unreachable..., but they are all so close once you start connecting with people. Your network is the key to a great internship, a great first job and basically kickstarting your career. Some think they can just finish school and then start, some think they don't need it in their job since they aren't in sales and others still believe that their university degree will do the work for them.

D - Your degree is just your ticket to play..., who you know and who knows you is what makes the difference.

EXERCISE

Take your structure or your slide deck and write D, N or A where you believe you need to change the emotion of the audience with your voice and movement. Practise your story out loud to see if it makes sense and has the right effect. If not, change the letter and try again.

If you did this for your own story, you have just completed the 6 steps to building any influential story. The 6 steps I recommend you go through every single time you need to speak. Keep doing these steps over and over for every important presentation, keynote or pitch you have and it will become your new comfort zone, your second nature. After a while you will no longer think about these steps, but your body will be trained and programmed to do this the moment you are asked to speak or process content. It will trickle into your everyday life, your conversations with friends will become more engaging, you will be asked to give speeches at weddings, you will be the person of choice to speak at company yearly kick-offs, you will be the most entertaining and valuable guest in panel discussions and you will know your business pitch will be 99% in the bag before you have even walked in. Let's list these 6 steps for future reference, to wrap up this content part of the book.

CHECKLIST

6 STEPS TO ANY GREAT STORY

What happens when you combine chapters 10, 11, 12, 13, 14 and 15? You have the 6 steps that will lead you to crafting any great story and bringing it across in the most powerful way. The way I recommend you prepare any pitch, keynote, internal presentation that you have to deliver.

1. DO THE GOAL AUDIENCE VALUE PREP

Determine your goal and gather all the necessary insights about your audience. Fill that backpack.

2. PUT IT IN THE FOUR-STEP STRUCTURE

Put these insights in the universal structure (relate - offer - explain - achieve).

3. LINK IT

Determine the points you want to make. Crystallize them and link them together. You can use words like 'because', 'therefore', 'but', 'that's why' and ' that's the reason that' to help you with the linking.

4. ADD CREATIVE SAUCE

Take your 1-minute story consisting of points and links. Engrain this core of your story and then add creative elements to amplify your points, making them more recognisable, simple, tangible and emotionally triggering.

5. VISUALISE IF NEEDED

Make slides for every point with its creative sauce if you deem it necessary to create a slide deck for this story.

6. DETERMINE AND PRACTISE STORY DNA

Now that you know what you are going to say, in which order, consisting of clear points that are linked together, amplified by creative elements and potential visual aids, you can now ask yourself at each part, "What do I want my audience to feel here?" Write a D, N or A next to this part or slide and practise bringing across your story using your body and voice in the right way.

CREDIBILITY
LEADING YOUR AUDIENCE IN DIFFICULT SITUATIONS

16
HOW DO I STAY IN CONTROL WHEN BEING CHALLENGED BY MY AUDIENCE?

THE SHORT ANSWER IS:
"STICK TO THE FACTS AND YOUR GOAL."

Big stage, small meeting, online, offline – an audience will not always agree with you. The better your preparation and adaptation of the previous chapters, the less probable it will be that you get challenged. But if you do get confronted with somebody giving you a hard time, interrupting your story or hijacking your meeting, there are techniques to stay in control and even turn these people into fans. The biggest heckler can become your biggest supporter if you play your cards right.

In comedy, heckling mostly comes from people who try to get a piece of your spotlight, feel insecure or who are just drunk. Safe behind their keyboard, online trolls bring others down just to feel good about themselves. People who stand out are easy targets. In an online or offline business context, I assume excessive use of alcohol will not be the reason for somebody speaking up. In most cases, they are projecting a 4/10 on the speaker, don't agree with your world view or feel they will be disadvantaged by what you are saying. The good news is that in almost all these cases, you can stay in control and keep your story on track.

Which is important, because speaking on big stages and being challenged can quickly sidetrack your entire presentation and make you lose credibility and the rest of the audience if you spend too much time, energy and attention on one person. While speaking in online or offline meetings, not knowing how to deal with challengers can also result in that same loss of credibility and attention or the complete loss of control over the goal and outcome of that meeting. It could even be that another person achieves their goal in your meeting on your time if you don't tighten the reins. Let's not go there – and become a frustrated speaker – but let's instead be one who knows exactly how to navigate the calm and the rough speaking seas.

The first step is determining the situation you are in:

What is the intention of my challenger?

- Is this person giving me a hard time because they are having a bad day and want to project this negativity on me?
- Is this person invested in my story, but concerned or misunderstanding the point that I'm making?
- Is this person invested in my story, but wants to test me to see if I know my topic well enough and have done my preparation?
- Does this person have a different agenda than me and wants to hijack my time frame for their own gain?

Note: We are talking about challengers here, not people just asking questions about your story, because they want to know more or pick your brain for insight and advice. That is not a challenge, but a compliment and a great way to get the interaction going, make people feel part of your story and learn more about what your audience cares about. This chapter is about people who make you a bit nervous with their question or are really pushing your buttons.

Who is my challenger?

- A random person in a big audience that is driven by one of the above points.
- A known person with lots of credibility in a big audience driven by, probably, point 1 or 2 in the above list.
- A person in a meeting that has no impact on the 'goal' of my story.
- A person in a meeting that has no impact on the 'goal' of my story, but has an influence on the people that do have an impact.
- The person in a meeting that I am trying to convince to act on what I am saying (e.g. approval, project go,...)

You will quickly know which category your challenger falls into and with what intentions he is coming at you. 'What' they are saying and 'how' they are saying it will signal the intentions (as seen in chapter 9). Your knowledge of the audience that you acquired during your preparation will tell you 'who' is talking. As you can read in the two lists, not every challenger has bad intentions and not every challenge should be avoided. It's okay to get some pushback occasionally. It keeps you sharp, fills your backpack with answers and confidence for similar encounters in the future. The way you are able to handle this pushback will increase your fear of speaking in front of a group or increase your credibility and confidence. Let's opt for the latter.

The second step is to be aware of the outcome you want and the time you want to spend on it:

- Is this person giving me a hard time because they are having a bad day and want to project this negativity on me?

  You want him to copy your energy, not the other way around. Your positivity will reflect his negativity like a mirror and make him aware of his state.

- Is this person invested in my story, but concerned or misunderstanding the point that I'm making?

  You will want to know more about where he is coming from. This concern or misunderstanding comes from a different world view. You need to understand that view first before you can realign your point with that view.

- Is this person invested in my story, but wants to test me to see if I know my topic well enough and have done my preparation?

  Most of these types of challenges come from the people that you need to convince or have a say in what you are talking about. This will be a moment to show your preparation and expertise. Time to be unshaken.

- Does this person have a different agenda than me and wants to hijack my timeframe for their own gain?

  Detect, contain and shut it down. This can be compared to a drunk heckler during a comedy show. Nothing good will come from it, it needs to be blocked or you will not achieve your goal, you will waste time, frustration will build and the challenger will use your loss of control to build themselves up.

- A random person in a big audience that is driven by one of the above points.

  Give it attention, but seeing you are on a big stage, quickly move on after one or two arguments have been exchanged.

- A known person with lots of credibility in a big audience driven by, probably, point 1 or 2 in the above list.

  Give it attention, a bit longer than with the previous point, because a great response to this person can increase your credibility and amplify the impact of your story.

- A person in a meeting who has no impact on the 'goal' of my story.

  Give it attention, but move on quickly if the challenge isn't an added value for your story.

- A person in a meeting who has no impact on the 'goal' of my story, but has an influence on the people that do have an impact.

  Give it attention and make sure, if the challenge is an added value to your story, that this person turns to your side, because their opinion affects the opinion of the decision maker.

- The person in a meeting that I am trying to convince to act on what I am saying (e.g. approval, project go,...)

  No matter how hard this person challenges you, deal with it. This is the one who will grant you your ask (your story goal). You need this person.

Note: Does this mean that every challenge from people that have an impact on your story needs to be addressed at length? No. You will always have to decide if the challenge links to your story and is added value to what you are trying to achieve. If the challenge risks sidetracking you and the rest of your audience, it also needs to be contained, even if the person challenging you is your decision maker. You are in control, you lead, the audience follows.

The third step is to then act accordingly and use many of the insights from the previous chapters as your weapons:

1. MASTER YOUR ENERGY

We have established this many times before throughout this book: the energy you give is the energy you receive. The same goes when somebody is sending you bad energy, anger or frustration. The pull of this kind of energy is strong and can easily bring your performance state down and trigger you into too much association with the person challenging you. "Cloud your mind, the dark side of the force will," Master Yoda would say. Keep your energy up at all times. Stay polite and respectful. Keep it up no matter what, and you will notice that the challenger will have to start copying your energy and behaviour or will just give up. It works as a mirror and the more positive you stay, the more the reflection of their bad energy will bounce back to them. At the same time, the audience will witness you standing your ground while staying constructive and positive despite the challenger bringing a 4/10. The challenger will feel he is losing his position in the audience and you are gaining sympathy.

Does this mean that you have to let people walk over you and be too soft on the challenger, risking losing control? No. Being in a performance state means you aren't a victim to your environment, can play with voice and body, come up with arguments and keep the story on track. Staying an 8 or a 9/10, positive and respectful, does not equate to not having a spine. It says, "I'm confident in my ability, I feel good, I will steer my environment, not the other way around. This is my stage and I will lead."

> *I asked the seasoned sales team in front of me what their expectations were for the training. The first response came from two gentlemen who immediately said, "Absolutely nothing and we hope this day will be over quickly." The team manager failed to tell me in the briefing call that some team members had experienced a horrible storytelling training two months before. I asked them about their experience, and it basically came down to them now feeling that storytelling is a waste of time with no added value to sales. I knew in those first minutes of the training that I was starting on -10 in credibility points. As we continued the check-in with*

the group, the two gentlemen kept jumping in and bashing everything I said. Even the rest of the team was becoming a bit uncomfortable, but these were clearly the most experienced and strongest personalities in the group. That they were huge guys didn't help either. What they didn't take into account was that this wasn't my first rodeo, and I had encountered worse hecklers in my comedy days. I looked at the team manager and he looked at me with an expression of, "I'm curious about how you are going to handle this, but deal with it in the way you see fit. I'm not stopping you." Yes, one glance can say a lot. So I started applying what I talked about in this chapter. I knew these gentlemen didn't have bad intentions; I was just paying for the frustration they had with the previous trainer.

To them, I was another slick coach who was going to tell them some mumbo jumbo. They had 60 years of sales experience between them, so who was I to tell them how to talk to their clients? I knew I had to address this and give it some attention. I started asking them about what they had hated about the previous training, focused on points I agreed with them on concerning the topic, and gave short quotes or reframed some of the things they said, as these comments frequently popped up in trainings. I made a few remarks myself in their direction, which put a smile on the team manager's face; he loved that these two had met their match. I wasn't trying to make them small, ridicule them or put myself above them, but I wanted to show them that they had valid points, I had a clear opinion about other points and I'm experienced and skilled enough to counter their banter. Instead of becoming angry, they started smiling and I saw them thinking, this guy is different, he seems to know what he is talking about, he is not shaken by our attacks.

After this, I cut off the connection, turned my eyes and body towards the others and continued, followed by a fun group exercise. In the beginning, the two gentlemen kept giving remarks and mocking the exercises. They had a reputation to uphold, but I stayed my 10/10 and kept motivating them. In my theory pieces that followed, I kept referring to what they had said earlier, linked to how they viewed storytelling, asked about their experience and connected them more to the group. I needed to keep them a part of the story. The more they warmed up to me, the more the rest of the group would enjoy the training and not get distracted. Close to noon, I did another exercise and asked for a volunteer. Guess who raised their hands?

We had lunch, and guess who said to their team manager, "This is a different training than we expected." At the end of the day, guess who came to shake my hand and literally said the words, "You did a really good job, the day flew by and I got value out of this training, thank you." They walked in ready to rumble, they walked out with a smile, insight, energy and a book.

Natalie and I went into a showroom to buy a new bathroom. Though there was nobody in the store, the sales lady who was present ignored us completely. After a stroll through the showroom, we started to talk to her. She was not having a great day. She was rushed and literally asked us, "What do you want?" I thought, take a guess. We came in for a bathroom, but most clients would have decided after this greeting that this was not the place they would buy and just walk out. Natalie and I saw it more as a project. We kept our positive energy and explained what we were looking for. She kept throwing remarks at us along the lines of "You have expensive taste, can you afford this?" "Please don't tell me you want that type of shower. It's not so trendy anymore." But through it all we kept giving her love and asked about her job and her interior architecture projects she was working on on the side. After a while, she started to become more positive, offered us a drink and really started showing us the good stuff in her showroom and portfolio. We eventually walked out with a great offer, and her befriending us on social media and buying my previous book.

2. STICK TO YOUR POINTS AND GOAL

If you are already familiar with the associating/dissociating concepts from chapter 9, then you will feel that your high performance state from point one will allow you to connect and disconnect with the challenger when needed. And probably be more inclined to dissociate. When you dissociate from the challenger, his energy, behaviour and words, you are not affected, you can determine what the intentions are, observe who is speaking and what is being said. You will have the space to assess the challenge and what is really being said. "Is this a valid point?" "Does going into this add value to my story?" "Does this have merit or is it just an opinion based on nothing?" Facts don't care about your feelings, so sticking to them and bringing every discussion back to the point you are making and the goal you are trying to achieve will deflect any challenge that has no value or merit. Your story maps out a clear path with a clear destination (your goal), that path needs to be guarded, and everything needs to get you and the audience to that destination. Dissociating yourself from the situation will allow you to keep a clear view on the way forward and bring back anybody who is trying to wander off the path. Dissociating in some of these challenging situations, while the eyes of the group are on you, is not easy. If you already feel too nervous, tired or frustrated, you are easy prey and will quickly find yourself associating and losing yourself in blabber and emotion.

Dissociate, answer a challenge when needed, but quickly follow it up with, "Let's discuss this afterwards, so we can continue with the presentation." "An interesting thought, but not the core focus of today, so let's park it for now." "No matter what the opinion or fear is around this topic, it will still come down to the point I'm making." "Since the goal of today's presentation is not X, but Y, I will address your point later, so I can continue." "You are saying exactly the same as me, but maybe I didn't explain myself correctly, as the point we apparently both agree on is..." "This is a valid concern to raise, but it's not today's focus, we only have limited time and the goal we want to achieve is... so allow me to continue."

If you have a clear goal when you walk into a room, you have prepared yourself for that specific goal and its audience and you know exactly what points you want to make and in what order. There will be very little that can shake your foundation while speaking. If this is not the case, anybody can hijack your presentation, determine a new direction, and you will be led astray.

3. GET SPECIFIC

Sticking to the facts and making a point doesn't only go for you as a speaker, but also for your challenger. People who challenge you are often in their association and will therefore challenge you with emotion, general statements or hearsay. When you are dissociated and not linked to this emotion, you will see these things for what they are: opinions, statements without any foundation or detail to them. Your response should be to get specific. You get challenged on something going wrong in the company, "What exactly?" "Give me a recent example?" "What data backs this up?" Instead of defending yourself or talking your way down, bounce back the challenge and get specific. In most cases, this will establish your control and make the other person nervous or stop pursuing the challenge. Many of the things we get challenged with in meetings, trainings, and keynotes are general ideas that seem difficult to overcome from up close, but become funny and easy to counter looked at from afar (dissociated). Or as Charlie Chaplin said it,

> ***"Life is a tragedy in close up, a comedy in long shot."***

Watch skilled politicians doing an interview with a reporter that is out for blood. A non-skilled politician will either repeat "no comment" and annoy the reporter and the audience watching. Or this politician will start defending himself, start explaining, but after reading chapter 12 you know, "Wer erklärt, verliert." If you explain, you lose. You need to control the narrative. Skilled politicians will relax, stay positive, dissociate and counter every generic challenge with, "Give me an example." "When and where exactly did I say that?" "What data are you basing this on?" "When did I use those words?" This will result in a stuttering reporter and a challenging interview that will quickly end. The same goes when you as a speaker get challenged during your talk or presentation.

4. USE THE POWER OF VOICE AND BODY

At point 2, you might have thought, "But Marnick, when I say 'let's discuss this afterwards, this is not the purpose of today' the challenger just keeps going." That could indeed happen, but that is where the beautiful instrument that is your body and voice plays a role. 90% of your speaking impact is voice and body. What happens when you are talking to somebody and they turn their head or focus on a different conversation? You feel disrespected, but you also automatically stop talking. When you lose eye contact and see a body turning away from you, the immediate response is to go silent.

I'm not saying you have to disrespect the people that challenge you, but you will use your voice and body to control the room and decide where this interaction is going. When somebody challenges me from the audience, I move towards them. They are sitting down, I'm standing up; that is already a power play. If I'm sitting down or in an online meeting, I will make sure my whole body is directed towards the challenger and frame the moment in such a way that the group knows that I'm going to direct my attention fully to this person. Combining moving closer with letting this person know all eyes are now on him signals, "You have my attention, you are now in the centre of it, tell me." Some challengers thrive on this, but most people back down a bit, because the spotlight is now completely on them.

When you are speaking for bigger crowds, most of the time you have a microphone and the audience doesn't. Don't give away your microphone or let a host give the mic. The one holding the microphone has the power; you as a speaker need to keep that power at all times. Repeat what the person is saying for the rest of the group, let the host hold on to the mic, but never hand it over.

You moved closer, you might have a microphone, you made sure the challenger and the crowd know that you want to address this. Now, it is time to use your voice. Dissociate, use a lower, slower voice, a voice that says, this is important to me, but I'm also confident enough to respond or park the interaction if needed. A lower slower voice radiates more confidence; combined with factual content, you will trigger the right emotion. If you lose yourself to the urge to be liked, you will get a higher pitched voice, more rambling, defending and explaining, which gives off the idea of being uncertain and too associated.

If the challenger is not impressed and keeps going, stay respectful and positive, wrap it up and instead of waiting for another response, turn your eyes and body away from the challenger and continue to the next point. 99% of the time, this person will go silent and let you continue. When they lose the direct line to you, when they lose the attention and the story continues, people go silent, and it is an effort to speak up again. If it happens and the challenger is persistent, see point 8. When you have the urge to be liked, your response will be to continue to give this person attention even if you just said that you wanted to park the conversation for later. That attention (eyes and body) keeps the line with the challenger open and will trigger a new response, so fight that urge.

5. FIGHT THE URGE TO BE LIKED

The biggest reason we tend to spend too much time on a challenger, and don't dare to cut it off or take back control, is our universal urge to be liked. No matter how hard you shout that you don't care about what other people think, you do. We all do to different degrees, but we love it when we are liked. It makes sense as an animal that is alone is easy prey; an animal that is liked, accepted and protected by the herd is safe. This urge is what tricks us into giving too much attention to a challenger, even if that challenger has no value, point or positive intent. Challengers feed on this.

There could be 20 people in a room, with 19 loving what you are saying and one grumpy person. Most people will get absorbed by that one person once he starts talking. Focus on the 19 others and keep that one person in check or turn him into a fan using the techniques in this chapter. However, if that one person is your target audience, then you need to give him attention and will need to reconsider your preparation (see next point). But in all other cases, focus on your fans, not your trolls.

6. RECONSIDER YOUR PREPARATION

What if the person I'm trying to convince or inspire is the one giving me a hard time? Well, you can't ignore him, because your goal is only achieved by action from this person. You will need to reconsider your preparation. It will not help you straight away, but it will for future talks. This decision maker is probably challenging you and getting frustrated because you didn't tailor your story to him. You are not relating, not making the right points, or not offering value. Or perhaps you are diving into the solution too late or too soon. It could be that this person is just having a really bad day, but most of the time this challenge comes from not connecting to what is said, due to incorrect preparation or a lack of it.

> *I had a client who said it was almost impossible to convince the CEO to go along with any of HR's ideas, so this new project proposal would be no different. "Challenge accepted," I said. We prepped the story together in function of this CEO according to what I shared with you in chapter 11. We prepared just for him, not for the entire board, since he alone would decide on this project. She did the 30-minute meeting and in a follow-up call she*

> *literally said the following, "He approved it all. He didn't challenge us on anything. He just went along with it, and we are already executing on the plan. This is crazy."*

Your preparation is everything. It's not a guarantee, as it is human to make mistakes or read certain people or situations wrong, but most of the tough encounters can be avoided by great preparation. So, next time a decision maker starts to make you sweat, don't get mad, but ask yourself if you are saying the right things or maybe made a mistake in your preparation. Adapt on the spot if you are quick on your feet and have a filled backpack. If not, ask questions, get insight, learn, rework it and secure a second chance.

7. FIND COMMON GROUND

No matter how much your world view and that of your challenger differ, there is always common ground to be found. You will always be able to find something you agree on. Going straight against what somebody is saying can escalate the situation and make you spend even more time on this challenge. Time you don't have, because you are speaking for a group, standing on stage, hosting a webinar and you need to be able to continue with the show. Find common ground first. Dissociate, maybe ask an additional question for better understanding and then find the part that you do agree on. Mention this and use it as the foundation for your counter or for respectfully parking the situation. People will connect with you more and let their guard down a bit if you make the effort to show them there are common opinions and ideas. As discussed before in this book, the more people get the feeling you are the same as them, the more they will trust you and give you attention.

8. TRUST THE COMMUNITY

Let's say none of the above insights work and your challenger just keeps asking for attention. Then just trust the community. When you stay positive, respectful, find common ground,... the audience's sympathy for you will grow and they will start to get annoyed with the challenger themselves. Just like in comedy or online, the community will turn against the heckler or troll if it goes on too long while the comedian, influencer, social media manager stands their ground using this chapter. Once a challenger feels they are standing alone, most of the time they will cave. They wanted attention, they wanted to lift themselves up, they wanted to make you sweat, but that is now resulting in you looking like the good person, and them as the bad person with an audience breathing down their neck saying, "Let the speaker move on with the story. Your remarks and behaviour are not relevant or appreciated." These extreme challengers are very rare, but I have had them in workshops a few times in the last decade. In the end, the group always stuck up for me. If you know this, you don't get extra nervous or waste unnecessary energy – you just patiently wait for the audience's patience-barrel to fill up and pop off when they have had enough.

9. KEEP ENGAGING THE CHALLENGER

When a challenger is just having a bad day or has a different world view, they aren't necessarily coming at you with bad intent. You still apply all the above, but while you contain the interaction and move on after a short interaction, keep engaging this challenger whenever you are saying something that links to his remark. This way you keep involving him, making him part of the story, giving him respect and some attention, while continuing your story. Don't overdo it, but refer to him two or three times at the right moments. No interaction, just acknowledging him and referring to what was said. This way you will turn that challenger into a fan by the end of your story. You must have some real negative energy and bad intent if you, as a challenger, can hold off a positive, respectful speaker, who, despite parking your remark, keeps involving you in a positive way throughout the story. I use this technique a lot myself and have turned the biggest hecklers into people who come to me after my talk and tell me they loved the presentation.

Most people will listen to your story with positive intent, but the business world can sometimes be hard. People are under pressure, stressed, have their own agendas, need to profile themselves,... Mix those things together and you can't avoid having a serious challenger in your audience once in a while. You are standing alone in front of a group, so you will be the target. The better you become at speaking and building your stories, the less you will encounter it, but there will always be someone to speak up down the road. This can be frustrating and energy consuming, but just like failure, you will learn the most from these challenging moments. Every one of these interactions will either teach you what not to do next time when you lose control or what really works if you did a good job. Put every technique, challenge and experience into your backpack for later. After a while, you will have so much experience that challenges are no longer challenges, because you have seen and heard most of it before and have the necessary content and ways of handling it ready. Your confidence will grow, you will prepare better, be less shaken and be more respected by the audience. They will be like, "Wow, I would have crumbled if I had been challenged like that on stage, but this speaker just stood his ground without breaking a sweat."

Focus
Give the challenger attention, move closer, stay positive and put the spotlight on you two.

Evaluate
Dissociate, determine the intention and role and stick to the facts.

Break
Respectfully wrap it up or park the conversation, break eye and body contact and move on with the story.

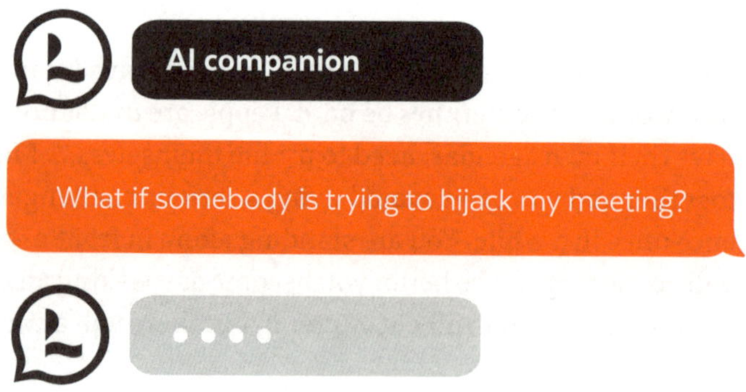

CORE INSIGHTS

- Always determine the intention and the role of your challenger first.
- Stay positive and respectful, no matter what. It will be your shield, it will be their mirror.
- Fight the urge to be liked. Limit the amount of attention and time you spend on the interaction. Don't forget about the rest of the audience.
- Dissociate and stick to the facts. Bring everything back to your point and your end goal. You must not stray from the path.
- You will learn the most from these challenging moments. Use them to fill your backpack and know that your biggest challenger can become your biggest fan.

17
WHAT IF I DON'T BELIEVE IN THE STORY I HAVE TO TELL?

THE SHORT ANSWER IS:
"DON'T TELL IT."

You realise deep down that you are going to tell a story that you haven't mastered or don't back and it is doomed to fail. Certainly, people have become good at cutting through fake stories. Which commercials do we still believe? What leadership speeches about the necessity of restructuring are still seen as credible? How many apologies of politicians are immediately parked as fake? As soon as we notice the person speaking doesn't fully stand behind their story, we check out. 90% of our speaking impact is determined by how we deliver the story – our voice, body language and energy. Unless you are a master of deception and body control, you will quickly reveal to the audience what your true stance is on the topic you are talking about. The body can't lie. Maybe you can somewhat get away with the way you deliver it, but due to your lack of conviction or knowledge about the matter, you will soon fall through the cracks. In these types of situations, it's dancing to a faint choir of credibility. You will feel the tension and pressure throughout your talk. Not a fun feeling and far from an added value.

"90% of your speaking impact is determined by voice and body. Only 10% is content."

In comedy, securing this needed credibility by only talking about what is true to you is called, 'telling jokes in function of your persona'. Does the audience believe what you say or are you, for example, a very young person getting those first pimples, but joking about your many sexual adventures? Or a very polite well-dressed person, joking about how you boldly stood up to law enforcement? You don't believe it, you didn't experience it and the audience sees, hears and feels that you are not credible. The same goes for all other stories being told in private and business life. So, "What if I don't believe the story I have to tell?" Don't tell it. That's the shortest and most logical answer, which you most likely agree with. The realistic answer is a bit more nuanced: as a professional, you do need to bring messages that you have doubts about, are not an expert in or just 'have to' communicate (e.g. budget cut, restructuring, strategy change, stricter safety regulations,...)

What do you do in those situations? I will define three possible scenarios for you:

1. NAME THE ELEPHANT IN THE ROOM

You must bring a message that you don't fully support. It has been laid on you by higher up – the message and the form, for example, team alteration, restructuring, change in working hours, postponing the anticipated project,... In this case, focus on 'naming the elephant in the room'. This means naming the things that are currently playing in the world and mind of your audience. The message is the message, but 'how' you deliver it is of importance for your own credibility and the landing of the story.

When you focus on 'recognition' (see chapter 10), the attention and trust will increase. People like to listen to somebody who seems to generally understand them, even if the message is tough and you don't fully agree. By naming these doubts, fears, concerns, challenges, they become less severe in the minds of your audience.

> *"The company had already said goodbye to two teams in two countries. Is a third country going to follow?" My client had to bring the story that the team could stay, but there were going to be some serious changes in roles and responsibilities. She far from agreed with the way things were being handled and how this was going to affect her audience. But the decision had been made and had to be communicated.*
>
> *She chose to start the meeting by naming, as objectively as possible (so no "I know how you feel, I understand your concern" = patronising) the things that had happened recently. No exaggerating or downsizing, no added emotion, but also no beating around the bush. The observations are what they are. Naming these elephants and immediately following it up with the fact that the team didn't risk unemployment immediately lowered walls and did wonders for the vibe of the meeting. She just, without literally saying it, signalled to the audience, "I'm also not happy with the current situation, but I am going to bring you the story you need to hear." Due to this opening, she could surf on that gained attention and trust and speak to the audience as an almost equal. Nothing made the audience like the situation more, but it did make sure she held her ground and credibility.*

2. ROOM FOR INTERPRETATION

You are not a parrot. Some 'obligatory' messages leave plenty of room for interpretation and reshaping, so they fit you more. These are messages I worked with the most in my corporate career. Something got decided on a European level. I didn't completely agree but had to translate it to my team. My preparation would then mainly focus on figuring out what the European goals were, what every decision was based on, and how it would affect my team.

The story that followed was not a lament or a literal translation of the message, but a view on how we as a team were going to deal with it, what we needed to take along and what we weren't going to do. As I said in chapter 11, people care about the end goal and the value that you bring, so you don't have to blindly follow and agree with everything.

Some situations allow you to reshape the stories you tell, so you can deliver them with more credibility and conviction, as long as they lead to achieving the bigger goal. There is also nothing wrong in calling out what you don't agree with, but immediately turn it around to "and this is what we are going to do about it".

> *A manager within a large multinational was tasked with announcing to all the sales teams that there was going to be a merger between different countries. The whole company was in a state of uncertainty. Nobody was certain of their job, manager or location. Many managers chose to just convey the decisions and plans as they were told to and tried to justify them. My client chose a different approach. I asked him a single question: "What is most important for your audience at the moment?" After some thought, he answered, "Well, the decision has been made, we can't change anything about that, and the teams aren't happy with it. But I believe the biggest insecurity now comes from not having a clear view on the new org chart."*
>
> *Great, that is what is currently playing in their minds, that is the world they live in. The only thing you must do is name this and clarify that org chart. He prepared a story that simply named the above, as something he has noticed and wanted to turn around by giving a clear view on who the new managers were going to be (as far as the current information would*

allow him). He even used a very creative and interactive approach to tell this story. What was going to be a very sensitive talk where the decisions were once more going to be laid upon the teams suddenly turned into a fun who-is-who-story. Of course it didn't take away all concerns, but that pinch of certainty in who was going to lead them, who they could talk to for what made a world of difference. He did a great job as a speaker and manager in front of a very tense audience.

3. FOCUS ONLY ON WHAT YOU KNOW

At the last minute, you have to take over the presentation of a colleague who called in sick or your manager asked you to explain something about a certain project that you are vaguely involved in. In these situations, the trouble is not in disagreeing with the message and backing it, but about not having enough knowledge about the topic. The short answer again should be, "Don't tell it." But you want to help, play your part, so these types of situations will present themselves. In that case, try to focus on what you do know. What is your current expertise that links to the topic or what can you get insight into at such short notice?

In my early career, I was asked to give a big talk on work culture. What did I know as a rookie, fresh out of college, about work culture? Instead of drafting a sketchy story and appearing in front of the audience with shaking knees, I decided to make it my own. I gave a talk about working with the new generation on the work floor and how they affected corporate culture. I was an expert on this versus all these middle-aged HR managers in the audience, I was 23 years old. I spoke only about what I knew, with complete conviction and insight and was asked to give this presentation many times across Europe, due to its great success. Until, of course, I was no longer part of the new generation.

This 'focus on what you know' technique can be applied to many types of messages. You need to give a training about a new tool, as you have a bit more experience with it than the rest of the team. Focus on what you know for sure, and leave out the rest for now. People can only grasp three points at a time anyway. You are taking over from a colleague for a project presentation. Prepare with that colleague, ask for the most important insights and use all this information to talk only about what you feel completely confident about. Leave out the rest.

The audience doesn't know what you are going to say, so they don't know what they are missing. If you get questions about things you have no expertise in, be honest and state that the goal of your talk is X and to move the project forward in the absence of your colleague. All in-depth questions will be taken along for this colleague to come back to (e.g. via mail) or in a follow-up meeting. It's more important to remain credible and leave a steady impression than to wobble your way through. The audience doesn't like fakes, uncertainty and being somewhat mislead. An audience likes credibility, so if that comes across, they will forgive and accept a lot.

A client of mine who is a marketing director had to speak at the company's yearly conference for all 800 employees. She was super nervous during our first coaching in preparation for this conference. Not so much about the speaking itself, but about the topic. The CEO had asked her to tell a story on the importance of brand strategy. She and her team were responsible for this, but it was far from her expertise and focus within the team. She feared making a weak impression as a director. She prepared a story for our session, but huffed and puffed her way through it. Her behaviour and face said it all, 'I don't want to deliver this story.' I was very aware of why she felt this way, but still I asked her, "Why do you feel such pressure for this talk?" She replied, "I have to bring a solid marketing story in front of 800 people and this is not my expertise or the thing I feel is the number one priority for this conference."

"What do you want to talk about? What would you talk about if you had carte blanche?"

She started talking with a sparkle in her eyes about the strategy for the new year. How certain decisions had already led to great outcomes and opened doors they could have never dreamed of for the company. How they increased the connection with their clients, which led to more leads.

"Then why don't you talk about this and how it eventually adds value to the overall brand?"
"Because the CEO wants me to talk about brand strategy."

> *"Does the CEO want you to talk about brand strategy or was it more a suggestion and does he just want you to give a good talk as a director and manifest your leadership role by inspiring the company? What do you think is most important to him?"*
>
> *She thought about it and realised that a strong marketing story was more important for the teams and her role than a forced story about brand strategy. A week later she returned for our next session with a new story. I barely had to give feedback on it. At the conference she took the stage without any slides and carried the audience along with the wonderful world of marketing for 30 minutes. What was the feedback of the CEO after the talk? "Well done, very nice story."*

I stay as far as possible from topics and messages that I don't completely own or support. The pressure, energy drain, doubt and eventual loss of credibility is too great. Chances of reaching one's goal are slim. I have it easy, as I work for myself and can choose which projects I want. But still, there were many trainings, coachings and talks in the past in which I knew I didn't master all aspects of the briefing. I took these projects but clearly stated to my clients that I would only train, coach or execute on the things that I completely own and support. They were free to not work with me or hire other people that had expertise in the other aspects. Result: I went to every session with confidence and excitement. Nobody ever complained about missing out on some parts and we closed yearlong trajectories with an 8 or 9 average audience satisfaction score.

Most people work within organisations and that complicates things. If you are in that situation, and you are still required to step up to the plate, remember the insights of this chapter.

CORE INSIGHTS:

- Avoid talks about topics you don't own or support.
- People see through you and your message within seconds if it is not genuine.
- 90% of your impact is made by 'how' you deliver it.
- Dare to name elephants in the minds of your audience so they become less severe.
- Observe, don't patronise. Leave it up to the audience to decide if they feel you understand them.
- Ask yourself what your audience really needs and wants to hear at a specific time.
- You are not a parrot. Read the room for artistic freedom and re-shape a story if possible or needed.
- Focus only on what you know. An audience will always prefer a credible story on 10% of the content over a wobbly story on 100% of the content.

18
WHAT IF I'M EXPECTED TO SEND SOMETHING TO MY AUDIENCE UPFRONT?

SHORT ANSWER:
"DON'T SEND IT."

This is a question I didn't plan on addressing when I was drafting the initial 21 questions that make up the chapters of this book, but it kept coming up in the months prior to writing it. It's a question that gives me the heebie-jeebies. A question that refers to those dreaded 'prereads'. I know I'm exaggerating the following a bit, but asking a speaker to send something upfront is like giving a child the table of contents at the dinner table for a fairy tale that will be told later that evening. Like reading the summary of a thriller movie before going to the cinema. Like asking a comedian to distribute all his punchlines as a hand-out before a show. For the performer, speaker or actor, it's not even worth starting.

I assume I don't have to convince you and I hope you are now nodding in front of your book in agreement. If this is the case, feel free to send this chapter to a colleague or manager that it applies to or use the insight from this chapter to kickstart a culture change when it comes to speaking within your work context. A company is not a theatre, a budget plan is not a fairy tale, but the impact of these stories should have the same effect on the audience as a great movie or captivating book. That is what strong stories do. What is the reason these prereads give me the heebie-jeebies, besides the fact that we both acknowledge that it's not the best way of working?

1. **MORE WORK:** It gives people who are already very busy (you) even more work.

2. **DEMOTIVATION:** It demotivates the speaker (you), as we both know everybody is as busy as you so chances are your pre-read will not be read.

3. **LACK OF TRUST:** It shows, probably unintentionally, a lack of confidence in your ability to speak and bring across the right content.

4. **NO SURPRISE:** It takes away the element of surprise, which is, as with a joke, a very important element of a story.

5. **NO CONTROL:** It takes away all your control over the narrative. Interpretations, assumptions and beliefs will be formed about your story at a time and place that you don't control (= missing the right context). The questions, challenges and misconceptions will build up before you have even had the chance to speak.

These five points result in a meeting where everybody already has an opinion or idea about your content. Nobody is really listening to your story anymore; they are ready to shoot or take over. Suddenly, the meeting turns into an interrogation or discussion completely besides the point. What should have been a nice presentation turned into disappointment. A meeting without action or decision. If you are now nodding in recognition, I can imagine your next question will be, "What can I do about it?"

There will be many nuances to what I'm about to share as possible solutions. But these are the four rules of thumb I used myself within my previous jobs and still apply to this day during client projects. When some of them make you feel uncomfortable or seem too bold, just remember what Elon Musk mentions as one of his ten efficiency commandments – principles that helped him get his Tesla factory production from 3.000 to 5.000 cars a week, against all odds. He applies the same at X and Space X.

> ***"Challenge every company requirement. The requirement can never come from a department. It must always come from a real person that came up with it. Then challenge that person. If this person can't come up with a valid explanation or there is no specific person linked to the requirement, change it and make it less stupid."***

1. KNOW WHAT REALLY MATTERS

What is the most important thing for your colleagues, managers, clients,...? That you deliver value, make plans and lead the team forward. At the end of the day, the amount of value you create for people and the company is all that matters. You have complete freedom in accomplishing this, as long as it stays within the law and the company code of conduct. Sending prereads is not in the law or any code of conduct (or you have a very special one). Everybody thinks that certain things are expected because they have evolved this way, have always been done or some random person initiated it, and nobody took the time to question its effects. Challenge these things. What is the worst that could happen? You lose your job, you get a warning,...? In the first case, maybe it's not a culture you want to be in. In the second case, maybe it's not a culture you want to be in.

I have been asked to send prereads over my entire career. I have always refused this, provided context, rocked the actual presentation and delivered value. I never got any complaints, angry reactions or clients refusing to work with me for not sending a preread. All people care about is that you deliver value. I danced on the desk of my former CEO with my colleagues, while dressed up as a cow, filmed it and spread it across the company. Everybody thought I was going to lose my job. The CEO showed this video with pride at an international conference in the New York head office as an example of a strong team culture. Go figure. This all might sound a bit exciting, bold or extreme. And I am not saying you should start dancing on office tables, but this is what I mean by 'stand up to stand out'. I am a fan of rules and guidelines. No game without rules, but if these rules don't add value to the game, slow the game down or demotivate the players, they need to be challenged. I agree with Arnold Schwarzenegger on this:

> ***"To achieve something in life, one must sometimes bend or break the rules."***

2. DETERMINE THE GOAL OF THE MEETING

Let's assume you will send them a preread or your entire slide deck. In that case, determine for yourself the goal of the meeting. Chances are you will end up in an interrogation. So, what is the goal of the meeting? Is it for the audience to hear your vision, plans, advice? Or is the preread the preparation for the audience and is the meeting there for debate, questions and taking away any concerns or doubts? Presenting might no longer be necessary, as everybody already has the whole story in their mailbox. When I feel that a presentation is no longer necessary, I will send the audience a strategically crafted document upfront and will use the meeting to run them through this document and let them speak. My personal speaking preparation will then be to list all the possible remarks, questions, challenges,... they might throw at me and have a great counter argument for all of them. You control the meeting; it will give you confidence and raise your credibility. You often only have ten to thirty minutes to make your mark; use those minutes in the most effective way in function of what you want to achieve.

3. SEND A TEASER

The urge to send something upfront is too big and you believe it is still useful to present something afterwards. Don't send the audience your entire deck or preparation. Make a teaser using the techniques from this book. A well composed trailer to the film that is your story. Give them enough so they are aware but leave out enough so they can't yet form an opinion or get distracted by details. Get them excited, eager to hear you, feed them enough information to be able to follow your story, but leave out all possible spoilers.

4. GIFT THEM THIS BOOK

If you are still somewhat uncomfortable with my strong view in this chapter, go for the culture change and gift your audience this book with a bookmark on this chapter. Let me do the evangelising for you.

> *A video call was scheduled by a regional Learning & Development manager of a large international manufacturing company. The purpose of the call was for me to meet the global lead of L&D, his direct boss, and convince him that I was the best man for their project.*
>
> Before the call: *"Marnick, my boss asked you to send him your pitch deck upfront, so he can read it before our call next week." I have nothing to send upfront. Let's just do the call; you can assure him that all his questions will be answered.*

At the start of the call, after some quick introductions: "*I assume you have some sort of pitch or an overview of your services. Feel free to share the screen.*"

I have no presentation. This meeting is for you to ask me any question you like or challenge me on how we would approach a project like yours. This way you can find out if there is a match and I know what will be, from our experience, the best way of working with a matching budget.
(Frowning look with a bit of surprise from the Global L&D manager and an anxious stare from the regional L&D manager.)

Global L&D manager: "Okay, well,... (starts explaining the project and the challenges in front of them)."

I answer all his questions, give examples of past projects that match his challenges, and elaborate on our way of working and what I believe is the best course of action. Thirty minutes later we end the call with a few laughs, and I send the budget proposal over that same day. A month later we were training their people from China, India, Australia, US,...

Note: There is a difference between being confident in your ability and experience and being cocky. I avoided a lot of unnecessary work that would not add value to the meeting for an audience I don't know enough about. I refused to give up control and comply with a way of working that I don't agree with and know is not efficient and effective. There were frowns, there was surprise, there was anxiety, but those quickly moved over for in depth conversation, understanding, inspiration and laughs. My goal is to get the client to sign the proposal and work with me. I control the way we get to that point. 'You lead, the audience follows.' Will this sit well with everybody? Probably not, but what is the worst that could happen? They won't work with me. This rarely happens and if you already need to comply with a certain way of working that you don't feel comfortable with to achieve your goal, imagine how the actual project will go. You will not be in the lead and will leak energy at every step.

WHAT ABOUT POST-READS?

A presentation you send upfront as a preread has no business being presented. A presentation that can be sent as a post-read or summary has no business being presented. If I can read your presentation afterwards as a complete reference work, your presentation holds too many details, too much information and vague points. More on slide building in chapter 15. I am not a fan of prereads, but I do send post-reads. There is value in post-reads, since people only remember 10% of your talk if you are lucky – no matter how great it was. This doesn't mean you need to send over your entire deck. Your presentation is built to support your talk, not to be used as the complete blueprint to your project. As we say in the professional speaker world, "A presentation that can be understood without hearing the speaker is a bad presentation."

"Prereads are a no no, post-reads are a go go."

Instead, I send over a well-designed summary with all my main points, which will serve as a reminder and guide in taking the expected action. I even send over videos that highlight my most important arguments, but this might go a bit far for most people's context. It's again about control. What do people need to remember, how easily can they retell your story and feel guided in taking the required action? Determine what should stick in the hearts and minds of your audience, during and after your talk. (This is not the same as sending over your presentation with an annex information dump attached to it for those who are interested in the details.) Distilling the main points and conclusions from your story won't take much extra time. You can even ask AI to do it for you.

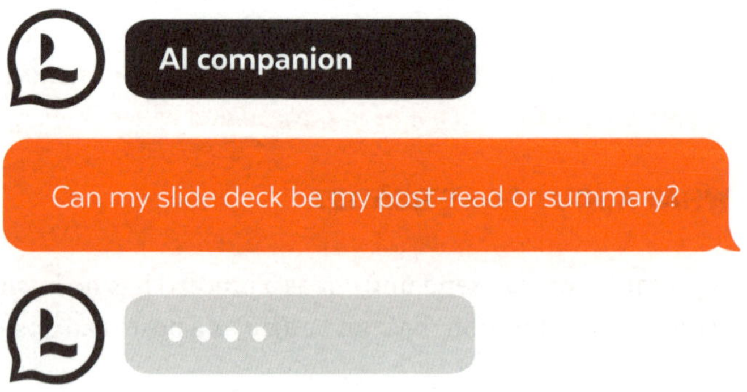

CORE INSIGHTS:

- People care about the value you bring, not about the preread you send. Dare to refuse.
- Prereads give away control over your goal and story.
- Prereads clutter, leave room for interpretation and questions about details that don't matter.
- Send a well composed teaser in function of your meeting goal.
- Still sending a preread or your entire deck? Change the goal of your meeting.
- Post-reads or summaries have value. People only remember 10% of what you say.
- Post-reads are not your actual presentation. They are a separate and strategically crafted summary of your most important points. They should help your audience retell your story afterwards or guide them in taking the expected action.

CONTEXT
SPEAKING IN A DIFFERENT SETTING OR ROLE

19
DO THESE INSIGHTS AND TECHNIQUES ALSO WORK IN FRONT OF A CAMERA OR IN A VIDEO CALL?

THE SHORT ANSWER IS:
"YES, THEY DO."

Almost every insight and technique in this book applies to a presentation in front of a camera or during a video call. There is very little difference between speaking via a screen or the real physical deal. If you agree with this bold statement, then this is the shortest chapter for you in the book. On to the next one. It could also be that you are now left with some reservations:

You aren't physically in the same room as your audience. That's different.
You can use your body less in the small frame you have to stay in during a video call.
Interacting with your audience is super hard, certainly when people turn off their camera.
People don't see you very well when you share your screen for a slide deck.
There is extra stress due to more technical issues that can occur.
Speaking to real people is easier than speaking to that camera lens.
Online video-presentations are always much more boring than real presentations.

Valid remarks – certainly the last one. In the past couple of years, I have had the honour of attending many online presentations where I almost couldn't control the urge to put on a movie or start answering my mails. Those types of presentations are abundant in the corporate world, but that isn't the fault of the meeting tool, the screen or the camera. I also admit that I prefer physical versus online, just as I like to watch a live comedy show instead of one on TV. But still, online doesn't have to be less engaging, entertaining, convincing or inspiring. I have done regular online meetings, and webinars for 200 people to all out virtual events for 30.000 people, and won awards for them. They all come down to the same principles.

So, what can you do to make sure you rock that camera just as much as you will rock your physical stage after reading this book? Just take everything you learned in this book and multiply it by two.

- **PREPARATION X2**
  You will have to take the audience even more by the hand during an online presentation. They can get easily distracted, can hide themselves and there is more technology involved that you must take into account. Preparation equals control. This goes for story structure, performance and for technology.

- **ENERGY + VOICE + BODY X2**
  Through a screen/camera, your energy will be cut in half. If you have recorded and watched yourself speaking, you will have noticed that what seemed to be a big play between body and intonation does not seem as big on screen. That's why you have to give it a little more. For some, it might seem 'too much', but it will come across as very normal on screen. Do your normal performance or less than normal and it will struggle to capture attention.

- **INTERACTION + SURPRISE X2**
  If your story, performance and technology are well prepped, you have offered yourself the opportunity to completely focus on the audience and how they will experience your presentation. Where interaction is an option during a physical talk, it is an absolute must during the online version – from small talk when the meeting is filling up, and reactions in the chat to picking up conversation with attendees during your story. Even when there are 500 people in the virtual room. People need to be stimulated to stay focused through these interactions, surprises in your story or by your visual support. The distance needs to be downsized as much as possible. The more people feel part of your talk, feel seen and engaged, the more they will stay attentive and the less stress you will have.

How can you double these elements?

1. CHECK THE TECH

Only work with technology that you fully understand and control. Technology that allows you to facilitate the desired experience for your audience. You want to be able to play with its functionalities without thinking and know it is reliable. If you can't choose the tool at your job, make a point of understanding it or, being the great speaker that you are, pitch a better tool.

I have my tool for day-to-day meetings. I have chosen this one, as it is the most used tool within the corporate world. I use this for regular meetings, pitching and coaching. I have another tool that I use for webinars, workshops and events. This tool offers easier ways to interact, more stable connection and easier ways to switch between chat, whiteboard, slides, video,...

I will be in the online room 15 minutes before a regular meeting and 30 to 60 minutes before a meeting where I have to present, give a webinar or host the meeting. I check the connection, computer battery, camera setup, lighting, check all the buttons for chat, allowing people in,... and will test the screen sharing and sound. It's not a guarantee that nothing will go wrong, it's still technology, but I want the comfort of knowing that I have checked and tested what I could, just as I do with physical meetings or conference talks. I often refer to this as, time – tech – trust. If you are on time, you have the room to check the necessary things and if you did that you will be able to trust the technology you use and boost your confidence.

(I consciously give you no tool names, because these platforms evolve so fast that by the time this book comes out it could be that a new one has hit the market.)

2. DON'T SIT, STAND

You need twice as much energy and focus during online presentations. Sitting in front of your screen all day and jumping from meeting to meeting isn't going to help with that. Move around between meetings, naturally inject yourself with the right hormones, give your brain a breather. Warm up your voice, walk around before the start of a meeting and only sit down when the first people show up or don't sit down and maximise your performance (voice/body) by standing while you speak.

I never sit before an important digital meeting or presentation. I make sure my tech and setup are tested way beforehand, so I only need to let people in when it is go-time and sit down at the last minute. This way I get myself in a performance state and make sure my brain and body don't doze off while waiting for the session to begin. I want to take that energy, focus and good feeling into the meeting when it starts, I need the audience to feel that they have just entered a fun, engaging and valuable online environment. People will get the feeling, "Okay, this session will be different than 99% of the online meetings we have. Maybe this will be worth my attention." Your energy will determine what people will be able to copy and will ensure that you can trust yourself and play with your voice and body. Remember, when you are truly you, your voice and body will know what to do. Online, in front of a camera it is even more important to be aware that you need to bring twice as much to the screen.

3. LOOK MOM, I'M ON TV

Don't see the frame your head is in as the frame of the online session. That frame is the TV-screen your audience is watching, you are the show, you are the presenter, even if you are talking about the quarterly results of a morgue. What is happening in this frame? Am I only watching a little head with a green screen background and a monotone voice? Or am I getting a face that moves, a body (hands) that support and a voice that plays with speed, volume and height? Even the background needs to play a role. What impulses are you giving people to stay engaged? Think about it and invest time and even money in getting it right. You are not presenting during an online call or webinar, you are making TV. Make it a show people want to watch.

4. INVEST IN YOUR BACKGROUND

As discussed in chapter 10, 'place' has an impact on the experience and memory of a story. This also applies to online presentations. Are you giving people a white wall as your background, a dodgy small meeting room or broom closet, because you forgot to reserve one? The same standard virtual backgrounds everybody uses. Or did you really think your background through and make the frame that is your TV screen totally feng shui? Offer your audience depth and diverse elements (without them distracting) to make your studio/background look more professional and engaging. A nice studio or background initiates questions, interest, attention and draws the audience in without you having said a word. The same with your lighting.

Make sure you are nicely lit; your face and eyes pop and you radiate through the camera. Don't forget to smile. Don't give the audience a face half in shadow, half overly lit due to the sun and don't disappear completely because you are sitting in front of a window. Bad lighting gives off a dodgy feel, distracts and makes it harder for your audience to read your facial expressions. What does your 'place' say? This story is going to be just as amateurish, rushed and unstructured as my surroundings? Or this story is going to be an experience, will add value and give depth to this topic.

If I'm working in function of a client event, there is a whole crew and studio to facilitate all the above. But for my regular online meetings, webinars and presentations, I use my home studio. It is nothing more than two LED lights, a camera, computer, desk and two stand up banners that make up the background. One with the 'stand up to stand out' quote and one with an art piece I made myself. Both in black and white, the colours of the company. It costs absolutely nothing to set this up. The lights light up my face and the whole frame as if it was a professional studio, so no matter the hour or weather, the feel is always light, welcoming and crisp. The banners, which you can't make out to be banners, are real and not virtual. They give depth to the room and as they are black and white, combined with a colourful T-shirt or sweater on my part. I pop even more, demanding attention. During small talk people always ask about the artwork and say, "That is a cool background you have." People like depth and getting the feeling they are peeking into the life of the speaker. It is a small thing, but 'place' adds to the experience and the memory of any story. The audience will unconsciously decide, this is going to be a good online experience.

5. STRAIGHT IN THE CAMERA

Look straight into the camera, as if you are a TV host. This will give the audience the feeling that you are communicating with them. See the camera not as a camera, but as the gate to your audience. The only way you have to communicate with them on the other side. Picture yourself standing at a door and the keyhole is the only way you can see and hear the person on the other side. You will focus all your attention on that keyhole. It's the same when talking to that black circle staring back at you that is the camera lens.

Keep this in the back of your mind while speaking and you will forget the world around you. There is only the camera and the audience that is sitting behind it. 'Be in love with the camera'. You have probably heard this before during fashion shoots on TV. That's what it is about. You are in love with the camera and there is only the camera. Very awkward in the beginning but, after a while, just another day at the virtual office. A great experience for your audience, because that camera focus comes across on their screen as, 'This person is speaking to me and only to me.' I apply this during virtual presentations, webinars, virtual conferences and video recordings. Also, don't forget to position the camera at eye level so you don't look down like an old man taking a selfie and so we can't count your nose hairs.

In a regular meeting or when I'm in an interaction, I also look at the person talking, because I want to pick up on their facial expressions.

At bigger events, you might be offered a teleprompter. If you decide to use it, don't worry about not looking into the camera. They are set up in such a way that it looks like you are looking straight into the camera. If you don't have a teleprompter and you are using speaker notes, read chapter 6 and don't use them. If they are on your desk, under your slides or next to the video-screen, the audience will see your eyes looking down or to the side. It's a very awkward sight, the audience doesn't feel appreciated, and you will probably start reading the notes anyway.

6. DON'T UNDERESTIMATE THE POWER OF SMALL TALK

Invest in small talk where possible. Make sure you are talking to people when others are entering or at least getting some early engagement in the chat. Everybody loves to walk into a cosy bar where there are people having a nice chat instead of an empty silent room. Even if you wait for everybody to join the lobby and let them enter all at once. People are still getting ready, getting some coffee, setting up their camera, so have some fun interaction with the people who are already fully present. It will focus the others, signal you have started and trigger people to join in. Try it, it's possible with two people and with 30.000 people. Make the room small. When you don't yet feel comfortable or it's better for the group size or the experience that the participant can't use their microphone, just interact without getting a response.

For example, I call out some people by name if I see that they are present, smiling or doing something that stands out. "I see John is completely ready in his fancy gaming chair." "I notice Sara is ready to rock, good morning, loving that smile." "Welcome everybody, also the people just sitting down with their coffee. Enjoy Tom."

7. NAME THE ELEPHANT IN THE ROOM

The elephant in the room has popped up in this book numerous times and it also plays a part in this chapter. Win the attention or regain it by naming things that are happening. You see people smiling, frowning, putting things in the chat, falling asleep, spilling their coffee, raising their hand,... Name what is going on once in a while. It lets people know they are seen. Even if it is a large group, they get surprised and triggered to refocus as they would when their teacher surprised them in class. People are curious creatures and want to be involved, "What just happened, what is going on in the chat?". It also gives them the opportunity to react and yourself a moment to breath.

The elephant also plays a part in guiding people through your talk. You will 'share your screen', 'they can put something in the chat', 'the poll is up', 'a mic is on mute', 'all mics need to be on mute', 'put your cameras on', 'we are still waiting for a few people to jump in',... Name what is going on, what is going to happen or what the audience needs to do. This is important during a physical talk, very important when hosting a physical meeting (see chapter 20) and also a vital part of guiding your audience when speaking during a virtual event.

8. EMBRACE THE SILENCE AND EMPHASISE THE EXPERIENCE

Let's paint the extreme picture of something that you have probably encountered once or twice in your career. You have to present during an online meeting, but everybody has turned their camera and mic off. You feel that the audience is just there to observe, if they are even there and not just logged on while actually eating cereal in the kitchen. Having the mics off with many people or when you are presenting can be a plus and a must, and you also don't need cameras on to deliver a great story. There are even webinar tools that don't offer the option so that they don't put too much pressure on the connection. But when it's a small group or you want to engage with the audience and see if your points are landing, seeing everybody helps. Dare to name this immediately and ask for it. An awkward silence will probably follow; maybe one or two people who feel your pain and pity you will comply. If you feel good, confident and have learned to embrace the silence, you can ask again and emphasise the value for their experience to put the camera on. In extreme cases when very few comply, I either start having some fun interactions with the people who have their camera on, to show that it is safe, and we are having a good time.

People will want to feel part of it. If nobody jumps in, not even out of pity, I'll just start my talk and own it. This situation is like playing music in the street. In the beginning you will be ignored, then some will notice that you are actually good, so they will stay and clap or give you money (put the camera on). Once you have those first followers, others will start to join in. If they really don't and you are confronted with a company culture where this is the norm, just give them your best and start with simple interactions in the chat. Maybe it is all you will get, or it will be a slow step towards trust and eventually cameras and full participation.

9. FOCUS ON YOU

People like to look at people. That's why your selfies work better than your other pictures on social media. So when you constantly share your slide deck and I only get a small frame in the top or bottom corner with you, I quickly get bored and distracted. And I certainly get bored when you tend to spend a lot of time on one slide, which is not recommended anyway (see chapter 15). The most important part of the experience is you, the speaker – the smallest thing on my screen. I want to see you speak and move; I want to be able to read your facial expressions. That's why I always switch between showing some slides and popping back to full screen. I rarely use slides, but when I use them, it's only in the strategic moments that they really add visual value. The rest of the time I want them looking at and engaging with me. I deliberately say 'strategic moments when they add value' as you don't want your presentation to become a pinball machine of an experience, of you flipping between full screen, screen share with slides, full screen, screen share with slides. At larger virtual events you therefore see the tech crew showing your face on one side of the screen and your visuals on the other side. People want to see you, hear you, not stare at some slides.

10. PRACTISE AND KNOW WHO YOU ARE

Practise using your technology, switching between the screen, engaging in the chat, setting up polls and experimenting with backgrounds. The more you do it, the more comfortable you will become and the more you will learn what works and what doesn't for the audience, you and the experience. But also practise your performance, the use of your voice and body in front of that camera in that little frame. As discussed in chapter 9, great speakers watch and listen to themselves a lot.

Until they know exactly how they look, sound, need to use their voice and body in the best possible way. They know how the audience perceives them every step of the way without seeing themselves during the presentation. You need to be able to picture how the audience sees and hears you through the camera, by practising and observing yourself a million times. Only this way will you be able to give them that TV experience they are hoping for. "Isn't a TV experience a bit extreme for a regular Monday morning team meeting?" I know my views in this book can sometimes be extreme, but if a meeting is not worth you preparing the best possible experience, the meeting shouldn't happen at all, as it is clearly unnecessary and could be an email. If it's not worth your time prepping your presentation in such a way, why should I spend my time showing up to your presentation and listening to it. Earn my attention. Your most valuable asset in life is time. Don't waste your own time, don't waste that of the audience. If you do ask the time of the audience, spend yours first on practice and preparation, so they feel it was worth theirs. Even if it's online.

Online presentations, webinars, virtual events, and remote meetings are very similar to the physical variants. The same techniques apply. The difference sits in the power of the screen and the camera. They make you work twice as hard for the attention and trust of your audience. They are gate keepers and only the true high performing speakers with engaging stories will be allowed through. Add to that the safe environment the audience sits in, where they can get distracted or can hide, and you now understand that you need to multiply everything by at least two. Take control, be prepared, speak, move, bring energy, make a TV show, interact, name what needs to be mentioned, add value and make sure the audience sees, hears and experiences the best online version of you.

NOTE. The above guidelines apply to speaking during virtual events and meetings. If you are planning to extend your speaking impact to recording videos for online purposes, most of the above still applies, but you will have to take one thing into account: online attention span is zero to none. Your 4-step structure from chapter 12 stays valid, but the relate/offer needs to be quicker and more triggering = your hook. For example, nervous for your next presentation? Here are 3 confidence boosters I wish I'd known earlier. OR Speaking for free? What if I told you that there is a way you can make 6 figures a year? People need to know within 2 seconds if the video is for them (relate) and if you have something they want, crave or fear missing out on. The greater the hook, the more chance you will go viral. The way attention is grabbed in online videos changes rapidly. What works today is old practice tomorrow.

People are currently using small microphones, speaking while eating something or holding a banana,... By the time you read this book, it could all have changed. All attention grabbers, just to make you stop scrolling and watch the video. During virtual presentations or offline speeches you also have to grab attention immediately, but you have a bit more time.

AI companion

What are the key do's and don'ts when speaking in front of a camera?

••••

CORE INSIGHTS:

- Online and offline speaking is not so different.
- Multiply everything by two – energy, focus, speaking, preparation, interaction,...
- Never underestimate the power of small talk.
- See online speaking as making a TV show. What are you offering the audience in your little virtual box?
- It's about you, your story and the experience, not about your slides.

20
HOW DO I HOST AN EVENT OR MEETING?

THE SHORT ANSWER IS:
"BY NOT BEING A MONKEY."

Your speaking is starting to stand out at events or within your organisation. This will sooner or later lead to the question, "Would you be willing to host our next event/webinar/meeting?" A very nice compliment to get, because hosting an event, interacting with the audience, watching over the flow of the entire event, giving speakers the right energy,... is a whole different ball game versus speaking for 30 minutes and walking off stage. It's a big responsibility and therefore not for everybody.

Is hosting then the logical next step in your successful speaking journey? Not at all. You should only host an event when you get energy out of it. Some speakers avoid it, and others love it so much that they turn it into their profession. You can only discover where you stand by doing it a couple of times. That you will get the question to host once your speaking becomes noticeable, I am sure of. This was no different for me. Once I started performing, I became the usual suspect for hosting internal events at my previous jobs and later in my Stand Up Company speaking career. I said 'yes' to the hosting question many years ago and that led to leading hundreds of internal meetings, webinars and small events to hosting TV shows, huge live streams and even a full stadium.

If you also got the question, you always dreamed of becoming a host, or you just want to test the water, use the following ten insights that I gathered over all those years to give yourself a head start. The audience and the speakers will be grateful, because hosting is not being a monkey that reads speaker names off a card.

"A host is not a monkey that just reads speaker names off a card. It's the person that makes or breaks your event."

The host or MC (master of ceremony), as it is also referred to, will often be seen as an inferior part of an event versus big name speakers and the catering. I'm not saying this out of frustration or bitterness; you will soon experience this yourself. People who have never hosted an event or aren't professionally involved in event management just see it as this monkey reading the cards and therefore something they must include in their organisation but doesn't seem of great value.

Companies regularly say, "I'll ask my cousin to host this internal event; he is always a smooth talker at family parties," while professional speakers and event organisers know that the host will make or break your entire event, no matter how delicious your afternoon snacks are. The host needs to be the first person they contact when planning an event. He will be the first to show up and the last person to leave. The host has such a responsibility that he needs to be the best speaker on stage, but can never be the best speaker on stage. This sentence will become clear in a second. Never underestimate the impact a host has on an event. The following insights will ensure that you can have that impact and be an added value to any event you MC.

> ***"The host needs to be the best speaker on stage, but can never be the best speaker on stage."***

1. THE CIRCLE IS ROUND

As we discussed in chapter 10, people love links, a red thread, a storyline that they can easily follow and help tie all the information together. One of the key tasks of a host is finding, creating and guarding that red thread between all the different speakers. This is the reason a host needs to be involved in the planning process early on. This way the host can help the organisation find the most logical build up and line up of all the speakers, workshops, panel discussions,... At the end of an event, the audience needs to feel that they didn't just hear a bunch of separate stories, but that each story, every speaker was carefully placed in the agenda, so the entire programme became one big story. It's the best compliment to get on surveys afterwards, "Wow, the entire event felt like one big whole where everything tied together nicely and came full circle at the end." Our brain loves it, and during your preparation and on the day itself, it is your job as a host to create and watch over this storyline with your announcements, interactions and in between bits, clearly emphasising the links and taking the audience by the hand from one speaker to the other.

Inexperienced hosts focus on the names, subjects and backgrounds of the speakers or workshop facilitators. No matter how harsh this sounds, nobody cares about that, besides some big ego speakers and the organisation. Make sure you pronounce the names right, and have a bit of interesting, attention grabbing information about the speaker or the talk (you can discuss this with the speaker upfront). Forget background, diploma, function, career,... the audience can read that on the website, brochure or in the event app. Focus on how this speaker's talk links to the previous talk or why this is the most logical way to start the day. There is where you make the difference as a host. Remember, you are not a monkey and the audience wants an experience, value and entertainment, not ego boosting biographies.

Now how do you remember all this information? By using speaker cards, preferably with a nice picture or logo at the back of the card, because that looks nice on pictures and video. The event organiser will be grateful. "But you said in chapter 6 that I couldn't use speaker cards?" As a speaker, yes, I'm against it. As a host, you need it. I'm pretty proud of my ability to remember large chunks of information, but even with an elephant memory it's still tough to remember all the names, all the talks, the panel questions,... Use speaker cards, nobody will mind if the host does this.

But as I said in that same chapter about using notes on the monitors, don't write down all the information in sentences or paragraphs; you won't have time to read it on stage. I use one card for every part of the show. For example, one card for the opening, one card for the first speaker, one card for lunch information,... and number my cards, because if you are nervous and drop them, you need to get them in order asap. I will write down any important names, the main points that I need to mention in bullet form, the time this section should last and the link to whatever came before or comes next.

This way, you don't have to read a lot, but you still have all the information in your hand, you can't get confused, and you just throw away the card or put it in the back of the deck once you have finished a part. When you are doing an online show or webinar, don't forget to write down the cues of bumper videos, camera movement,... that you discussed with the tech crew and director (at bigger live streams) during a possible dry run. In this environment, you can also rely on teleprompters for your notes. I don't use them, because they still urge you to read a bit, but that is just my style. Do what works for you, but in each case, cards, monitor, prompter, no full sentences or text, you won't have the time, you will only have seconds to glance at the information. Of course you can read names or titles; nobody expects you to memorise all those names. In an international environment, certain names can definitely be quite the challenge.

2. MASTER OF ENERGY

Besides linking it all together, the most important task of a host is energy management. Online or offline, there is no difference. This means sending energy into the room in the beginning of the day. Making sure people feel welcome, have something to look forward to, are ready to listen attentively and already like the person that is currently speaking – you. You are going to put people at ease, explain how everything is going to unfold and trigger that first dopamine. The warm energy bath that you create will be the one the first speaker can step into. As I said before, people use the beginning to rate the experience, so your opening and the first speaker ready to rock surfing on that energy, will have the audience wanting more. The host needs to be involved upfront (see point one), as this first speaker needs to be good and able to use your energy setup. The start is essential, so don't put a risky or unexperienced speaker first. You have to start and end with a bang.

The audience needs to realise that the more energy they give the speakers, the better they will perform and the better their entire experience will become. After that first setup and speaker, it will be your job to assess the energy at every point during the event. If a speaker absolutely blew the roof off, you will need to lower the energy a bit, because the expectation and excitement is too high within the audience, so the next speaker doesn't have a fair chance and the audience will likely be disappointed. In a comedy line-up show where different comedians perform that night, they then say, "That comedian destroyed the room." Meaning he was so good everybody else will be less funny to the audience. A good MC/host knows to lower the vibe a bit before announcing a new speaker.

The same goes when somebody destroyed the room in a bad way. Let's say you worked up the crowd to a nice energy level, but a speaker is boring and is making the audience fall asleep or become annoyed. It's your job to reinject the energy, make the audience forget this speaker and realise a new one is coming on. If you don't, the next speaker will have to work hard to keep the attention. I have had many events in my career where I wasn't involved in the agenda and speaker planning and multiple bad speakers were lined up. This is a hosting hell, as you literally have to save the event, reinjecting new energy after every talk, to carry the audience through the day, only to see it being destroyed by the next speaker and the next speaker. I can guarantee you, after those events you curl up into a ball on the couch and cry with exhaustion. A bit exaggerated, of course, but I want you to feel that pain, because you will encounter it too. When a speaker does well and the atmosphere in the room is on point, keep your bit as short as possible and let the next speaker leverage the ambiance. In those moments you need to give yourself a break as a host and let it all flow.

AUDIENCE ENERGY LOW = HOST BRINGS IT UP TO GOOD
AUDIENCE ENERGY NEUTRAL = HOST BRINGS IT UP TO GOOD
AUDIENCE ENERGY GOOD = HOST LIMITS HIS INTERVENTION
AUDIENCE ENERGY HIGH = HOST LOWERS ENERGY TO GOOD

This energy management is the same during a webinar or live stream event. The only difference is that, besides a chat, you won't get much response from the audience. You as a host need to feel the vibe in the room you are presenting in, and make an estimate of how people are experiencing the show. Trust me, when a speaker is talking, you can feel if this is resonating with the online audience or not. You don't have to see the audience to know. Plus, in front of a screen, the energy you send needs to be twice as much, because so much is lost through a screen; see chapter 19. You literally have to radiate through their monitors.

That energy management, feeling the vibe, increasing, lowering, holding, is the reason why hosting is not something that can be done by anybody. You have to bring your 10/10 energy and focus (see chapter 8), you interact, you move around, you insert entertaining stories, you do exercises with the audience (if that is your thing) and ask for applause regularly. You are the drug dealer, handing out dopamine. You need to be the best speaker to be able to manage all this and step up to the plate when it is needed. You are responsible for keeping the audience engaged throughout the entire event, no matter how good or bad the speakers are. Not every speaker is able to do that; it takes a very skilled speaker to host.

3. TIME, TECH, TRUST

There is probably somebody behind the conference or internal event that you are expected to host, but still, you are ultimately responsible. You are the person the audience will see the whole time; you will become their friend and will have to come to the rescue when things go wrong. You will also, even if it is not your fault, be seen as the one responsible when things go south. The life of a host is being the saviour in distress, getting the blame when it falls apart and being forgotten in the credits when the event becomes a success. Again, I'm not writing this out of frustration – just giving you the reality you will step into as a host.

> ***"The more fires you prevent from starting when the room is empty, the fewer fires you will have to put out when the room is full."***

So, make sure you are on time. Give yourself the time to get acquainted with the environment. Check in with the tech crew and the organisation. Test microphones (even if the tech crew said they have already done this) and light positioning on stage, make sure there is water for the speakers, find out how people need to walk on and off the stage, what the walking range is of microphones to avoid feedback of the speakers, etc... You need to check everything and then check it again.

Not because you want to be perceived as a micromanager, but because, as I said earlier, you will be the one having to solve the problems when things fail. The more fires you prevent from starting when the room is empty, the fewer fires you will have to put out when the room is full.

It will boost your confidence and that of the organisation in you. The smoother the event runs due to your preparation, the more you will be able to focus on the audience, the linking, the experience and the energy management. There will be a lot of things (e.g. testing mics) where you will think, "But that is the responsibility of..." and it will be, but in my experience there few people who take their job as seriously as you. So, for your own peace of mind, check and double check. Because when it's go time, it is you and only you that the audience sees. The tech crew will be cosy backstage, the organisation in the audience and the speakers will look at you for help.

These speakers, no matter how professional, will sometimes run around like headless chickens backstage. Guide them and make sure that they are ready to perform, that they know where everything is, how to walk on and off the stage, where the water is, where the best spot to stand is,... This is of course their responsibility, but not every speaker is as experienced, some are divas and others would forget their head if it wasn't tied to their body. It takes a village to raise a child; it takes a dedicated host to raise an awesome event.

4. PLAYING WITH DISTANCE AND MOVEMENT

Move as a host, use the entire stage. If it's a live stream, though, they will ask you to stand on the spot where they put the duct tape cross. Give the audience the feeling you are there for everybody and not just the people in the middle part of the room or in the front row. In a smaller meeting this is of course not applicable; addressing all the people in the room is enough and much easier. It's your job to build rapport with the audience as quickly as possible. You need to become the friend of the audience, their trusted guide and the one that 'invited' some of his friends who happen to tell great stories. You are the director of this show, big or small.

Besides the content insights from this entire book, which are also valid in hosting, the fastest way to make a connection is by playing with your movement:

DON'T FORGET THE BACK ROWS: Don't only address the first rows, but also the back rows, to include them and make the room feel a bit smaller for everybody.

FIND ALLIES: Find and create your allies as we discussed in chapter 4.

SHORTEN THE DISTANCE: Move more to the front when interacting to shorten the distance between you and the audience. They will be more likely to respond and even dare venture into the audience when the room allows it and it feels it could add value to the interaction.

RELOCATE THE ATTENTION: Move from one side to the other if you want excitement and want to involve everybody in what you are saying. Move back to the middle to tone it down a bit and share some important information.

GUIDE THEIR EYES: Guide the eyes of the audience by sticking out your arm to the place where the speaker will enter when you announce him. This way the audience knows where to look. When you want them to answer a question by raising their hand, raise your hand first.

Use the knowledge that the audience will look and follow where you look, move to or point. Guide them with your movement to where you want their focus to be. Like a magician who uses his hands to distract you from what he doesn't want you to see, guide the audience as a host to what you want the audience to see, hear or experience. They move as a collective, so it is up to you to guide them, like a conductor guides his orchestra. You don't have to overdo it. Everybody has their own style. I use every part of the space I am granted, but there are many professional hosts who rock the stage with less movement, without ignoring what I just said in this part. Give the audience the feeling that there is something happening in front of them, it's an experience, their attention and interest is triggered, and they are being engaged. The more engaged an audience, the better the connection with you and the speakers, the better the energy, the more feedback you will get from them.

5. ELEPHANT IN THE ROOM

The audience is very smart, but also very dumb. They know very well what they like and dislike. If they're being fooled or not. However, they do need to be taken by the hand and guided through the story and to literally hear what is being expected from them. If you want them to be quiet, become quiet yourself. If you want them to clap, literally ask for it, "Give it up for... "A big round of applause for..." If you want to interact with somebody, make sure through your movement (see previous point) that this person knows you are talking to them. Is something going wrong or is there a disturbance? Call it out. Do they have a 30-minute lunch? Mention this. When they can go, when they need to come back. Where and when their next workshop is. You need answers in the chat? Ask for them. And so on.

The same goes for the speakers. Where do they need to walk off or walk on? After the Q&A, if the speaker needs to stay seated on stage, make sure they know. Mention it even if you discussed it backstage. Leave nothing to chance, repeat and call it out. The audience and the speakers are one big herd, and you are the sheepdog. I'm not saying the audience and speakers are sheep, but it is a human trait that when we are in group, we stop thinking, because we count on somebody else in the group to pay attention. The same happens at events; you need to be that person who is paying attention. This doesn't mean that you belittle the audience and treat them like little children. Nobody likes a micro-manager or a patronising teacher. Do it in a fun, open way. You are their friend making sure they get the best experience, and you offer them friendly, but firm guidance. You lead, the audience follows. Do this with the right flair and conviction and the audience will accept and appreciate it.

6. DON'T JUST ASK QUESTIONS

As a host you will also be asked to lead debates or panel discussions. People often think you need to be an expert in the content of the event to be able to guide these interactions. It helps of course, but is not a necessity. I have led panels around JavaScript, robotics and financial control – topics I know very little about and still it went smoothly. If you do have the expertise, that is a plus, but can sometimes be a pitfall, because hosts who have a link to the topic tend to feel like they also need to share their opinion and expertise. That is not your role; you are there to make the others shine.

The responsibility of the host is to ask questions, but also to link all the answers together and to ensure that everything is discussed in a logical order. It needs to feel like a spontaneous conversation with a clear structure. Not just question-answer, question-answer. This is largely achieved through strong preparation, but also by listening and reading between the lines. Who are you going to pose which question to? (=preparation) Who do you notice is willing to react to something that was said or challenge it? When is a question hollowed out and does the conversation need to move on? You are in control at all times, without people experiencing it that way.

Ask extra questions, ask for extra clarification, call out laughter or frowning from other panel members to trigger a response and keep things interesting. These things will keep the conversation fresh and spontaneous. Even if you know very little of the topic, you will know enough to guide people through it and ask these extra questions, due to your preparation with the speakers up front. Here the role of the host upfront flares up again. Make sure you don't have a debate or panel where everybody agrees with each other. Those get boring quickly. People like frictions, clash of opinions. You don't have to start a fight or heated discussions, but a mix of different views makes for a tastier knowledge cocktail.

You will notice that it can even be an advantage to be a novice in the topic, because this gives you an open, non-biased look at it and allows you to ask the simple questions. The questions the audience likes, because we all know children ask the most pressing questions due to their unapologetic honesty. You are that kid in the panel discussion. Of course, the questions add value and aren't just dumb.

It's also your job to check in with the audience from time to time. A debate or panel is not a cosy tea party with the speakers. It's a show for the audience; they need to feel part of the conversation even if they are mostly listening. If they have questions, let them ask them or put them in the chat. Ask for a collective reaction to a point (cheer, applause, raise of hands,...) and make sure the speakers know they need to talk to the audience and not just to each other. Nobody likes to stand outside a group of people talking and not feel included. Your questions, speaker answers, wrap-ups of points made – all of this is for the audience, so make sure they experience it that way.

7. BE THE LIFEBUOY

I personally find that the most demanding part of hosting is not having the luxury of shutting off. You are there first, you leave last and you can't lose your focus for a second, because you never know what will occur – a mic that dies, a presentation that goes dark, a speaker who blacks out, people can't re-enter the live stream,... You name it and I have seen it in my hosting career. Experienced speakers, the tech crew and organisations know what to do, but you are the single point of contact for the audience, and even professional speakers struggle sometimes to fill up the time to fix a problem, keep the audience engaged and get back on track.

Whatever happens, it can't come back to the speaker or the organisation; they need to keep their credibility. The more you manage the situation in a fun and calm manner, the less the audience will notice of the little hiccup and the more grateful the speaker, tech crew and organisation will be. In these moments you really earn your stripes as a host. Build up experience and you will have scripts/stock lines (as discussed in chapter 7) for every scenario, because you have seen it many times before.

Do it right and you will notice that the audience enjoys the hiccups even more than the talks. It isn't the goal, but manage such a situation well and it becomes a show in itself. I once had to re-introduce a speaker three times, because his crucial video opening failed to work. It became a funny play between speaker, audience and host. It was voted most entertaining part of the event; people thought it was part of the talk and the speaker got great ratings. But if you don't pay attention or you are chitchatting in the lobby during a talk, you will be surprised many times and miss these crucial moments for you to step in as a host.

8. CHOOSE A LANGUAGE

You will be asked to present in different languages. I don't know how many languages you have mastered, but I recommend that you only speak and host in a language that is native or that you have mastered as if you are a native speaker. For me this is Dutch and English. As a Belgian I also speak German and French, but these are good for travel or normal meetings; I will never host or speak in these languages. To really entertain, manage energy and guide an audience, you can't be thinking about what verb and what adjective goes were. It needs to come fluently.

When they ask you to speak in two languages, which is done a lot at international events, that is, native language and English, refuse it. Not because I don't think you have mastered the languages you chose, but because it is hell for the audience. Your job is to entertain, manage energy, link, guide speakers, put out fires,... Your main focus should not be to remember to switch languages every three sentences. Very annoying for you and very annoying for the audience. It's mostly a request from event organisers that are more concerned with internal politics and keeping certain parties happy than actually constructing a great experience for the audience.

The solution that mostly pops up then is duo-hosting. You are free to do whatever you want, but most professional hosts will also tell you to run away from that. You see it on TV, but most of the time the energy between the hosts is cringey. One person is more skilled and liked than the other. The styles differ too much, and you can't really build 'your' show. I'm not against it, but I know few hosts that go about life saying, "Duo-hosting, it's the best!" This language point is also applicable to your regular presentations.

9. YOU CAN'T WIN

Hosting is a noble, but hard profession. You need to be the most skilled speaker on the physical or virtual stage. You must constantly be on alert, put out fires, manage energy, ask good questions and make others shine. Do this right, and the audience will adore you and you will make events. But you can never 'be' the best speaker, because an event is about the speakers, workshop facilitators and panel members. You are at their service. If you shine brighter than them, you didn't do your job right. In comedy they taught me that an MC needs to be funny, but can never be more funny than the comedians.

You are not in the role of a comedian that night, you are the MC, supporting the comedians. Put your ego aside and perform in function of your speakers. If you can't do this, that is perfectly fine, but then maybe hosting isn't for you. I have been voted best speaker at an event many times after hosting. A great ego boost, but you notice backstage that speakers feel intimidated and know, 'I will not perform to this level'. That was my mistake and not something you want. Use your skills to make them shine. It doesn't mean falsely doing a lesser job. It means working in function of the line-up instead of putting yourself in front. Like a helper in cycling who might be faster or fitter during a race than his team leader, but instead of showing off his skills to win, he directs it to helping his lead win the race. That is hosting. Of course, the speakers are responsible for showing up prepared, professional and ready to rock.

If you are at an event where all the speakers are boring or unprofessional and you need to pull all the tricks out of your hat to keep the audience going, you have a hall pass and my blessing to rock the stage completely and be voted best speaker of the conference.

10. CHOOSE, BUT CHOOSE WISELY

Let's say your colleagues have given you the opportunity to host a couple of internal events, some event organisers have booked you as their conference host and you got a taste of what it is to host an event instead of being one of the presenters. If you do it right, you will get a lot more requests, because good hosts are very rare. But no matter how successful you were, you will have to decide at some point whether you want to be a host or a speaker. After many years, I have chosen to be a speaker and leave the hosting world. Speaking is better for my business, I have more fun doing it and offers me more credibility in my profession. Why can't you just be both, you may ask. This is going to sound sad, but once you are a host, you will always be the host. A great profession, but once you carry that label, you will be booked as the host and even if you have found the cure for cancer, you will not be asked to speak about it at the next big pharma conference, you will be asked to host that conference. The same goes for comedy: if you want to be a successful comedian, don't be an MC.

Hosting is a great way to build up experience. I don't think I would have been able to write two books on speaking if I wasn't carrying all this hosting experience in my backpack, but I couldn't stay there. My speaking career really started booming when I decided to say goodbye to hosting. Once in a while, I will still do one as a favour to a friend or client, but that's all.

Do you like hosting and find hosting a podcast, a New Year's kick off or conference a welcome change in your agenda? Great, do it and do it well. If you want to further develop as a speaker, then host, pay your dues, get that experience, but know you will have to let go at some point. If you think this applies only to speakers who have professional ambitions, I coach plenty of clients who are very good at their job, but rarely share insights at internal events, because they are so good at hosting and are therefore only asked to host by their leadership instead of sharing their expertise.

Hosting is a profession, and it is a beautiful profession. Something few master. But if you are that person who loves it, gets energy out of it and wants to pursue it in your organisation or as an independent worker, then go all in. Audiences, event organisers and speakers around the world will be grateful.

BONUS CONTENT

What about doing exercises with the audience to keep the energy and focus throughout the day?

You don't have to do exercises with the audience to be a great host. A lot of people don't like getting up and doing something; they come for the content and want to listen from the comfort of their seat. But sometimes the organisation expects it or the event demands it, because the day is too long or the speakers, too boring. If you then decide to do some fun exercises with the audience, make sure the audience feels comfortable doing them, make sure you are fully committed, bring it with conviction and take the lead. Any doubt in your body language or voice and the audience won't follow. Doing the exercise yourself first or doing it with the audience also helps as an audience will be more likely to follow and accept the exercise than if a host just commands the audience to do things, while not participating at all. The audience thinks, we jump, you jump first. We have to shout something, you do it first, dear host. If you are able to do that, then you could try one of the following exercises. They are my favourite ones from when I still hosted a lot of events:

- The Mexican wave: I adapt this wave to the location I am in, for example, the Amsterdam wave where they don't say 'heyyyyy', but 'hoyyyyyy'. I start at one end of the room and run with the wave to the other end and ask the audience to return. Once they have returned the wave, I ask them to end with applause. A very simple, low entry level exercise, but it delivers great content for the after movie and people generally enjoy doing it.
- Three times applause: An exercise often used in audience warm ups by comedy MCs. You ask the audience to show you what applause would sound like if a speaker is very bad. Then you ask them what it would sound like if the speaker was okay, not great, but okay. And then you ask them to show you what applause would sound like if they had just experienced the best talk in the world. Then you urge them to give this same amount of energy to the next speaker.
- Bibedibop: It's a well known game in Scouts – a bit like Simon Says. You ask the audience to stand up and to react appropriately when you say something. When you say bibedibop, they have to say bop before you reach your bop. When you say bop, they need to stay silent. When you say toaster they need to start jumping like bread jumping out of the toaster and when you say James Bond, they need to hold up their hand to form a gun. You then run through all of these at a fast pace and try to trick the audience. They will jump, make mistakes, laugh and to this day it's the most popular exercise. Audiences even request it, if they have seen me hosting before.
- Split the room: Divide the room in two by saying there is an invisible line in the middle. You take the name of the next speaker and let one

part say one part of the name and the other part of the room the last part of the name. When you point at them, they say their part. Go back and forth so the room shouts the speaker name. Mix it up, so they make a mistake, and this will always get a laugh. Speed it up and when at full speed, announce the speaker and ask for big applause. A variation is to split the room and throw big plastic balls into the audience and tell each side that they have to keep the balls out of their camp. Then start some pumping music and watch people go berserk tapping the balls from one side to the other.

- Take a picture: Get the audience to stand up. Ask the photographer to come on stage. Say you are going to take three pictures and the audience needs to have their picture taken as the thing you call out. For example, you are an audience of monsters, 3...2...1 click. The whole audience tries to express themselves as a monster. Then you ask them to be an audience of flamingos, 3....2...1...click. This is a very funny sight, people laugh and it delivers original event pictures.
- Creative announcement: Announce the speaker in a creative way. Look up something about them that stands out, have him share something cool with you upfront that you can use or just play with the way you announce him. For example, I sometimes announce speakers in a movie trailer voice, because I feel their name sounds like that of an action hero. I play some theatre or tell a personal funny anecdote that links to the topic of the speaker.

Scan the qr-code to watch the video:

There are hundreds of these types of exercises online for big and small groups: rock, paper, scissors, counting exercises, associating exercises, a lot of improvisation theatre, warm up exercises, you name it. The key is to take the ones you feel comfortable with organising, are low key for the audience, don't become awkward and are quickly set up. Too complicated, too out of the comfort zone, too long and the audience will not follow or quickly protest. Exercises like massaging or touching the person next to you, switching clothes or phones (yes I know, weird, but it happens more often than you think) are a no go for me, too cringe, too into your personal space and no added value to the energy of the audience. It will lower the mood instead of boosting it. Stay away from those. Have fun with the rest, get creative and sense what you think a specific audience needs or will be up for. But as I said, good hosting doesn't need these exercises, they are a bonus.

BONUS CONTENT

What if I have to do a duo presentation or I choose to do a duo hosting? How do I hand over to the other speaker?

Just like with the video presentations in chapter 19, all the techniques in this book also apply when you are sharing the stage with someone. However there are some pointers to keep in mind when preparing and speaking to make things go as smoothly as possible:

- **YOU ARE NOT IN SCHOOL:** Avoid handing over your presentation the school-like way: "I now give the word to..." "I will now hand over to..." "I will give the stage to..." It's not wrong, but it feels amateurish and can create an awkward vibe.

- **ONE STORY, DIFFERENT SECTIONS:** Prepare your presentation together instead of mixing two separate stories into one. See it as one story and then divide that story up in a logical way. Preferably with each speaker doing a section that revolves around one topic or point. Speaker 1 will talk about point A, speaker 2 about point B , speaker 1 returns with point C. This way it remains one story, the switches are clear for the speakers and the audience enjoys the idea that every speaker brings a new insight and builds further on what the other speaker previously said.

- **LINK IT ALL TOGETHER:** Don't only divide the presentation into logical sections, but also double down on getting the links between these sections right (see chapter 13). These links will be your transitions between speakers. E.g. speaker 1 wraps up point A and instead of saying in a school-like way, "I will now hand over to...", speaker 1 says his last sentence and remains silent. Speaker 2 knows his section B starts and what the link is between A and B, so he will use that link as his entry and jump in the moment speaker A finishes. This creates a very smooth and professional feel. When speaker 2 finishes, speaker 1 jumps back in with the link to point C and starts his section of the story. The audience will experience you as a well oiled tag team.

- **DON'T STAND ON STAGE, DO BUILD CHEMISTRY:** The length of each section determines whether you stay on stage or not. If you are duo-hosting and have a part of the event, you only come on stage when you are up. When you are asked to stand on stage together and cover shorter sections, it's ok to remain on stage, but do acknowledge each other and focus on creating a nice chemistry between you two, like two friends who are eager to share their experiences with the audience. When in a duo presentation, the same goes. Are your sections a normal length? Then feel free to stay in front of the audience together. Are the sections longer (e.g. 10 minutes each)? Then stay backstage or sit down in the first row or on a stool at the side of the stage. It becomes very awkward for you and the audience when one speaker is just standing there for a longer period of time. The moment you know your section is about to start, move to the stage, ready to jump in and continue like a professional.

- **DON'T ADD MORE PRESSURE:** Avoid sections that are too short. Imagine being nervous or not yet that experienced and besides rocking your performance you also have to remember all the transitions. Some duo speakers switch every few sentences or switch languages. That can cause a lot of stress, tends to become messy or overly rehearsed. It's not fun for the speakers and the audience. Let every speaker cover a logical section of the story you prepared together.

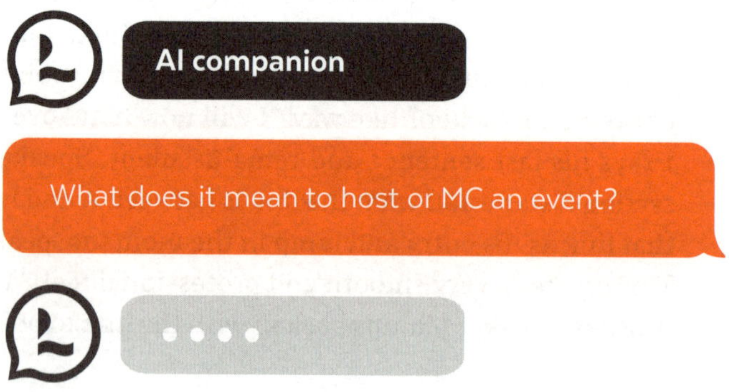

CORE INSIGHTS:

- Hosting is a profession and more than just reading names off a speaker card.
- Energy management and linking everything together are your main tasks.
- You are the backbone of an event. You are the first in and the last one out.
- You want to become the friend of the audience as fast as possible.

AI
USING TECHNOLOGY TO YOUR ADVANTAGE

21
CAN'T I JUST LET AI DO EVERYTHING FOR ME?

THE SHORT ANSWER IS:
"YES, YOU CAN."

By the time I finish writing this chapter, the capabilities of AI will have evolved exponentially. I can't predict the future so I am unable to know where AI will be in its evolution at the time that you read this book. Maybe you are a fully self-aware robot. But we can be sure that AI is already playing and will play a major part in our future way of living and working. I just got back from a conference in Slovakia where a speaker wrote and published a full book on the history of the British empire in 30 minutes. I have been chewing on my book for months, because I wanted to write it entirely myself. Seeing AI accomplish in half an hour what only a few people in the world will endeavour, due to the intensity and time investment, is astonishing. The world keeps changing faster and faster and in that world where AI can speak, write, paint, design, code,... it's logical for clients in workshops to ask me, "Marnick, why should I invest so much time in mastering everything from this book? I can just ask AI to build my story, create my slides and get my avatar to tell it for me." You could indeed and who am I to stop you?

The reason I write my books myself, build my presentations myself and keep working on my stories in a way that some might already consider old school, is because the biggest and most important computer that I want to see evolving is my own brain. I'm a fan of AI, Amplifying your own Intelligence. It's the reason I also still write my notes and thoughts on real paper. Not because I'm against digital tools, but because the act of writing, the motion, the brain power that comes with it, is a way to train the brain, process information better and potentially counter mental diseases like Alzheimer's. My maternal grandfather, who I dedicated this book to on the first page, lived until he was 92. He was 92 and walked and talked like he was in his 20s. His memory was spot on, and he could easily beat you in a debate. His secret was reading, writing and staying curious every single day. My paternal grandmother passed away at 91 and had the same elephant memory – you couldn't fool her to her last day. She shared the same passion for reading, writing letters and being curious. They aren't related, didn't share the same genes or eating patterns and still lived to their last day in full control over their body and mind. They did share one thing and that was their commitment to their own development.

"I am a fan of AI, Amplifying your own Intelligence."

We live in a world where everything is being designed for humans to do as little as possible, as easily as possible, which I can encourage to a certain degree. The less time we lose with pointless or frustrating tasks the better, but art, writing, building and telling stories that inspire people, and trigger emotion are not pointless or frustrating tasks, they are the things that give our life meaning, create legacy, expand our mind and establish culture. Outsource all of that and we basically have no purpose for being here besides consuming food and turning air into CO_2.

This last part might sound a bit harsh, but am I far from the truth if you look at currently developments? I'm not against AI; if I was, there wouldn't be an AI companion included with this book. I am for AI if it helps to Amplify your Intelligence. I use AI agents as a sounding board, to check spelling, do translations, to inspire me to think differently or give me an answer to a question I have no time to research myself. But despite that companionship and other great adaptations in other sectors like the car industry, health care,.. I still urge you to not ignore your own growth.

I have noticed in meetings with younger generations that they are kids of their time and were born with technology. That is their world, but take away the tech and some become very nervous. In a workshop, they immediately take their phone or laptop and start asking AI to help them with their story. Proudly they show me generic text that has the charisma of a mop. They get challenged on a few points and choke up. If you have a text, this doesn't mean that it therefore identifies as a great story, just like talking without much effort in front of a group doesn't mean you are a great speaker. I challenge them to come up with the best story for their audience, and they use AI. I use my own brain and the techniques I have shared in this book. It might sound cocky, but I beat AI every time, in impact and in time to come up with the story. After that moment, the laptops are closed and the group takes out markers and paper and starts building their story. It's a big claim and maybe I will say something different in the years to come, but the human brain is a supercomputer and we have only explored a tiny fraction of it.

So, do I want you to ignore AI and embrace my viewpoint, which makes me sound like a technology-averse grumpy old man? No. I do recommend that you use AI for...

- **BUILDING SLIDES:** Use your 10-15 point skeleton story with the creative sauce elements as your prompt and you will get beautiful slides for every part in no time.
- **VISUAL GENERATION AND DATA VISUALISATION:** Can't find the visual that you need to best express the point you are trying to make or need a bundle of data visualised for better understanding? Just use one of the many image generators and pick the best one.
- **RUBBER DUCKING:** Struggling with your GAV preparation and no colleagues or friends around? Just use AI to challenge yourself, as a sounding board or to give you new insights about your audience. The answers will be generic, but it might just trigger you to come up with some valuable insights.
- **RESEARCHING AND SUMMARISING:** You need data, the right names of people or places, you wonder if there is research available about your topic. All these questions can be put to an AI agent instead of losing a lot of time crawling search engines. You need a summary of a book and the highlights from a certain chapter, but don't have the time to read it, just ask AI.
- **SPELLING, STRUCTURE CONTROL AND TRANSLATION:** I check things with my wife, but if you need to check certain spelling or grammar or you need to double check whether your structure, points and links make sense, just ask an AI agent to do a review of your work. Or if you need to switch your story from Dutch to English and don't want to put in the work or hire a translator, AI will do it in seconds.

Yes. That is what the AI companion of this book and many other even more advanced agents are for. But in all that AI help, treat your own brain, body, voice and skill as the number one priority. It will make you a sharp cookie in meetings, it will allow you to detect the value in other people's talks, it will have you turn any message into a story in seconds and will fill your mental backpack with so much knowledge and experience that you can pop out at any given time. You will be confident, credible, skilled and inspiring. You will have AI to speed things up, rubber duck or challenge you, but you will always know it's a support. Just like you are always the story and not your slide deck.

Another reason I urge you to train yourself in mastering the skill of speaking with real impact is to make sure AI avatars don't make fools of themselves in the future. AI mimics what it is trained and fed. If you go to a conference with ten speakers, you will be lucky if one or two speakers actually know what they are doing. The skill of speaking is so valuable, so powerful, but at the same time so rare that people who master it possess gold. But if the vast majority are tone deaf or have limited speaking capability, these boring speakers and presentations will be the biggest chunk of training material for AI to work with. This is why the avatars currently available for videos and online presentations are just as boring and uninspiring as the speakers that fed the information. So, please do not only yourself but also the future of AI a favour by putting in the work and really becoming good at speaking. You will rock your internal and external stages, open the door to opportunities across the world and if AI uses your skill to train itself for future avatars, at least we know these avatars will speak with impact, tell stories instead of transferring information and trigger emotion.

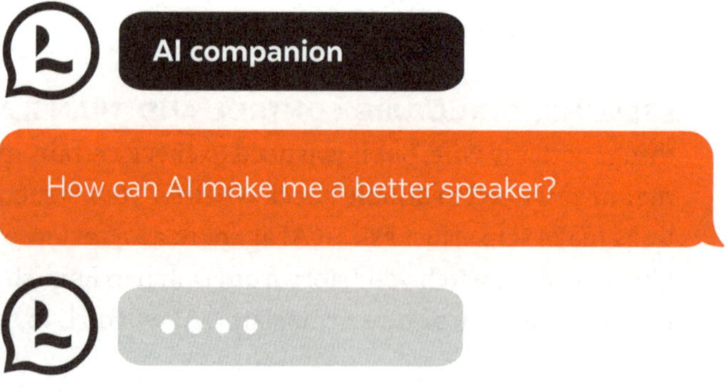

CORE INSIGHTS

- Speaking, triggering emotion and connecting with people through the power of stories is what makes us human and offers us value, comfort and inspiration.
- AI will continue to evolve at a rapid pace and the possibilities seem to become endless. Don't be blind to it, use it to your advantage.
- Keep Amplifying your own Intelligence so you remain the story and when AI organises their own conferences in the future, you will be asked as a keynote speaker.
- Use AI to support you in research, translations, structuring, brainstorming, visualisation.
- Do current and future AI avatars a favour and become a great speaker so it can learn from the best.

AND SO IT BEGINS...

Let me end this book with the same question for you, which I used to kick it off:

> *"How much dopamine are you triggering when you speak?"*

Are you just transferring a message, or literally changing the emotional and physical state of your audience, leaving them thinking, "I understand it, I feel it and I want more of it!"

After reading and applying the insights from this book, I'm convinced you will become that drug dealer and you will no longer think, "Fuck, I have to speak!", because you now know exactly what to say and do. You have all the answers to the 21 most frequently asked questions. Time for you to stand up for your ideas and stand out in life and business by the way you share them with the world. Your audience will be grateful.

I hope you enjoyed the read, that you will embrace the continued journey of practising, improving, filling that backpack and have already welcomed the applause into your life. You are now well on your way to mastering the world's most valued skill, public speaking.

SOURCES

I KINDLY ASK YOU TO

Steven Bartlett, *The Diary of a CEO – The 33 laws of business and life*, Penguin Random House UK, 2023

THE QUESTION THAT STARTED IT ALL

Daniel Z. Liebermann, MD & Michael E. Long, *The molecule of more*, BenBella Books, Inc., 2019

Chris Williamson (host) & Jimmy Carr (guest), episode #691 – *The secret hacks for living a fulfilled life, Modern Wisdom podcast*, 2023

Millionaire Move Club, Jeff Bezos quote from interview, https://youtube.com/shorts/ESTSlh5fsCY?si=zm82dOE9dL1n4GtT

1. WHY SHOULD I LEARN TO SPEAK BETTER? I'M NOT IN SALES

Sofia Vergara, quote from TV-show 'Modern Family'

Carmine Gallo, *The Bezos Blueprint*, Macmillan Business, 2023

Dale Carnegie, *How to win friends and influence people*, Vermilion London, 2006

Warren Buffet, Interview – *Advice for young professionals* (Linkedin post), 2019

Successful Genius, Jordan Peterson quote from interview, https://youtu.be/YziYMgGnJOA?si=6PGwrxqVhgtP6IoN

2. IS IT SOMETHING YOU CAN LEARN OR IS IT JUST A GIFT SOME PEOPLE HAVE?

Marnick Vandebroek, *Stand Up to Stand Out*, Die Keure, 2019

Katia Malecki, *Casa Nardo Music*, 2023

Dale Carnegie, *How to win friends and influence people*, Vermilion London, 2006

Jordan Belfort, *Way of the Wolf*, John Murray Business, 2022

Billionaire Secrets, quote Simon Sinek from interview, https://youtu.be/TA5W1bjq2Qg?si=L759Amf8T1W9qJZk

Netflix, documentary, Live to 100: secrets of the Blue Zones, 2023

3. HOW CAN I TELL STORIES WHEN EVERYTHING IN MY COMPANY HAS TO BE TO THE POINT?

Bas Birker, *Online Comedy Course*, Comedy Tunes, 2024

Stijn Vantilt, *60 second pitch for BlooLoc*, 2022

Rener Gracie, QuikFlip Apparel – Shark Tank pitch, season 10 – episode 4, https://youtu.be/9iOdIt8iR2U?si=PypHxfDg5H91vTAq

4. HOW CAN I BECOME LESS NERVOUS?

Sascha Del Sal, *The Mental Edge*, 2024

Marnick Vandebroek, *Stand Up to Stand Out*, Die Keure, 2019

Chris Voss, *Never split the difference*, New York, Simon & Schuster, 2013

Stefanie Van Moen, *Mastering your keynote*, 2024

Steven Bartlett, *The Diary of a CEO – The 33 laws of business and life*, Penguin Random House UK, 2023

Het Ontwikkelingsinstituut, NLP Practitioner Course, Mechelen, 2018

Jordan Belfort, Way of the Wolf, John Murray Business, 2022

5. HOW DO I AVOID USING FILLER WORDS?

Matt Ellis, What are filler words and how do you cut them?, https://www.grammarly.com/blog/grammar/how-we-use-filler-words/#:~:text=Filler%20words%20are%20often%20unintentional,if%20you%20avoid%20using%20them. , Grammarly, 2022

Taran Hughes, Mastery of your voice, https://medium.com/@iamtaranhughes/mastery-of-your-voice-217d95aea63a , Medium, 2023

6. SHOULD I USE SPEAKER NOTES?

Roy Slenders, *Cyber Security in Insurance*, Kantoor Van Hees, Master Communicator Intensive Program, 2024

7. HOW CAN I BE FUNNY?

Bas Birker, *Online Comedy Course*, Comedy Tunes, 2024

Gabriel Tremblay – Sept24, *Employer Branding Reinmagined*, World Employer Branding Day, 2024

Bas Birker, *Comedy Academy*, Antwerp, 2013

Dale Carnegie, *How to win friends and influence people*, Vermilion London, 2006

8. HOW DO I MANAGE MY ENERGY, EVEN ON A BAD DAY?

Marnick Vandebroek, *Stand Up to Stand Out*, Die Keure, 2019

Jordan Belfort, *Way of the Wolf*, John Murray Business, 2022

Het Ontwikkelingsinstituut, NLP Practitioner Course, Mechelen, 2018

Chris Williamson (host) & Jocko Willink (guest), *Extreme Ownership: The key to fixing your life*, Modern Wisdom podcast, 2022 https://youtu.be/lCiZ2G2GSY4?si=MZPKsOGOnYYyciCo

Matthew Mcconaughey, *The Art of Livin'* Virtual Event, 24th of April, 2023

Stephen R. Covey, 7 *habits of highly effective people*, Simon & Schuster, 2020

9. HOW DO I SPEAK WITH MORE CONFIDENCE AND ENTHUSIASM WITHING BEING SEEN AS FAKE?

Het Ontwikkelingsinstituut, NLP Practitioner Course, Mechelen, 2018

Vinh Giang, Youtube video, https://youtu.be/9eAB-mX7gkc?si=Dgrb6D-vVm1L33qIJ, 2024

Erik Scherder, *Singing in the brain Light*, Athenaeum, 2018

Marnick Vandebroek, *Stand Up to Stand Out*, Die Keure, 2019

Will Stephen, *How to sound smart in a TEDx talk*, TedX New York, https://youtu.be/8SoFDjFBj8o?si=XUxIXgcpSf1uOCvY, 2015

Mohammed Qahtani, *The power of words*, https://youtu.be/xwbI8VOsD-To?si=jFUGRdbs-U_i04zV, 2019

GQ, Gerard Butler interview – His most iconic characters, https://youtu.be/-3rtedLsJFw?si=jTgQxOooA5XHiO6I , 2019

10. HOW CAN I CAPTURE THE AUDIENCE'S ATTENTION?

Pocket Marketing/nXt, quote Herman Konings – trendwatcher, 2018

Netflix Explained Series, *The Mind – Memory*, season 1 episode 1, 2019

Carmine Gallo, *The Bezos Blueprint*, Macmillan Business, 2023

Jurgen Mangelschots, Strain2Data pitch, 2020

Benjamin Maes, *Story Coaching* – BIM keynote, 2023

Brecht Van der Vliet, *Data scientist*, 2023

Jordan Belfort, *Way of the Wolf*, John Murray Business, 2022

ChatGPT, prompt 'What causes an earworm?', 2024

11. HOW DO I PREPARE MY PRESENTATION?

Stephen R. Covey, *7 habits of highly effective people*, Simon & Schuster, 2020

Rubber Ducking, https://en.wikipedia.org/wiki/Rubber_duck_debugging

Eminem, Lose Yourself, Shady Records, 2002 – https://youtu.be/xFYQQPAOz7Y?si=qwxTn6NMqMo18Fpw

Dale Carnegie, *How to win friends and influence people*, Vermilion London, 2006

Dr. Hermina Van Coillie, *How to communicate with impact: speak the ABC-language and make deeper connections with your employees*, 2023

Bain & Company, *Elements of Value pyramid*, https://media.bain.com/elements-of-value/#

Lieze Geebelen, *CEO Proactify, networking presentation example*, 2022

12. HOW DO I STRUCTURE MY PRESENTATION?

Joseph Campbell, *The Hero Journey*, https://en.wikipedia.org/wiki/Hero%27s_journey

Julius van de Laar, *Story campaigning workshop*, Berlin, 2024

Lieze Geebelen, CEO Proactify, networking presentation example, 2022

13. HOW DO I TURN MY MESSAGE INTO AN ACTUAL STORY?

Trey Parker and Matt Stone, *Writing advice from Matt Stone & Trey Parker* @NYU, https://youtu.be/vGUNqq3jVLg?si=Avb_mnSy9IKf6MF4

Bas Birker, Comedy Academy, Antwerp, 2013

14. HOW DO I INTERACT WITH MY AUDIENCE AND POSE GOOD QUESTIONS?

Carmine Gallo, *The Bezos Blueprint*, Macmillan Business, 2023

Sonja Tielen, SOTI pitch, mentorship, 2019

Zara Altair, *Analogy vs Metaphor: understand the differences*, https://prowritingaid.com/analogy-vs-metaphor#:~:text=The%20best%20way%20to%20identify,a%20thing%20is%20another%20thing. , 2022

Steven Van Belleghem, my favorite customer experience metaphor ever, https://youtu.be/lW3_9G3Hc2w?si=xtw5cDJ9kjk4iZAs , 2022

15. HOW DO I BUILD A POWERFUL SLIDE DECK?

Guy Kawasaki, *World Creativity Forum speech*, 2014

Michael Humblet, *Mastering your keynote*, Chaomatic, 2024

BONUS CHAPTER – COMING FULL CIRCLE

Katia Malecki, *Casa Nardo Music*, 2023

16. HOW DO I STAY IN CONTROL WHEN BEING CHALLENGED BY MY AUDIENCE?

Outstanding Screenplays, Rowan Atkinson explains Charlie Chaplin quote, https://youtu.be/KcBfhzby_jI?si=bHY0NofC1ayVQiax , 2024

Marnick Vandebroek, *Stand Up to Stand Out*, Die Keure, 2019

Julius van de Laar, *Story campaigning workshop*, Berlin, 2024

Young America's Foundation, Ben Shapiro – *Facts don't care about your feelings*, https://youtu.be/bGG8i10VJhw?si=IlvQeFdN8GVrIPwb , 2018

17. WHAT IF I DON'T BELIEVE IN THE STORY I HAVE TO TELL?

Chris Voss, *Never split the difference*, New York, Simon & Schuster, 2013

18. WHAT IF I'M EXPECTED TO SEND SOMETHING TO MY AUDIENCE UPFRONT?

Walter Isaacson, *Elon Musk*, Spectrum, Amsterdam, 2023

Arnold Schwarzenegger, *The speech that broke the internet*, Mulligan Brothers, https://youtu.be/u_ktRTWMX3M?si=pp3X_eapN4TWuxU_ , 2019

19. DO THESE INSIGHTS AND TECHNIQUES ALSO WORK IN FRONT OF A CAMERA OR IN A VIDEO CALL?

Marnick Vandebroek, *Stand Up to Stand Out*, Die Keure, 2019

Viral Video Club, https://www.instagram.com/viralvideo.club/ , 2024

20. HOW DO I HOST AN EVENT OR MEETING?

Bas Birker, MC masterclass, Antwerp, 2019

Jeron Dewulf, improv masterclass, Antwerp, 2013

Marnick Vandebroek, *Stand Up to Stand Out*, Die Keure, 2019

21. CAN'T I JUST ASK AI TO DO EVERYTHING FOR ME?

ChatGPT, prompt 'What is the impact of physical writing on the brain and the effect on preventing diseases like Alzheimer?", 2024

WHO IS MARNICK VANDEBROEK?

Marnick Vandebroek is an internationally awarded speaker, communication expert and founder of Stand Up Company. He has trained +2.000 entrepreneurs and professionals across Europe. He is the author of the book, Stand Up to Stand Out: Expressing yourself in the most powerful way, and has over 15 years' experience in marketing and communication, which has resulted in more than 10 marcom awards.

In addition to marketing and communication, Marnick's background includes neuro-linguistic programming, stand-up comedy and stage performances.

He loves to read, draw, play the piano, ride his Harley Davidson and pump iron in the gym. He has two lovely cats, Blinx and Zarra, and is happily married to his college sweetheart, Natalie.

Linkedin: www.linkedin.com/in/marnickvandebroek
www.youtube.com/marnickvandebroek
www.standupcompany.com

D/2025/45/72 – ISBN 978 94 209 3630 8 – NUR 800

Cover and interior design: Joost van Lierop
Photograph cover and page 324: Matija Habljak - PIXSELL

LannooCampus Publishers is a subsidiary of Lannoo Publishers, the book and multimedia division of Lannoo Publishers nv.

LannooCampus Publishers
Vaartkom 41 box 01.02
3000 Leuven
Belgium
www.lannoocampus.com

P.O. Box 23202
1100 DS Amsterdam
The Netherlands